Civil Society

EUROPEAN CIVIL SOCIETY
Editors: **Dieter Gosewinkel** and **Jürgen Kocka**

Civil society represents one of the most ambitious projects and influential concepts relating to the study of modern societies. It encapsulates their structures and their gradual restructuring as well as their changing polities and cultures. Scholars working in this field aim to secure greater equality of opportunity, democratic participation, individual freedom, and societal self-organization against both the overbearing and overburdening powers of the modern state as well as the social deficits of globalizing neo-liberalism. This series deals with the multiple languages, different layers, and diverse practices of existing and emerging civil societies in Europe. Its leitmotif is to analyse whether and how far the renewed interest in the concept can contribute to the gradual evolution of a larger European civil society.

Volume 1
The Languages of Civil Society
Peter Wagner

Volume 2
Civil Society: Berlin Perspectives
John Keane

Volume 3
State and Civil Society in Northern Europe:
The Swedish Model Reconsidered
Edited by Lars Trägårdh

CIVIL SOCIETY

BERLIN PERSPECTIVES

Edited by
John Keane

Berghahn Books
New York • Oxford

First published in 2006 by

Berghahn Books

www.berghahnbooks.com
First paperback edition published in 2007

Library of Congress Cataloging-in-Publication Data

Civil society : Berlin perspectives / edited by John Keane.
  p. cm. -- (European civil society ; 2)
  Includes bibliographical references and index.
  ISBN 1-84545-064-7 (hardback : alk. paper)
  1. Civil society--Germany--Berlin. I. Keane, John H. (John
Horacio), 1959-

JC337.C535 2006
300.943'155--dc22

2006018072

British Library Cataloguing in Publication Data

A catalogue record for this book is available from
the British Library.

Printed in the United States on acid-free paper

ISBN 978-1-84545-064-9 hardback
ISBN 978-1-84545-357-2 paperback

CONTENTS

EDITORS' PREFACE

Is there a 'European civil society' which cuts across national borders and spreads, though unevenly, through the continent? Does it help to form a European identity from below? Can it be seen as an answer to the obvious democratic deficit of the European Union?

For two and a half years, more than 40 political scientists, sociologists, historians and other scholars from 15 research institutions in 10 different countries have worked together on the project 'Towards a European Civil Society'. They were supported within the 5th Framework Programme of the EU. The network was coordinated by the Social Science Research Center Berlin. The results of the project are published in the volumes of this series which include studies by other authors as well.

'Civil society' means many things. The concept varies and oscillates. To give a working definition: 'civil society' refers (a) to the community of associations, initiatives, movements and networks in a social space related to, but distinguished from, government, business and the private sphere; (b) to a type of social action which takes place in the public sphere and is characterized by non-violence, discourse, self-organisation, recognition of plurality and orientation towards general goals and civility; (c) a project with socially and geographically limited origins and universalistic claims which changes while it tends to expand, socially and geographically.

Civil society is a deeply historical concept. For a quarter of a century, the concept of 'civil society' has experienced a remarkable career in several languages. Having a long tradition of many centuries, it had nearly disappeared during most of the twentieth century before being rediscovered and reinforced in the 1970s and 1980s when the concept became attractive again in the fight against dictatorship, particularly against communist rule in East Central Europe. But in non-dictatorial parts of the world the term and its promise responded to widely spread needs as well. Western Europe can be taken as an example.

Civil society as a political concept of our time has come to formulate critique of a broad variety of problems in contemporary society. To name three tendencies: first, the concept emphasizes social self-organisation as well as individual responsibilities, reflecting the wide-spread scepticism towards being spoon-fed by the state. Second, 'civil society', as demonstrated by the phrase's use by present-day anti-globalization movements, promises an alternative to the unbridled capitalism that has been developing so victoriously across the world. The term thus reflects a new kind of capitalist critique, since the logic of 'civil society', as determined by public discourse, conflict and agreement, promises solutions different from those of the logic of the market which is based on competition, exchange and the maximization of individual benefits. Thirdly, civic involvement and efforts to achieve common goals are specific to 'civil society', no matter how differently the goals may be defined. In the highly individualized and partly fragmented societies of the present time, 'civil society' promises an answer to the pressing question of what holds our societies together at all.

On the basis of broad empirical evidence, the project has analysed a large number of core problems of 'civil society', among them the complicated relation between markets and civil society; the impact of a European civil society on a European polity and vice versa; the importance of family and household for the ups and downs of civil society. The project has dealt with resources, dynamics and actors of civil society. It has dealt with questions of gender and other forms of inequality. It has compared developments in different European regions. It has begun to open up the perspective towards the non-European conditions, consequences and correlates of European civil society. It has reconstructed the language of civil society, including different semantic strategies in the context of tradition, ideology and power which explain the multiple uses of the concept for different practical purposes. These are some of the topics dealt with in the volumes of this series. The authors combine a long historical perspective with broad and systematic comparison.

What does it mean to speak of a 'European' civil society? It implies a certain common European development, a parallel or even convergent trend towards the emergence of civil society in Europe. Such a development may be based on the activities of civil society groups. From the eighteenth to the twentieth century, civil society circles, associations, networks and institutions largely evolved in local, regional and national frameworks. Trans-national variants, however, which might contribute to the emergence of trans-national coherence and similarities remained secondary. It is in the second half of the twentieth century that the quality of the process changed. In this phase, the development of civil society in Europe increasingly assumed trans-national, 'European' and sometimes global dimensions. This is a basic hypothesis of research in this series of studies. 'European Civil Society' will concentrate on trans-national dimensions of civil society in Europe by comparing and reconstructing interrelations.

The evolution of a European civil society in the process of trans-nationalization is based on actors as well as on mobile concepts. The ideas and practices of civil society have evolved in a very uneven way, starting to emerge mainly in Western Europe, where it was initially restricted to a few proponents and to specific circles. In the course of its development, civil society spread to other parts of Europe (and into other parts of the world) and gained support within broader social spheres. As they expanded into widening social and spatial environments, the ideas and realities of civil society changed. Thus, the potential of an approach is explored which takes civil society as a geographically and socially mobile phenomenon with a good deal of travelling potential and with the propensity to become a European-wide concept.

'European Civil Society' focuses on Europe in a broad, not merely geographical, sense. This includes comparing European developments with developments in other parts of the world, as well as analyzing processes of (mutual) transfer and entanglement. Europe in this sense transcends the institutional and spatial realm of the European Union. Yet, studying the emergence and dynamics, the perspectives and problems, of civil society in Europe may produce insights into the historical process of European integration, a process which is underway, but far from complete, and presently in crisis.

'European Civil Society' is a common endeavour of European and non-European scholars. It centres around a topic which is both the object of scientific analysis and political efforts. The political success cannot be taken for granted. Scientific analysis, however, may help to work out the conditions under which the utopia of civil society in Europe has a chance of realization.

Dieter Gosewinkel
Jürgen Kocka

Introduction

CITIES AND CIVIL SOCIETY

John Keane

Sanctuaries of Freedom

Among the sadly neglected themes within recent research on civil societies is their intimate connection with urban life. Its absence from the literature on civil society is odd, if only because classical and early modern images of civil society (*societas civilis*) are tightly dependent in a linguistic sense upon a family of terms associated with cities. Such old-fashioned words as *civitas* (the inhabitant of a city), *civis* (a citizen of a town, as in *civis Romanus*), *civilis* (befitting a citizen, or becoming a citizen) and *civilitas* (politeness or civility) today live a vibrant life within all European languages of civil society. The interdependence of cities and civil societies is, however, not just a linguistic phenomenon, as important as that is in shaping the way we think about the institutions and norms of civil society. The patterns of interdependence between cities and civil society run wider and deeper – towards a history of institutional practices that have shaped and transformed the ways we experience and judge fields of power, whether in the spheres of governmental or non-governmental institutions.

Historically speaking, the influence of European cities was out of all proportion to their numbers of inhabitants. Around the year 1500 – census data are unreliable and far from comprehensive – only one tenth of Europe's population lived in towns, most of which were small by today's standards. There were only three or four cities with populations of more than 100,000 – Naples was the largest – and only about 500 cities with more than 5,000 inhabitants, most of them shadowed constantly by death caused by harvest crises or epidemic diseases. Yet despite their limited numbers and small populations, cities functioned as places for the articulation of particular and collective desires, for invention, commerce, creative experimentation and emancipation from cramping ties – in fields as diverse as architecture and theatre, fairs and markets, and the production and consumption of new commodities. Whatever freedoms cities enjoyed were usually licensed by political rulers who granted them charters in return for (monetary) benefits, including taxes. Cities were often granted permission to protect themselves by walls punctuated by gates and watchtowers; some cities even had elaborate systems of fortifications, with bastions and outer works. Cities were strongholds, and that – ironically – enabled them to become sanctuaries of freedom from arbitrary exercises of power (Weber 1978: chap. 17). The city states of the ancient world spawned the invention of democracy, the self-government of equals. The towns and cities of medieval and early modern Europe, hemmed in by a much 'denser' and more complex framework of estates and political and spiritual power – sometimes to the point where cities functioned as appendages of courts or cathedrals – were, in contrast, the birthplace of civil societies. The great urban revival that began in the eleventh century, and that was symbolized by towns like Bruges, Genoa, Nuremberg and London, nurtured new spaces of non-governmental freedom and pluralism, on a scale and in ways never before experienced.

How exactly did this happen? The short answer is that the first sparks of civil society in Europe resulted from a combustible mixture of urban life, conciliar government, Protestant sects and market trade and commerce. The first chemical reactions were evident in urban spaces like Magdeburg and Nuremberg (whose local government opened the city gates to Calvinist merchants and artisans from the Netherlands, and even offered tax breaks to attract them). It was in such towns, around 3,000 of them in the German-speaking lands alone, that something like a counter-power to the established order was created (Collinson 2004: chaps 5, 6). These towns resembled levers used to turn the old Christian feudal world upside down, initially by raising basic questions about who was entitled to get what, when and how on earth. The inversions that took place – another irony – were helped along by the old and (for the most part) conservative conciliar structures of urban politics. European cities were initially not havens of open government. They rather resembled self-supporting oligarchies. Cities were typically governed by single councils that were equipped with combined executive, legislative and judicial powers; cities like Venice and Strasburg, which had complex systems of interlocking councils, were rare. City mayors sometimes rotated in and out of office, but council members generally served for life. Occasionally, councillors were elected and sometimes a certain number of seats were reserved for particular constituencies, such as guilds and neighbourhoods. But in most cases, when a seat on a council became vacant through death or retirement, the existing councillors themselves decided the replacement. Research on the social composition of these urban councils also shows that the end result was usually the same: council members were typically among the wealthiest members of the city.

The pattern of conciliar government was set from the time of the rebirth of towns during the eleventh century, but the growing influence of market wealth rather than pedigree changed the composition of the councils. Whereas late medieval councils were typically composed of merchants and wealthy craftsmen, by 1550 rentiers and lawyers came to occupy council seats. In some Protestant cities, so too did the clergy, who sat with council members on consistories that defined and enforced policies about marriage arrangements and personal conduct. Virtually all councils were male preserves; city women could inherit and sometimes own property and engage in certain forms of economic enterprise, but they were normally excluded both from decision making in the guilds and from membership in any of the governing councils. The net effect of all these factors ensured that the urban councils of early modern Europe were highly conservative institutions. But that did not make them invulnerable to inside and outside pressures, especially when state rulers tried to poke their noses into municipal government, for instance by installing their own people or extracting new taxes (Mackeney 1989). During the Middle Ages, urban leaders had struggled to assert their autonomy from kings and princes. But, by the sixteenth and seventeenth centuries, the growing fiscal and military resources of rulers tempted them to assert or reassert their authority over local urban bodies. A few cities, such as Venice, Geneva and the free cities of the Holy Roman Empire, vigorously resisted. Elsewhere urban oligarchs often saw the advantages of cooperation with princely governments, sometimes to the point where the two groups were fused into a single urban oligarchy of households run by wealthy and well-educated men.

Sometimes, things did not run smoothly for oligarchs. Since city governments never had a professional police at their disposal, instead employing a few constables or beadles, they often depended upon the cooperation of civic militias and neighbourhood watches organized by citizens. The existence of an armed citizenry that expected to be treated decently, with respect, functioned as a major constraint on the exercise of arbitrary power. Most magistrates and councillors feared an armed crowd of citizens in the marketplace, and they knew that they could govern effectively only by heeding the interests of the rest of the citizen householders. Striking a balance proved difficult. There were times when excessive taxes or unwelcome policies caused uprisings. Council members were given a serious fright; or they were actually thrown out in the name of the right of resistance to arbitrary government. For that resistance, the citizens of some cities sometimes paid heavily, as illustrated by the fate of the 10,000 Huguenots slaughtered in the August 1572 Massacre of St Bartholomew. Other believers were luckier and more successful, and it is to them – especially the Dutch and English revolutionaries clustered in towns like Amsterdam and London – that we owe some basic constitutional principles that would later feed the wellsprings of civil society. The right to resist tyranny, the abolition of monarchy, constitutional conventions, written constitutions, popular election, limited terms of office: such principles of government are virtually unthinkable without noting their roots in early modern urban life.

But the early European towns spawned something else: traditions of *civil liberty*. In the struggles and counter-struggles that clawed at the heart of the towns of Reformation Europe, the faithful on both sides at first clung with all their might to the canon that the ruler determines the religion of his state (*cuius regio, eius religio*). In this way, ironically, the friends and enemies of Reformation helped to discredit political abuses of religion. They saw the possibility that religion and despotism could hold hands, that faith and force could be confused, with evil effects. Out of this recognition sprang the efforts of Philipp Melanchthon and other sixteenth-century Protestant thinkers to rescue and defend the ideal of a *societas civilis* (Colas 1992). This ideal was only a few steps away from the realization that cities could function as templates of religious compromise among confessionally divided communities. There were religious dissenters who went even further. Prominent figures like George Buchanan (tutor to James VI) and John Milton (a great champion of liberty of the press) came to identify with the project of limiting the scope of governmental power. Freedom of the printing press from government control was often high on the agenda; cities were the pacesetters for the diffusion of print culture throughout Europe – such that, by the end of the eighteenth century, at least in north-western Europe and Germany, the great majority of men and women in cities were able to read and write. They spotted the importance of nurturing non-governmental spaces – families, schools, church congregations, scientific and literary clubs – protected by good laws. From the time of the American Revolution, these spaces would be called *civil society* – an old term branded with a meaning that was entirely different from that of the classical term *societas civilis* (a well-governed political community) that it superseded (Keane 1988). This new form of urban society was a religious – not a secular – invention designed to promote the active toleration of different faiths, and to check governments prone to popish cruelty.

Yet European towns spawned more than new religious interactions and new forms of government charged with civilizing potential. They were simultaneously places where new forms of market exchange blossomed (Mundy and Riesenberg 1958; Braudel 1981: chap. 8). Towns nurtured socio-economic interactions in strange combinations of proximity and distance, new money-driven networks and encounters among many different actors, within specific times and places. They carved up old forms of *communitas* into a thousand pieces by activating new modes of money-fuelled mobility, long-distance trade and other forms of market-driven social interaction, the combined effect of which was to link together the quite different Europes of (say) the Mediterranean, the Atlantic and the Baltic regions. From the outset – this point is obvious when the historical evidence is carefully examined – the local development of towns and their civil societies within the wider framework of territorial states and empires also contained the seeds of their own interpenetration through space and time. Within the European region, even the most local civil societies were more than local. The rebirth of towns marked the beginning of the continent's rise to world eminence – and its contribution to the laying of the material foundations of what later came to be called a global civil society (Keane 2003).

Although the distribution of these European towns was highly uneven, with the weakest patterns of urbanization in Russia and the strongest in the Low Countries, they were typically linked to each other in networks, or archipelagos stretching across vast distances (de Vries 1984; Hohenberg and Lees 1985). In opposition to feudal lords and princes, cities had a self-interest in mutual cooperation. Barcelona was a good example: during the thirteenth century, it cultivated long-distance networks that stretched through the western Mediterranean, with settlements in Sicily, Sardinia and the Balearics and consulates in Oran, Tunis and Bougie (Blockmans 1997: 139–49). Wherever these urban archipelagos thrived, they functioned like magnets that attracted strangers fascinated by their well-lit complexity, higher wages and real or imagined freedom. Cities attracted outlaws, who swore oaths, *coniurationes* ('swearing together') confirming that they would commit themselves to mutual social support within a hostile political order. The escape of many from serfdom added to the feeling that cities were unusual clumps of people engaged in many different tasks, living in houses close together, often joined wall to wall with buildings like churches, chapels, city halls, granaries, warehouses, hospitals and almshouses. Their architectural pluralism did not automatically make them havens of social pluralism, freedom and equality. They contained visible social elites, normally comprising merchants and some professionals, notably lawyers; large cities, such as Nuremberg and Venice, even had a higher stratum of patrician families, whose members were no longer active in trade but lived off their investments and thought of themselves as aristocrats. Yet the towns that sprang up in Europe resembled some new kind of tension-producing engine. They seemed to recharge life by adding motion to its elements.

Town-dwellers seemed to be perpetually on the move. They travelled regularly to and fro among built-up areas and regularly spent only part of their lives there: during harvest-times, for instance, artisans and others typically abandoned their trades and houses for work in fields elsewhere. The constant rumble of wheeled carriages, the weekly or daily markets and the numerous trades added to the sense of motion through space: town-dwellers encountered water-carriers, floor polishers, sawyers, porters and chair-carriers, pedlars, rabbit-skin merchants, wig-makers, barbers, cobblers, domestic servants and a floating population of paupers and thieves and unskilled labourers, who lived in small rented quarters and supported themselves by performing the menial tasks – carrying, digging, transporting and animal tending – that abounded in a pre-mechanized society. All these occupations, together with ethnic and religious minorities, rubbed shoulders with members of the upper middle classes: merchants, some of them very rich, masters, mercenaries, engineers, ships' captains, doctors, professors, painters, architects, all of whom knew what it meant to travel through time and space.

The winding, twisting layout of towns added to their appearance of geographical and social dynamism. Medieval and early Europe was one of only two civilizations – the other was Islam – that fashioned large towns with an irregular maze of streets (Hodgson 1974, vol. 2: 105–31). What was probably different about the medieval and early modern European towns was their unparalleled civil and political freedom from the well-armed political authorities of the emerging territorial states and empires. Local merchants, traders, craft guilds, manufacturers, and bankers, many of whom were Protestants, formed the backbone of a long-distance money economy endowed with the power to dictate the terms and conditions on which state and local governments ruled. Seen in this way, urban markets were the cuckoo's egg laid in the little nests of the medieval towns. These nests were woven from a complex plurality of non-governmental institutions, such as households, religious sects and guilds. Self-organized guilds were especially important sources of the new freedoms. Although they sometimes had religious purposes, and despite the obvious fact that their major aim was to control the production and exchange of commodities, for instance by regulating the process through which apprentices became journeymen and journeymen became masters, and by preventing the manufacture of goods by non-member craftsmen and merchants in the surrounding countryside or within the city itself, the guilds in fact achieved much more than protecting their members' livelihoods. Like other non-governmental 'societies' rooted in market structures, the guilds nurtured something new: unfettered and unbounded social space within which the absolutist state could be checked, criticized and generally held at arm's length from citizens who no longer considered themselves the property of others.

The Metropolis

The birth of urbane civil societies in the modern European sense did not simply lay the foundations for 'strongly connected national civil societies living in a system of many states' (Peterson 1992: 388). Historically speaking, the institutions of civil society were never exclusively 'national' or constituted by their exclusive relationship to the territorial state. Civil societies, both past and present, have always been structured and linked by tangled webs of common and overlapping threads, operating at a distance, across borders. Cities and their civil societies have horizon-stretching effects, as the Berlin-born scholar Georg Simmel (1858–1918) spotted with great clarity more than a century ago. His influential writings on the 'microscopic-molecular' processes of modern urban life were guided by analytical methods that were among the first civil society-centred approaches in the human sciences. Simmel structured his observations with various conceptual rules: the obligation upon researchers to reject mindless empiricism and openly to admit their linguistic habit of selecting and interpreting certain historically specific phenomena from the world of infinite flux ('cognitive representations of things are not poured into us like nuts into a sack', he once remarked (Simmel 1965: 290; translation altered)); his emphasis on the restless, self-directing qualities of social actors, whose powers to shape civil society ensure that its institutions are restless, open, fractured and conflict-ridden; and his adamant rejection of false hopes that one day, in spite of everything, conflict-producing, conflict-resolving civil societies could be overcome in some higher-order political totality that would secure and protect a single-minded version of the common good.

In all but name, Simmel's approach to analysing modern urban life supposed its close links with civil society. 'We are continually circulating over a number of different planes,' he wrote. 'Each presents the world totality according to a different formula; but at any given time our life carries with it only a fragment from each' (Simmel 1918: 37). Modern cities were for him dynamic bundles of stimuli that have profound effects upon the internal and external lives of their inhabitants. The large metropolis – he clearly had his native Berlin in mind – is above all a school of social difference. It comprises 'a highly diversified plurality of achievements' (Simmel 1903: 336). With every crossing of the street, every glance at strangers whom one may never again see and every transaction in the marketplace of emotional, occupational and business life, city living stimulates awareness of the deep contrast between the slower-paced rhythms of small town and rural existence. Cities stimulate the desire to be different – to make oneself noticeable in the presence of others. Strange 'eccentricities' and 'metropolitan extravagances' are the result, Simmel claimed. They reinforce the shared sense that life is structured by the differences between future expectations, present experiences and those that have preceded them. Urban life also stimulates consumer needs, which is unsurprising considering that cities are the seat of the many-sided money economy, in which sellers are compelled to whet 'new and unique needs' of consumers. Within the urban market economy, the spirit of 'calculating exactness' flourishes. So too does a matter-of-fact attitude towards people and things, a certain 'hardness' of the emotions, a mutual reserve and indifference matched by a deep dependence upon the pocket watch and the grandfather clock. 'If all the watches in Berlin suddenly went wrong in different ways, even only as much as an hour,' noted Simmel, 'its entire economic and commercial life would be derailed for some time.' But city life – Simmel here dissents from Marx's economic reductionism – is more than commodified punctuality, calculability and exactness. While appearing to cultivate dissociation, cities stimulate a vast mosaic of dynamic social interactions. Cities comprise colourful, constantly moving kaleidoscopes of social action structured by institutions (*Gebilde*) that are continually altered by the choices, judgements, desires and actions of their inhabitants. 'The relationships and concerns of the typical metropolitan resident are so manifold and complex that, especially as a result of the agglomeration of so many persons with such differentiated interests, their relationships and activities intertwine with one another into a many-membered organism.'

Simmel emphasized that the multiple relationships and activities of the urban organism extended well beyond a metropolis like Berlin. The civil relations of the large city are not coterminous with its geographical boundaries. Cities are more than the simple sum of their territorially based and defined social relations. They rather comprise complex webs of civil society institutions that are joined together in complex chains of interdependence that operate and have effects far and wide. Cities and their civil societies stretch the horizons of their inhabitants. Their lives are 'extended in a wave-like motion over a broader national or international area'. Simmel put his finger on the 'cosmopolitanism' of all cities: in the European case, the birth of local civil societies within local urban areas heralded the dawn of what has been called universal history, marked by the constant reciprocal interaction between local and far-distant events (Aron 1978). Universal history so understood is *not* the clichéd story of the one-way spreading of a bundle of 'Western' urban ideals to the rest of the world, whose contribution is a non-history of non-contributions, or what has been called a 'history of absences' (Mamdani 1996). It is universal in a more complex and messier sense: the local and the beyond are interrelated recursively, through power-ridden processes of entangled pasts and presents. So, for instance, it can be said that the eighteenth-century vision of cosmopolitanism defended by Vattel, Kant and others was a child of local civil societies; it can also be said that that very cosmopolitanism was the privilege of those whose lives were already anchored in the non-governmental activities of local civil societies. The other-regarding, outward-looking openness of these local urban civil societies – their glimpse of themselves as part of a wider, complex world, their capacity to see space and time not as part of the bare bones of the world, but as constructions – constantly tempted them to engage and to transform that world. Their stocks of social and political skills, their capacities for commercial enterprise, technical innovation, freedom of communication, for self-government, learning languages and saving souls in independently minded churches: all these qualities fed the developing worldliness associated with civil societies, as well as laying the foundations for both their Europeanization – the formation of a European civil society – and, later, their globalization.

Hegel's Berlin

It is, of course, easy to get carried away with the positively appealing effects of modern urban life. Simmel himself cast doubt upon one-eyed, progressivist views of the city. He was an ironist who supposed that modern city-based civil societies were neither governed by universal world-historical processes nor susceptible of a single interpretative scheme that supposed, for instance, that civil life could be analysed – its true meaning grasped – through dialectical conceptions of the social totality or through universally applicable categories. As a style of thinking about civil society, Simmel's approach remains admirable and important, even if time has rendered many of his observations less relevant. Simmel recognized that modern urban life produces flux, indeterminacy, uncertainty and conflict. He noted the 'tragic' quality of cities: their tendency to produce self-destructive dynamics. He concluded, with an air of troubled resignation, that modern cities and civil societies spawn formlessness: feelings of indifference and worthlessness, even outbreaks of aggression. That conclusion rather understates the *political* problems attending civil societies as we have come to know them, for the historical fact is that in modern times the face of urban life has been inscribed with the experience of power struggles, humiliation and powerlessness. Cities have indeed functioned as havens of self-government, market freedom and religious equality and solidarity. But they have also been spaces of injustice and destruction: sites of bitter social conflict, uncivilized aggression towards others, scenes of bizarre cruelty and blood-curdling violence.

Founded during the early thirteenth century AD by traders from the Rhine, the modern city of Berlin stands out as a symbol of these two radically different faces of modern urban life. Its civil society was born of a tortuous history. Once a partner in the Hanseatic League of free-trading European cities, which included Hamburg and London (1359), it was conquered by Friedrich of Hohenzollern and drawn into the Holy Roman Empire (1411). That prompted an uprising of its citizens (in the so-called Berlin Indignation of 1447–48) and, during the Thirty Years War (1618–48), it suffered occupation and population decline caused by military intervention, pestilence and the collapse of its trading links. Under the Prussian rule that followed, Berlin again suffered war and repeated occupation by outside troops; but from the end of the seventeenth century, when one-fifth of its population spoke French (thanks to the presence of large numbers of Huguenot refugees), its reputation as a great cosmopolitan city of trade and industry and culture was also consolidated (Gerteis 1986). Following the Napoleonic invasions (1806–12) and the subsequent reforms of the Prussian state, the town that was founded originally on a swamp had become the fourth largest city in Europe. With a population of around 400,000 in 1840, it had a vibrant civil society that was an instrument of God-fearing bourgeois circles (*Bürgertum*) that lived a new conception of social relations. Merchants, bankers and industrialists, together with doctors, professors, lawyers and other members of the educated, professional strata (*Bildungsbürgertum*), valued hard work and achievement and thought that material success in the market – not feudal privilege based on birth – should determine the distribution of wealth, status and power. These circles favoured the protection of property rights and public freedoms (above all, *habeas corpus* and liberty of the press) through constitutional government and parliamentary representation. They championed agrarian reforms, commercial expansion and vigorous industrial growth; and they supposed perforce that 'society' should enjoy power over the inferior natural world. The middle classes also thought in terms of the division between private and public life, as well as defending a particular version of family life as the space marked by a strictly defined hierarchy of differences between the sexes, a household economy of emotions in which children should be inducted into bourgeois personal norms like individual self-discipline, cleanliness and educated manners (Kocka 1997).

This lived vision of *bürgerliche Gesellschaft* did not usually regard itself as limited by time and space. It saw itself as universally significant, as a model of social and political order that *all* groups could and should eventually adopt. Something of this universalizing spirit of civil society was captured in G.W.F. Hegel's path-breaking *Grundlinien der Philosophie des Rechts* (Hegel 1821). First presented as university lectures in the city of Berlin, Hegel's reflections on civil society were the most advanced of their time. They argued for an original thesis: 'The creation of civil society (*bürgerliche Gesellschaft*) is the achievement of the modern world.' With Berlin in mind, he noted that civil society was not a natural condition of freedom but a *historically produced* sphere of ethical life anchored between the simple world of the patriarchal household and the complex governing institutions of the modern state. Civil society is the grazing ground of the middle class of male property-owning citizens (*Bürgerstand*). It includes the market economy, social classes, corporations and institutions concerned with the administration of 'welfare' (*Polizei*) and civil law. Civil society is a mosaic of private individuals, classes, groups and institutions whose multiple transactions are regulated by civil law and, as such, are not directly dependent upon the political state itself.

Hegel emphasized that civil society in this sense is not a pre-given and invariable substratum of 'natural life'. It is rather the outcome of a long and complex process of historical transformation, which he associated with the rise of the modern West. Civil society denatures the human condition; it reminds its participants that they are part of a historical experiment. The 'system of needs' it nurtures represents a decisive break with the natural environment. The modern bourgeois economy, for instance, is a dynamic system of commodity production by means of commodities. It greatly increases the level of specialization and mechanization of human labour. Nature is thereby transformed into an instrument for the satisfaction of human needs, which multiply and diversify and can therefore no longer be understood as 'natural'.

Hegel's critique of naturalistic conceptions of civil society had important theoretical consequences. He was so impressed by its restless dynamism and 'de-naturing' of human needs that he was led to explore the proposition that there is no necessary identity or harmony among the various elements of civil society. Harmony nourished by unadulterated love is an essential characteristic of the patriarchal family, Hegel claimed. Described by him in glowing patriarchal terms as the 'first ethical root of the state', the family is an immediate, unreflecting unity whose members (especially women, who are guided by intuition and feeling and therefore destined for love and marriage) understand themselves as 'accidents' and not as competitive individuals bound together by contract. In civil society, things are otherwise. Its multiple forms of interaction are often incommensurable, fragile and subject to serious conflict; its manifold elements (its 'societies') do not merge spontaneously and harmoniously, as if governed by the invisible hands of benevolent Nature. Modern civil society rather resembles a restless battlefield where private (male) interest meets private (male) interest. It unfolds and develops in a blind, arbitrary, quasi-spontaneous manner. This means not only that it cannot overcome its own particularities; according to Hegel, civil society also tends to cripple and destroy its own pluralism.

The subdivision of civil society into classes (or *Stände*) is a principal reason why it is gripped by an inner restlessness – and why the exuberant development of one part of civil society often impedes or oppresses its other parts. Hegel recognized a variety of classes or class fragments – civil servants, landowners, peasantry, intellectuals, lawyers, doctors and clergymen – but he located the moving principle of civil society primarily in the *Bürgerstand*. He argued that this class of burghers (in which he included workers) is defined, paradoxically, by its selfish individualism. The burgher class certainly depends upon the corporations – municipal, trade, educational, religious, professional and other state-authorized forms of collective associations – which function as its 'second home', as a shelter that protects it from the vicissitudes of life in civil society and familiarizes it with a higher level of ethical (or public-spirited) form of life. The selfish actions of the burgher class and those of its unintended child, the 'rabble of paupers', are further restrained by the civil 'administration of justice' and by the various regulations and moral improvements secured by the 'policing' agencies of civil society. Nevertheless, the burgher class tends to struggle against the restrictions imposed by the corporations, civil administration and police. It tries to turn them into means of furthering its particular interests through commercial transactions. The burgher is less a public-spirited *citoyen* than a self-serving *bourgeois* who prefers to keep others at arm's length. He is an apolitical man who likes to stand on his own two feet. He is impatient with traditional privileges, shows little genuine interest in public affairs and is concerned only with his self-enrichment through the exercise of his private property. He views his freedom as abstract – as the freedom to act within the bounds of externally enforced laws that safeguard his property and enforce contracts. In this way – here Hegel would exert a decisive influence on Marx – modern civil society becomes a complex system of transacting individuals whose livelihoods, legal status and happiness are mutually interwoven. But it is precisely this universal selfishness – here Hegel rejected all assertions about the natural sociability of the human species – which turns civil society into a blind and unstable field of economic competition among private non-citizens.

A Universal State?

Hegel was understandably suspicious of those who expressed unbridled enthusiasm for civil society. In practice, just as he predicted, the bourgeois version of civil society was to meet stiff resistance, from within and from all sides. From below and outside, the rise of Berlin as the workshop of continental Europe and the corresponding formation of a self-conscious industrial working class caused trouble for private property-centred understandings of civil society. In the Berlin scene, the power of organized labour was manifested in the beaten-up revolution of 1848–49 and in the formation of independent workers' parties in the 1860s – early by European standards – and in direct challenges to middle-class institutions in the form of socialist cooperatives, strike action and the rejection of 'bourgeois' freedoms in the name of democratic and Marxian communist principles. Banned for nearly two decades, the Social Democratic Party won more than 70 per cent of the adult male vote in Berlin in the 1912 German election. Four years later, the party took a stand against war and refused to pass Berlin's budget. In *Rotes Berlin* and elsewhere in the country, civil society meanwhile also came under siege from within. Although on balance an open and tolerant city that was politically out of step with some other parts of Germany, Berlin's spirit of civility was diluted by the poisonous gases of xenophobia, anti-Semitism, unemployment, militaristic nationalism and ugly outbreaks of violence, early symbols of which were the murder of Rosa Luxemburg and Karl Liebknecht and the right-wing putsch (March 1920) staged in Berlin by Wolfgang Kapp. Meanwhile, by the last years of the nineteenth century, support for the project of civil society began to crumble within those parts of the middle class nervously convinced of the *Kaiserreich* strategy of maintaining an alliance between the old elites, the nobility, the state bureaucracy and the military – a governing strategy that Hegel himself had first sketched and recommended earlier that century.

Hegel was restrained in his enthusiasm for civil society because he viewed it as a self-crippling entity in constant need of state supervision and control. He noted its darker sides: for instance, its subdivision into classes (or *Stände)* and the corresponding selfishness of the middle classes and their humiliation of a 'rabble of paupers'. Such problems, he thought, demonstrate that modern civil society is incapable of overcoming its own particularity and resolving its own fundamental conflicts. Civil society cannot remain 'civil' unless it is ordered politically, subjected to 'the higher surveillance of the state'. Only a supreme public authority – Hegel had in mind a type of constitutional state managed by the monarchy, the civil service and the Estates – could in his view effectively remedy its injustices and synthesize its particular interests into a universal political community of freedom. From this perspective, Hegel criticized modern natural law theory for confusing civil society and the state, for supposing the latter to be a mere partnership of its subjects and thus for challenging the 'absolutely divine principle of the state, together with its majesty and absolute authority'. The ideal state is not a radical negation of a natural condition in perpetual war (Hobbes, Spinoza), an instrument for conserving and completing natural society (Locke, Pufendorf) or a simple mechanism for administering a naturally given, automatically self-governing civil society (Georg Forster). Hegel rather conceived the state as a new moment that contains, preserves and synthesizes the conflicting elements of civil society into a higher ethical entity.

The state represents society in its unity. Under its tutelary powers, civil society is *aufgehoben*: it is at the same time preserved and overcome as a necessary but subordinate aspect of a more complex and higher community that is organized politically. According to Hegel, if the state demands from civil society only what is necessary for itself, and if it limits itself to guaranteeing this necessary minimum, then beyond this limit the state can and should permit considerable scope for the freedom of male individuals and groups acting within civil society. This means, on the one hand, that the state should not be considered as a central superintendent that directs the life of all other institutions (a type of state which Hegel identified in oriental despotism and in the Prussian state of Frederick the Great and his successor, Friedrich Wilhelm II). On the other hand, Hegel urged that the public authority could not take the form of an administrative body that rarely interferes with the conduct of civil society. He proposed that both points of view must and can be satisfied politically: the freedom of the members of civil society can be guaranteed and synthesized with the state's articulation and defence of the universal interest.

Although Hegel consequently recommended against dissolving the separation of civil society from the state, he was quite clear that the degree to which civil society is differentiated from the state could not be fixed through hard and fast general rules. From his perspective, the practical relationship of state and society can be determined only by weighing up, from the standpoint of political reason, the advantages and disadvantages of restricting the independence, abstract freedom and competitive pluralism of civil society in favour of universal state prerogatives. Hegel supposed two conditions under which state intervention (in his words, the state's 'purging of privileges and wrongs') is legitimate. First, the state may intervene in order to remedy injustices or inequalities within civil society – for instance, the domination of one or more classes by another, the pauperization of whole groups or the establishment of local oligarchies (within a region or municipality, for example). Secondly, he thought (especially in his later writings, such as *Über die englische Reformbill* (1831) that the supreme public power is justified in intervening directly in the affairs of civil society to protect and further the universal interest of the population – which of course the state itself defines! The activity of the corporations was for him an important case in point: although they require autonomy to facilitate their members' development of *Sittlichkeit*, it is precisely because of their (potential) 'public' character that they require subjection to the 'higher surveillance' of the state, lest they degenerate into its rivals. Thus, while Hegel defended the need for 'particularity ... to develop and expand in all directions' within civil society, he insisted at the same time that the universal state has 'the right to prove itself as the ground and necessary form of particularity, as well as the power which stands over it as its final purpose'.

Considered together, these two conditions constitute a very broad licence indeed for state regulation of social life. The fear of despotism that had motivated, say, Montesquieu's reflections on power is in Hegel's writings drastically weakened in favour of a deep trust in state regulation (Keane 1998: 46–47). Despotism was seen by Hegel as a preoccupation of earlier times, which is why, in his work, the perennial problem of how, and under which conditions, male citizens can question, reconsider and resist state power falsely claiming to be universal – the problem of political power sharing and active public monitoring of power – fell into obscurity. Simply stated, if the requirements of the public good set limits upon the autonomy of civil society, and if the state itself – a monarchic one at that – is ultimately responsible for determining these requirements, how can its interventions possibly be identified and prevented as illegitimate?

Hegel's failure to deal adequately with this quintessentially modern problem of (democratic) checks and balances on the universal state – his assumption that the monarchic state is in the last instance sovereign *vis-à-vis* all relationships within the family and civil society – weakened, even contradicted, his claims on behalf of an independent civil society that guarantees the 'living freedom' of individuals and groups. From the perspective of Hegel's metaphysics, indeed, the ideal of the universal state is understood as 'absolutely rational'. It is the highest and concluding moment of a process of historical development in which reason actively works itself into the existing world. The universal state is the concrete human embodiment of the ethical Idea. It is mind (*Geist*) developing from a stage of immediate, undifferentiated unity (the family), through that of explicit difference and particularity (civil society), to the concrete unity and synthesis of the particular in the state. Given that the process of human history is in this sense 'the movement of God in the world', the universal state conceived by Hegel must be regarded as a secular deity. It is a body whose claims upon its male citizens and female and other subjects are always for their benefit and, ultimately, unquestionable and irresistible.

After Hegel

Through nasty twists of unreasonable cunning, the city of Berlin was later nearly destroyed by such presumptions about the supremacy of political power. Neither Hegel nor Simmel – two of the greatest Berlin-based theorists of civil society – could possibly have imagined the political originality and destructiveness of what happened. Touched by the deadening hand of several forms of state power, the twentieth century was unkind to Berlin and its civil society. The lives of Berliners were racked by the first all-European war (1914–18), which left 20 million Europeans dead, and by the humiliation inflicted by the military defeat of Germany and the outbreak and failure of a communist revolution (November 1918). The daily lives of Berliners were then badly damaged by random violence and civil war (1919–20) and the unemployment and hyperinflation that together conspired to destroy the Weimar constitutional state and its struggling civil society. The subsequent seizure of power by a criminal fascist regime and the Stalinist occupation and encirclement of half the city left permanent scars on the bodies and souls of its inhabitants. Two totalitarian forms of the so-called universal state proceeded to rip the guts out of the city – leaving its demoralized inhabitants shattered, disgraced and divided for nearly half a century.

The scale and depth of destruction inflicted on the city by state power remains almost unimaginable to our eyes. During the Second World War, its population was reduced from 4.3 million to 2.8 million inhabitants. A mountain of rubble (an estimated 80 million cubic metres) was left behind by the utter destruction of one-fifth of total dwelling space and heavy damage to the remaining half. As fascism died and the red flag of victory was hoisted over the city, more than 100,000 women were gang-raped by Soviet soldiers. An estimated 10,000 victims and some of their families committed suicide. It was a Hobbesian city governed by the rule of each for themselves. In the version portrayed in Roberto Rossellini's classic neo-realist film, *Germania, Anno Zero* (1947), Berlin looked to some outsiders like a sterile non-city of shocked, indifferent zombies. Law-abiding citizens were meanwhile turned into looters of shops and storerooms. As markets gave way to plunder and bartering, it was each and every civilian for themselves: a stick of dry sausage for a loaf of bread, a torch battery for a bottle of schnapps.

When looking back on these events, the sad conclusion is obvious: Berlin is a piteous city. Berliners have lived like guinea pigs through both the rapid growth and the violent destruction of the institutions of civil society, several times over. In today's Berlin, the ghosts of these experiments have been left behind in abundance, like Hitler's buried and unmarked bunker or the line of bricks in the road that marks the route of the Berlin Wall through Potsdamerplatz. Yet – despite everything – Berlin is today rebuilding itself. It is becoming a great European city with a vibrant civil society protected by parliamentary government and the rule of law. Thanks to the geopolitical and socio-economic successes of the Federal Republic, Berliners now enjoy a vibrant civil society, which nevertheless has strong, shared memories of every imaginable trajectory of the contradictory experiences that we now call 'modern' (Kocka 1979; Wehler 2001). It is probable that Simmel would have been left speechless by the strange brew of triumphs and tragedies. The lives of Berliners have been shaped by religious struggles and by the growth of industrial and consumer markets linked to worldwide trade. They have witnessed the projection of rural idylls and intense ecological awareness; after 1800, Berlin was even known as the 'City of Romanticism', thanks to the writings of aristocratic-bourgeois rebels such as Tieck, Kleist and Arnim. Berlin established itself as the home of the *flâneur*, as a great metropolis with enough street life, galleries, museums, opera houses, restaurants, theatres, cinemas, bars and cafes – an invention of the nobility, perfected by middle-class taste – to last anybody a whole lifetime. It has been a city blighted by pauperization and by the rapid growth, following the industrialization of the 1860s, of a distinctive and no-nonsense proletarian culture. It is the city that witnessed the aestheticization of politics and violence in the laboratories of fascism – a development captured in Alexander Döblin's great novel, *Berlin Alexanderplatz*. It has experienced the death of fascism, by force of arms. It is a city that has been defined by grand architecture in styles ranging from Schinkel's neoclassicism and art nouveau through to the handsome, tree-lined Unter den Linden and the present-day commercial glitz symbolized by the glass temples of Potsdamer Platz. Berlin is a city in which high bourgeois politeness and proletarian good humour have simultaneously flourished, at various times. It is a city that has spawned terrible incivility; witnessed organized rape and cold-blooded murder by uniformed troops; and suffered under total war that virtually destroyed the local civil society and left the city in chaos.

Part of the strange appeal of today's Berlin to its citizens and strangers alike lies in its contradictoriness. A sickly song from the post-1945 years repeats the cliché that Berlin is still Berlin, but the truth is that the city is changing itself faster than any other European city, and in ways that ensure that Berlin is never quite at one with itself. The city that was once physically wrecked by war and scarred by partition now feels like a place where 1989 is mere history and pre-1939 just archaeology, or almost so. The Reichstag building, topped by Norman Foster's glass dome, sports not only the words 'To the German People' but also, behind glass panels, samples of the angry and obscene graffiti scrawled by invading Red Army soldiers. Just around the corner stands a cluster of private banks, including Frank Gehry's DG Bank building, together with the pastiche bourgeois atmosphere of the city's most expensive hotel, the copper-roofed Adlon. Proof positive of the power of private capital in shaping the local civil society is further evident in the rejuvenated Friedrichstrasse, stuffed with arcades and galleries and designer shops that mask the fact that Berlin has the lowest per capita income of any major city in Germany. Meanwhile, opposite Berlin's central park, the Tiergarten, stands not only the Brandenburg Gate, a historical symbol of public freedom and joy, but also a new memorial to the murdered Jews of Europe. Not far away is Daniel

Libeskind's Jewish Museum, whose complex but visceral narrative of signs and spaces, including the Stair of Continuity, which in essence leads nowhere, defies simple expectations of victimhood, which seems right and proper for a city with the fastest-growing Jewish community in Europe.

The push–pull spirit of contradictoriness of Berlin's civil society – an invigorating, in-the-face civil society with many different faces – makes its presence felt in *Civil Society: Berlin Perspectives*. Drawing upon a great volume of scholarship that is directly or indirectly traceable to Hegel and Simmel, its contributors treat the subject of civil society with a sophisticated sense of nuance that comes from both historical wisdom and the experience of living in a city that has seen it all. *Civil Society: Berlin Perspectives* certainly bears the birthmarks of the city. It presents, for the first time in English, a sample of the best, recently written essays on the subject of contemporary civil societies produced by scholars who were born in Berlin or currently live in Berlin, or who have had a long-standing relationship with the city. Their contributions are bound together by a strong preoccupation with contemporary civil societies, their structural problems and their uncertain future. Guided by the symbolic connection between cities and the rise and decline of civil societies under modern conditions, the book aims to introduce readers to the kind of innovative work that is currently being done in the city of Berlin. Some of the contributors are well-established scholars who enjoy a wide reputation outside Germany; others are young scholars whose work is locally celebrated and likely to become known elsewhere in the coming years. The contributions have a path-breaking feel about them: for the first time in the history of modern civil society discussions, a city is represented intellectually as worthy of attention by others. Individual contributions cross-refer to each other – some of them were written by scholars who work together closely – and in their own particular ways all of them strain to situate and to bind their concerns and to present them as exemplars of the outstanding scholarship that is earning contemporary Berlin a – deserved – reputation as a vibrant and exciting city.

The book is deliberately varied in style, discipline and content – in this it mirrors the dynamism and heterogeneity of Berlin itself – but it might be described as a paean to G.W.F. Hegel. It is bound together by a single concern: to keep alive and to nurture the discourse of what was once called *bürgerliche Gesellschaft* and is now called *Zivilgesellschaft* – an old eighteenth-century word that was re-minted in the oppositional scene of West Berlin in the early 1970s. Jürgen Kocka's opening reflections on the changing historical meanings and uses of the category of civil society usefully introduce a range of key propositions in need of further research. He points out that in the Federal Republic of Germany, whose current Chancellor has even spoken of the importance of civil society, the term enjoys considerable popularity, as it does elsewhere around the world.

With the wisdom befitting a distinguished social historian, Kocka cautions against simple-minded definitions of the term. He points to the great temporal and spatial variations of its meaning, and he notes the wide variety of social agents who have spoken its language and defended its institutions. In Poland, during the nineteenth century, there was a close connection between civil society and parts of the gentry. In France and Britain, the conjoining of the gentry and middle classes ensured that civil society institutions enjoyed broader social foundations. In Russia, prior to the First World War, civil society institutions were far weaker, due to the political isolation of the urban middle classes, in whose petit bourgeois strata the norms of civil society nevertheless enjoyed support, especially in local urban politics. Meanwhile, in Germany, Kocka points out that from the end of the eighteenth century the project of nurturing a civil society (*bürgerliche Gesellschaft* or *Bürgergesellschaft*) was firmly in the hands of the *Bürgertum*, made up of industrialists, bankers, academically educated civil servants, professors, teachers, lawyers and journalists. Parts of this social class subsequently turned their back on civil society, although today, Kocka emphasizes, the social patterns of identification with civil society have broadened to the point where civil society institutions and norms enjoy something of a post-class popularity.

Such popularity makes it incumbent upon social scientists and others to exercise care when wielding the term for either normative or analytical-descriptive purposes. In Kocka's hands, the concept of civil society refers to a historically specific mode of social action that is structured by a cluster of interdependent rules, including individual independence and collective social self-organization, the suspicion of state spoon-feeding and 'governmentality', the open and non-violent recognition of plurality, difference, conflict and compromise, and actors' public preoccupation with various and conflicting opinions of the 'common good'. Kocka emphasizes that social action marked by these rules is never fully actualized, that civil society stands for something like 'a comprehensive project' with utopian qualities. The fact and vision of a civil society stand in opposition to unbridled capitalism, to an all-permeating state control, to violence, even to the mentality ingrained in Lenin's remark that trust is good, but control is better.

Kocka is aware that, when civil society is seen in this way, 'boundary' questions arise. The relationships between civil society and households and markets, for instance, become contingent and contestable. Calling for further comparative research, Kocka offers the example of the tension between markets and civil societies. Cross-national historical comparisons show that during the early modern period there were many parallels between the two sets of institutions. The successful emergence of market economies was conditional upon the trust and social capital produced by civil societies, while (conversely) the market de-concentration of capital investment, production and exchange proved vital for the formation and nurturing of civil society institutions. Kocka admits that there are forms of capitalism and capitalist ventures – today's global finance capitalism, for instance – that are parasitic upon the tissues of civil society, and even threatening of its health and strength. But that is not to say that civil society and the market are contradictory opposites. It is better to say that their relationship is complex and ambivalent, as present-day controversies about 'corporate citizenship' show. 'Not every form of patronage by wealthy individuals should be celebrated as civil society engagement,' says Kocka. 'But conversely, it would be just as false to dismiss every case of "corporate citizenship" as a mere manifestation of purely individual interests veiled in ideology.'

Susanne-Sophia Spiliotis takes up this point. She raises theoretically interesting and politically important questions about the function of shared wealth and shared memories in civil societies. Within these societies, she points out, stocks of memories are continually fixed and unfixed, on a more or less openly contested basis. In a complex and power-ridden world containing an infinite number of items potentially to be remembered, the trouble is not only that these social memories are always selective; it is, rather, that within civil societies there is constantly the danger that awareness of present-day or recent injustices will fade into the mists of time and so be forgotten by all but a few who are burdened by the pains of memory. So-called 'facts' do not survive because they are 'facts'; whether or not details of events that happened are themselves remembered is entirely contingent upon active efforts by governments, journalists, historians and other civic actors to keep alive memories of these events.

Spiliotis notes the growing role of historical themes in recent public life, but she points out that for the most part the political process of coming to terms with past injustices – what she calls 'justice in time' – has been heavily guided, sometimes controlled by states. The examples are familiar to our world: official state-led apologies for deeds done or not done; government-organized truth and reconciliation commissions; and compensation packages for the victims of state policies. Spiliotis contends that the 1999 German Business Foundation Initiative for the compensation of former forced and slave labourers during the Nazi regime is an important recent exception to this trend. The Initiative breaks the rule that corporations only admit of their wrongs when dragged before state courts. It provides – Spiliotis claims – a pacesetting example of the tendency of some business corporations to see themselves as publicly responsible actors *within* civil society. Launched by companies such as Siemens, DaimlerChrysler, Commerzbank, Bayer and Robert Bosch, the Initiative eventually attracted support from only a small minority of private German companies. Its material and symbolic significance has nevertheless been important, Spiliotis emphasizes. Compensation payments have been made to more than 1.5 million former forced and slave labourers. A so-called Future Fund has also been established in support of projects whose aim is to nurture human rights, global understanding and democracy. Overall, the Initiative has drawn attention to hard questions about corporate responsibility for past injustices – thereby helping to lay the foundations for a 'corporate civil society' in which companies abide by the best normative rules of *civility* backed by social freedom and equality.

Paul Nolte expresses – sympathetically – doubts about the viability of corporate definitions of civil society. Drawing especially upon nineteenth- and twentieth-century German historical experiences, he points to the tense relationship between the originally 'bourgeois' institutions of civil society and the normative ideal of social equality. Symptomatic of this tension is the long modern history of claims that either recognize or assert that a functioning civil society requires a measure of social inequality. One version of this is the Marxian condemnation of *bürgerliche Gesellschaft* as fundamentally a class-divided society that produces class domination. In the Scottish Enlightenment, Adam Smith and others had earlier noted the same problem: market societies can only become 'civil societies' if and when they cultivate norms of politeness and moral improvement through policies of charity and welfare towards the poor. The experience of fascism negatively confirmed the same tension: the political effort to eliminate class-based inequality, along with the 'Other' defined in racial, religious and other grounds – the quest for a *Volksgemeinschaft* – in practice resulted in the violent destruction of civil society.

Nolte tries to break new ground, at first by contextualizing the modern history of social inequality. He is particularly concerned with the manner in which the widespread 'nervousness' produced by the class inequalities and conflicts of the Weimar Republic enabled Nazism to attract support by promising that that society would be 'levelled' and 'pacified', and with how the hollowing out and destruction of civil society was consolidated by the Party-dominated state of East Germany and repaired only slowly, and with great difficulty, through several crises, in the Federal Republic. Nolte points out that the recent renaissance of civil society has been accompanied by new forms of social inequality defined by new class structures, structural unemployment, 'underclass' poverty and the cultural segregation of southern European, Turkish and other immigrants. That is why, according to Nolte, Germany is today on the cusp of a new debate on the social foundations of civil society. There is much talk of the importance of 'civic spirit' and 'social capital' – and of poverty, exclusion and social inequality. It is against this backdrop that Nolte poses some difficult questions. Can social inequality within a civil society be reduced without destroying its best civil society qualities? Can the concept of social inequality combine the principles of recognition and redistribution by reaching beyond matters of class to include other inequalities based (for instance) on gender difference and ethnic, cultural and religious differentiation? If individualization is an indispensable prerequisite of civil society, then how can it be channelled towards the cultivation of 'trust', 'justice', 'responsibility' and other civil society virtues? And in intellectual and policy terms – Hegel's question – what does it mean to overcome egoism, hedonistic consumerism and the ethos of '*Ich-AG*' (roughly, 'Me Inc.') by developing social bonding forces or 'ligatures'?

During a period of intense restructuring of the Keynesian welfare state in Germany, Herfried Münkler also considers whether civil society institutions can play a vital strategic and normative role. He warns against instrumental or opportunistic uses of the language of civil society by politicians and other policymakers; and – against wishful thinkers – he doubts whether policies geared to strengthening civil society somehow automatically produce social and political tranquillity. The contemporary significance of civil society lies elsewhere: it promises (in theory) that positive effects can result from the recognition that state institutions cannot and should not fully control and integrate the political order. From a neo-republican perspective, Münkler views the subject of civil society as up for grabs, politically speaking. 'The political crisis within the Left and the semantic success of civil society are two sides of the same coin.' While drawing attention to the political dangers linked to the overuse and abuse of the term, he proposes that a politics of civil society can draw attention to the fact that market mechanisms produce social dysfunctions, and that the best antidote to both these social dysfunctions and governmental sclerosis is the 'willingness of citizens to display social solidarity and political engagement'. Münkler is interested in the 'active' or 'competent' citizen, in the politically aware actor endowed with a capacity for making political judgements in the company of others – or what the classical republican tradition called the 'good citizen'. He asks difficult questions about the social and legal preconditions of citizenship. He agrees with those who insist that citizenship cannot be viewed as a 'natural' or ontologically given substratum of a political community. When civic engagement is considered as a political resource, he also agrees with those who say that it is fragile and potentially narcissistic; civic action can indeed lapse into single-issue or 'not in my backyard' concerns. Yet he goes on to challenge the well-known theory of Ernst Wolfgang Böckenforde that civic spirit resembles a stock of food that is easily consumed by the organs of government, but is not easily replenished (Böckenforde 1976: 112ff.). Münkler sees that civic spirit can be nurtured for the good of all citizens of a political community. He insists that serious efforts to trim down state power without at the same time reducing social security cannot succeed unless citizens are encouraged, perhaps even required, to busy themselves in civic affairs, within the social spaces of civil society. Whether or not its cultivation should be a citizen's *duty* – in the form of a compulsory social year for both young men and women, for instance – is a question he raises, without answering. He instead takes the example of locally based, social welfare initiatives that are controlled neither by state power nor by the profit-centred rules of market competition. So long as they are protected by welfare state arrangements and market economy solutions, such initiatives can transform 'administered solidarity' and 'legal regulations' into 'real, experienced solidarity'. They can generate 'a common good orientation and civic spirit', which in turn can serve to complement the representative mechanisms of political democracy with new sites of participation – thus acting as a brake on the well-known dangers of populism, a constant companion of democratic orders.

Münkler's concern for the nurturing of civic spirit for the good of all citizens of a political community inevitably raises questions about the wellsprings of such 'community spirit'. Concentrating on the German case, Hans Joas and Frank Adloff cast doubt on those pessimistic 'communitarian' critics who lament the decline of community and community spirit. Joas and Adloff begin by reciting the findings of surveys of German citizens' involvement in civil associations such as clubs and societies, religious communities and informal networks, self-help groups and social movements. The aggregate figures show no overall decrease of 'social capital'; somewhere between 300,000 and 500,000 informal and private-law organizations currently exist in German today. Yet, when the figures are analysed more carefully, a different picture emerges. Participation in civil associations is strongly correlated with higher income, religious commitment, formal educational qualifications and midlife (the years between 30 and 59). One consequence is that participation 'holes' have opened up in zones of high unemployment and among people with low income and low education. It also seems likely that non-governmental advocate groups are no longer membership organizations that are locally entrenched (as was true historically, say, for the labour movement or the Catholic church). Times have changed. These groups are increasingly led by professionals and highly educated experts, who pay more attention to media coverage than to the cultivation of active membership.

Such trends prompt the suspicion, for the case of Germany, that the civil and citizens' society (*Bürgergesellschaft*) is a middle-class affair. Joas and Adloff resist this conclusion. Drawing on the concept of 'social milieu' first used by Émile Durkheim, they are concerned to map the dynamic formation of everyday social nests within which social actors weave together and make sense of their lives, using the many branches and sticks of intersecting and overlapping social traditions. They note all sorts of contemporary trends in the everyday life of German citizens: the de-proletarianization of labour due to such trends as the doubling of the real wages of West German workers during the years between 1950 and 1965; the abolition of traditional Prussian conservatism by the Sovietization of its power base in the East Elbian estates; the widening access of young people to university life; the decline of church attendance and the intensification of religiosity in some circles; the rapid regrowth of Jewish communities; and the growth of new social milieux associated with the new social movements and the Green Party. From these observations, Joas and Adloff extract the conclusion that while traditional social milieux have undergone considerable disintegration, the trend is by no means a one-way street. The forces of trade union membership, church attendance and involvement in political parties have indeed waned. But Christian communities, conservative traditions and working-class organizations remain very much alive. New immigrant communities – based on language, ethnicity and religion – have mushroomed on German soil. There are signs as well of the spread of self-reflexive, self-determining behaviour, especially among the young. Considered together, these trends not only raise questions about how surviving social milieux can be stabilized and bridges built among them. They prompt a much more difficult but politically vital question: under conditions of growing social diversity, how can value commitments to particular social milieux become more self-reflexive and more modest – more respectful of their own and each other's particularity – without losing their intensity?

This question poses another, darker query: if civil societies comprise a kaleidoscope of different and potentially irritable social milieux, then how can they retain their civility? The topic of civility is at the centre of the contribution of Sven Reichardt, who explores in fresh ways, by means of fresh questions, the complex historical relationships between violence and civil societies, past and present. He casts doubt upon excessively normative and positive appraisals of life in civil societies as we have so far known them. He does so by pointing to their historical affinities with violence, understood as any act of unwanted interference with the bodies of others such that it causes them mental and/or bodily harm. Civil societies generate different and sometimes opposed life plans, and therefore a multiplicity of conflicts. Reichardt also shows that violence has been stripped of its violent appearance: victims can be defined and denigrated as 'rude' or 'barbaric'; violence itself can be camouflaged using terms such as 'education', 'reform' or 'improvement'; and violence can be judged a necessary, if unpleasant, means for the nurturing and protection of political democracy and a free and equal civil society. Seen together in this way, civil societies have so far failed to live up to their promise of non-violence. Reichardt argues that it is therefore important not to exoticize and trivialize violence as some kind of prehistoric relic, say, from the days before 'civilized' democracy took root. He cites Claus Offe's interpretation of the twentieth century's barbarity as 'post-civilized barbarity' (Offe 1996), and goes on to define several problem areas of research that need further attention.

Most familiar is the problematic historical relationship between civil societies and the modern territorial state's monopoly of the means of violence. Although 'sovereign' states are supposed to be the precondition of peaceful order in civil society, it turns out that the relationship is fraught. Reichardt shows that the history of public lynching in the United States shows what can happen when the state does not exercise a monopoly of the means of violence. But the inverse relationship has also applied: as the experience of military dictatorships in Latin America and totalitarianism in Europe has shown, territorial states have a bad record in the defence of civil societies. Drawing on the path-breaking work of Ute Frevert (2001), Reichardt illustrates the point with reference to conscription in the German *Kaiserreich*. In line with the principle of (male) equality in arms, conscription injected civil society with militaristic virtues, such as the willingness to use lethal weapons, to obey the principles of violent command, to overcome the fear of death. The ideal of peaceful civic engagement was distorted and thrown off balance by a form of 'social militarism' that came equipped with a gun and a penis. War has exacerbated these tensions between civil societies and their states. There are recorded cases where the mass mobilization dictated by total war proved to be the catalyst of the democratization of civil society, for instance, through the extension of the franchise, the strengthening of civil rights and social insurance innovations. But war has equally dealt death blows to civil societies – quite literally, as in the 1918–45 period, when worldwide only a handful of functioning civil societies and political democracies survived. Reichardt also shows that the extension of hard-won democratic rights to organize and to agitate was not always synonymous with 'civil disobedience' and peaceful self-organization. Sometimes – as happened in quite a number of civil societies after the First World War – democratization turned out to be a precondition of violent mass movements and the rise of authoritarian populist politics. Democracy enabled the self-brutalization of civil society by spawning the growth – as happened in Italy and Weimar Germany – to a politics of *vivere pericolosamente*, which saw itself as pitted against the 'ponderous reformism' and bureaucratic boredom of parliamentary government. Something of the same tension is evident in the apparent flourishing of terrorist violence in democratic civil societies. Reichardt asks whether there is empirical evidence that guaranteed basic rights to freedom provide fertile soil for terrorist acts, and whether it could be that the peacefulness of violence-sensitive civil societies makes them equally sensitive to media coverage of terrorist threats and actions, which have a strongly 'communicative' function, in that they serve as warnings from the terrorists to the whole civil society that its peaceful routines can easily be disrupted.

On balance, Reichardt's historically informed reflections on violence and civil society draw some paradoxical conclusions: violence is not merely the normative antithesis of civility and civil society. There have been times when violence has served as a functional prerequisite, sometimes unintended, of the emergence of civil societies: as when violent protests kick-started the defence and/or elaboration of civil freedoms; when the call to arms reinforces the promise of political participation and social self-organization; or when civil society institutions are renewed by the experience of violent catastrophes, as was the case in the early years of the Federal Republic of Germany.

Claus Offe considers the intriguing possibility that the deep winter of European violence may have helped prepare the way for a recent springtime of civil society institutions that have begun to spread across state borders, to form something like a European civil society. His consideration of whether a *European* civil society is thinkable and possible is as path-breaking as it is controversial. Offe points out one unique feature of the civilization that is called Europe: that its history is marked simultaneously by the worst political crimes and the most elaborate standards for institutionally condemning those crimes. Among the key mechanisms of self-critical scrutiny is the institutional division between society and state; through time this division has been designed to guarantee that states earn their entitlement and privilege to govern their citizens and guarantee their social security and social entitlements by exercising such political powers as the right to extract taxation, to educate the young and to wield the (threat of) violence of the police and army.

Offe is especially interested in dysfunctional cases or 'disarticulations' of the state-society relationship. Historical examples include the collapse of regimes (such as the Soviet Union) that have eroded the foundations of their social support; cases, like the former Yugoslavia, where deep social divisions based on ethno-national, linguistic or historical cleavages wreck the governing ability of state institutions; and regimes that are paralysed when their geographical scope becomes too great because of (say) political takeovers and military conquests. The current long-term experiment in European integration is potentially an example of this last-mentioned case, or so Offe claims. Watched by important parts of the world, Europeans are attempting to do something never before achieved in Europe: to apply to itself 'the logic of the circular creation of state and society that shaped the modern history of European countries'.

Offe's contribution here brings into play the problem-spotting perspective for which his work has justly become famous during the past three decades. He does not investigate the growing evidence that a number of interconnected *non-governmental* processes – such as the Europeanization of telecommunications, markets, sports competitions and city life – seem to be nurturing the growth of cross-border social relations. He instead emphasizes the lack of 'stateness' of the emerging European polity, in particular the deep tensions between its member states and its supranational political and legal institutions. The cluster of institutions known as the European Union is so far not well equipped to make, enforce and adjudicate the types of political rule exercised by territorial states. In contrast to earlier times, in which (for instance) the leaders of the Italian *risorgimento* boasted that after making Italy they would proceed to make Italians, the European Union is incapable of acting as if it were a state capable of making Europeans. Until now, says Offe, '"Brussels" lacks the capacities that have played a critical role in the formation of the societies of nation states, namely the capacity to impose military conscription and action, to impose educational standards and curricular powers, and to directly extract taxes from (what only then would be) a "European people".'

Meanwhile, the prospects for developing a European-wide 'society' are correspondingly dim, Offe claims. There is no European idiom and no European-wide public sphere sustained by Europe-wide communication media and audiences. If societies can be partly understood as products of state-sponsored civility, then the European project faces an uphill struggle to ward off the incivilities that are likely to result from tensions produced by such factors as job losses, uneven prosperity and structural unemployment. Most of all, the grip of nationhood upon the various peoples of the region is strong. States in Europe have helped create their own societies – their own *demos* – by imposing not only strictly defined territorial borders. They have also imposed their own judicial, economic, religious, pedagogic and other rules upon pre-existing patchwork quilts of local and regional cultures and political units, such as cities, kingdoms and principalities. Within the European project, in contrast, no formula currently exists for removing the sting from conflicting senses of nationhood by alternative or hybrid identities. Hence the inference: for the time being, the vision of a 'European society' remains utopian.

If that is so, then what are the chances of the successful formation of civil society relations that stretch beyond the borders of Europe, perhaps to the four corners of the planet? Dieter Rucht answers: the new phase of globalization of markets presently championed by neoliberal governments has generated a backlash of social protest organized on a global scale. Rucht points out that, while this process did not begin with the 'Battle for Seattle' in December 1999 – over a decade earlier, on the streets of West Berlin, 80,000 people had demonstrated against the policies of the World Bank and the IMF – the events in Seattle gave a big boost to the rebirth of civic actions that tend to grow into social movements, on a global scale. Not only did the protests bring the meeting to an undignified halt after more than 50,000 demonstrators mounted blockades and publicly criticized transnational corporations, 'corporate censorship' and global consumerism in the streets. Not only, in addition, did the protests raise more specific global concerns, like the protection of rainforests, job losses, the need for cheaper AIDS drugs, bans on genetically modified food and concerns about the destruction of biodiversity, symbolized by dying turtles trapped in commercial shrimp nets. The ultimate achievement of the Seattle protests symbolized something bigger: it signalled the birth of a (misnamed) 'anti-globalization movement'.

Rucht emphasizes that these movements should not be thought of as (coalescing into) one big, world movement. There is in fact a wide variety of such movements, whose activists specialize in publicizing their experiences and applying their campaigning skills in particular policy areas as diverse as sexual politics, trade rules, religiosity, corporate power, post-war reconstruction, clean water, education and human rights. The targets of these movements are equally variable: they take aim at a whole spectrum of opponents and potential allies, from local institutions that have global effects to global institutions that have local effects. The spectrum of political loyalties within these movements is also very broad, ranging from deep-green ecologists to Christian pacifists, social democrats, Muslim activists, Buddhist meditators and anarcho-syndicalists. Their participants, contrary to some prevailing stereotypes, are not all rich, middle-class, Northern kids. Calculated by numbers alone, activists from the South tend to be in the ascendancy. The inner architecture of these movements is also complex and marked by a variable geometry. Most of their sympathizers and supporters are part-time. Full-time activists and professional workers are in a definite minority within the movements, which have no globally recognized spokesperson or leader or secretariat, and for that reason do not speak in one voice, with one point of view.

Rucht points out that *simulated* unity momentarily appears during organized public protests: for instance, in the Intercontinental Caravan 99, a tour through North America and Europe by nearly 400 activists, from Nepal, India, Mexico, Bangladesh and Brazil, campaigning on behalf of fishermen and farmers threatened by the aggressive marketing of pesticides, genetically modified seeds and neoliberal policies. The same unity was evident in the successful alliance between the Uganda Debt Network and the Jubilee 2000 debt relief campaign, and in the remarkably self-disciplined and peaceful gathering of 500,000 protesters in Barcelona during a European Union summit in the spring of 2002. Such unity is *exceptional* and *mobilized*: it always rests upon months or even years of hard planning, preparatory meetings, seminars and teachings. And in every case it draws upon movements that have strongly decentralized, constantly evolving, kaleidoscopic structures. The global movements comprise a clutter of intersecting forms: face-to-face encounters, spider-web-like networks, pyramid-shaped organizations, hub-and-spoke structures, bridges and organizational chains, charismatic personalities. Action takes place at multiple levels – from the micro-local through to the macro-global – and sometimes movement organizations create vertical alliances for the purpose of communication and synchronization. The well-known nodal organizations of these movements – the Global Action Project, Earthwatch, WEED (World Economy, Ecology and Development), Jubilee 2000 – display a remarkable awareness of the need for striking a balance between common and particular concerns by means of a variety of decentralized, non-hierarchical and yet coordinated initiatives. Using advanced means of communication – such as the reliance upon the Internet by the Mexican Zapatistas in their global campaign for human rights – these nodal organizations are typically in touch, on a horizontal and spreadeagled basis, with many other initiatives and groups, which are themselves in touch with other initiatives, groups and individuals. Sometimes, as in the global campaign against landmines, conscious efforts to build a 'network of networks' prove to be a vital condition of campaigning success. Because these acephalous social movements are marked by hyper-complexity, some organizations concentrate on the task of heightening the movements' self-conscious commitments to networked and coordinated pluralism. They specialize in spreading the medium, not just the message – by encouraging others to embrace the techniques of participatory research, sophisticated policy analysis and continuous organizational learning. Rucht points out that the Association for the Taxation of Financial Transactions for the Aid of Citizens (ATTAC) similarly understands itself as a global platform for pluralism in support of the taxation of stock market transactions. And at the front line of action, some networked, semi-professional groups, like the Wombles and the Ruckus Society, operate facilities for training groups and individuals in the arts of non-violent direct action and civil disobedience.

Although these various self-organizing efforts do not (and cannot) overcome the heterogeneity of the movements, Rucht argues that it is important to see that they have more in common than their variable architecture. These movements are marked by a cross-border mentality. It is highly misleading to dub them 'anti-globalization movements', if only because each assumes the form of links and chains of non-governmental solidarity and contestation spanning vast spaces stretching to the four corners of the earth. Their participants, most of whom are part-time sympathizers and not full-time activists, do not see their concerns as restricted within a strictly bounded community or locality.

They are convinced that toxic chemicals, human rights, debt relief and compassion for those whose dignity has been violated know no borders. For them the world is one world. So they nurture their identities and publicize their concerns in what has been called 'translocalities', as if they were global citizens. They think of themselves as building cross-border cooperation in a variety of ways among a variety of potential supporters around a variety of shared goals, including efforts to apply the emergency brake (as in anti-nuclear protest and debt relief) and to effect positive social changes in the lives of women and men, regardless of where they are living on the face of the earth. In the name of inclusive forms of globalization, movement activists take advantage of global communication networks. They share technical and strategic information, coordinate parallel activities and plan joint actions, often by putting direct pressure on governmental institutions and corporate actors – and by risking tear gas, baton charges, bullets and criminal proceedings – under the halogen lamps of media publicity. In this way, Rucht concludes, the social movements pose a brand new question: can the ideals of civil society and democracy, once thought to be a utopian dream incapable of realization at the nation-state level, be extended to global institutions?

In the penultimate contribution, Shalini Randeria deals with the fundamental objection that the present-day language of civil society speaks with a Western accent. As we have seen, the development of long-distance social relations, of the kind fostered by towns and cities in Europe, had the effect of spreading the norms and institutions that would later be named civil society in the modern sense. Yet even a cursory glance at the historical record shows that this diffusion of the institutions and language of civil society everywhere encountered resistance – sometimes (as in parts of the East African mainland, during the Christian missions of the 1840s (Curtin 2000: chap. 7) armed hostility, followed by a fight to the death. Such resistance has led some critics to conclude that 'civil society' is not just a geographically specific concept with pseudo-universal pretensions; they are convinced as well that it has a strong elective affinity with 'the West', and even potentially plays the role of an agent of Western power and influence in the world.

Might talk of a civil society, even a *global* civil society, be a wooden horse of European domination? Are there indeed good reasons 'to send back the concept of civil society to where … it properly belongs – the provincialism of European social philosophy' (Chatterjee 1990)? Given the *prima facie* evidence, the suspicion that the language of civil society is mixed up in the nasty businesses of hubris and blood has to be taken seriously, and Randeria is certainly aware that any contemporary use of the phrase needs to be highly sensitive to what is conceptually and politically at stake. Sensitivity presupposes and requires clean hands. For one of the bitter truths lurking within the contemporary popularity of the language of civil society is the fact that European talk of civil society originally presupposed and required the disempowerment or outright crushing of others elsewhere in the world. Hence the commonplace contrast drawn by early modern advocates of civil society between 'civil society' and 'the Asiatic' region, in which, or so it was said, civil societies had manifestly failed to appear. 'Among the Hindus, according to the Asiatic model,' wrote James Mill with India in mind, 'the government was monarchical, and, with the usual exception of religion and its ministers, absolute. No idea of any system of rule, different from the will of a single person, appears to have entered the minds of them or their legislators' (Mill 1817, vol. 1: 122). Marx and Engels, who were otherwise no friends of modern civil society (*bürgerliche Gesellschaft*), similarly observed that in the East the 'first basic condition of bourgeois acquisition is lacking: the security of the person and the property of the trader' (Marx and Engels 1953: 40). And, along parallel lines, Tocqueville noted that, whereas in America the spirit of Christianity enabled the growth of a civil society and democratic institutions, the Muslim faith and manners had heaped materialism and fatalism onto its believers. The chronic decadence of Islam meant that 'the great violence of conquest' initially carried out by Europeans in countries like Algeria would need to be supplemented by 'smaller violences'. He considered that 'there have been few religions in the world as deadly to men as that of Mohammed', and he was sure that it was 'the principal cause of the decadence so visible today in the Muslim world'. Civil society was impossible in Muslim societies. Their pacification required a two-tier political order: a ruling group based on the principles of Christian civilization, and a ruled group of natives who would continue to live by the laws of the Koran (Tocqueville 1951: 69; Jardin 1988: 318).

According to Randeria, the friends of civil society must today be willing to ask tough questions of such views. They should also note a strange irony: an originally European way of life, some of whose members set out brutally to colonize the world in the name of a civil society, helped lay the foundations for its own universal appeal and, with that, strengthened civil resistance to colonizing forms of power and prejudice originally traceable to the European region. Proof positive of this trend, she argues, is the reception by scholars and activists alike of the idea and ideal of civil society in the Indian subcontinent. In recent years, this reception has been driven by renewed interest in indigenous traditions of civility, widespread disappointment with the post-colonial state, market reforms and the defence of civil and political rights against religious nationalism and authoritarian state policies.

Randeria points out that three different versions of the case for civil society vie for attention. The *traditionalist* approach criticizes state violence and calls for 'humane governance' based upon strengthened indigenous traditions of mutual aid and conflict resolution. Others reject this traditionalist approach as nostalgia for traditions that harbour inequality and individual unfreedom – and produce instability within modern institutions. These *modernist* critics prefer instead to reach a different understanding of civil society as a distinctively modern sphere of voluntary associations, some of them of colonial origin, that stand as buffer zones between the individual and governmental institutions. Constitutional democracy in India is seen to require a *modern* civil society: a plurality of secular and inclusive institutions that enjoy considerable autonomy from state power.

Some who are otherwise sympathetic to this modernist approach doubt its implied teleology: they point out that such 'civil-social' institutions are in short supply, that they are confined to well-to-do strata, and that this lack of modern civil associations in a society dominated by caste and religious ties is the key indicator of the post-colonial condition. Randeria questions this interpretation of post-colonialism in order to develop a third – *anthropological* – approach. It seeks to cut through the pre-colonial/post-colonial dualism by pointing to the ways in which castes and religious communities deserve to be included in any descriptive-analytical account of civil society. Randeria denies that castes and religious communities are (or were ever) describable as traditional 'organic bonds of kinship', as standard accounts of the tradition/modernity divide have supposed. She points out that the social groupings within pre-colonial India, castes included, were typically multiple, flexible and fluid, rather than rigid and exclusive in outlook. The Gujarati community of Mole-Salam Garasia Rajputs, which until recently assigned a Hindu and Muslim name to each one of its members, is an example of this dynamic heterogeneity, which evidently survived colonial conquest: in the 1911 census, nearly a quarter of a million Indians still described themselves as 'Mohammedan Hindus'.

Randeria acknowledges that colonial administration, which sought to map and control Indian society, was responsible for the refashioning of territorially defined castes into enumerated communities through bureaucratic definition: for the purposes of census classification and counting, employment in the colonial administration and the allocation of seats in representative bodies, colonial administrators twisted social identities like religion and caste (*samaj*, or society, in Gujarati) into political categories. Social ties that had been multiple, fluid and dynamic – 'fuzzy' – tended to become monolithic, enumerated and homogeneous. Randeria notes that these bureaucratic classifications had profound political and social effects, so that by the early decades of the twentieth century, caste organizations and communal parties were mobilizing to define and protect their interests on an India-wide basis. Yet she goes on to point out – against politically loaded, nationalist claims on behalf of a homogeneous Hindu majority – that, despite their ascriptive qualities, most lower castes, including the so-called 'untouchable castes', continue to be largely self-governing local collectivities. They enjoy a measure of self-conscious jurisdiction and authority over their members – a power that is often jealously guarded against state intrusions. Castes are far from being kinship groups with unalterable customs and procedures. Their assemblies (the *panchayat*), comprising all the adult members of a local caste unit (*paraganu*), are sites of deliberations about rules and the contestation of norms that are vital for maintaining the patterns of solidarity and belonging – and for resisting unwanted state intervention in such matters as the rules of marriage, divorce and remarriage, the exchange of food, and care arrangements for children.

Randeria points out that the European language of civil society first travelled to India during the nineteenth century. With the founding of the colonial state, the civil sphere – often not named as such – took the form of spaces of social life either untouched by colonial rulers or established through the resistance to their power by colonial subjects themselves. Randeria shows that the subsequent debates about civil society in India have come to interact with different European images of civil society, so highlighting not only their travelling potential but also the ways in which 'foreign' or 'imported' languages both resonate within local contexts and are often (heavily) refashioned as a result. They then become subject to 're-export', back to the context from which they originally came, in consequence of which the language of civil society is both *pluralized* and *globalized*. The impressive cooperation between the coalition called Narmada Bachao Andolan (formed in 1988) and international non-governmental organizations (INGOs) – like Oxfam and the Environment Defence Fund – in campaigns in support of the right of people *not* to be displaced by dam construction in western India illustrates what Randeria has in mind. The profound theoretical implication of her point should not be missed: *multiple*, *multi-dimensional* and *entangled* languages of civil society now contribute to the definition of the world in which we live. Contrary to other scholars, including Ernest Gellner (1994), Randeria's conclusion is that civil society is not a uniquely Western achievement.

In returning to the theme of Europe, Ralf Dahrendorf has the final word in this volume. Concentrating on the small handful of European intellectuals whose work can be said to be basic for the late twentieth-century revival of interest in civil society, he poses some disturbing questions: why did so many public intellectuals allow themselves to be seduced by totalitarianism? Why did they regard figures like Lenin, Mussolini, Stalin and Hitler as promising symbols of a new paradise on earth? And why were others – Norbert Bobbio, for instance – prepared, under pressure and for the purpose of furthering their careers, to do deals with totalitarians?

Dahrendorf tackles these questions in an unusual way, by examining the personal and intellectual trajectory of a small handful of 'dissident' intellectuals – figures such as Raymond Aron, Hannah Arendt, Karl Popper and Isaiah Berlin – who actively refused the temptations of totalitarian power. Dahrendorf notes that, despite various important differences of intellectual trajectory, these latter-day 'Erasmus intellectuals' shared at least four virtues. These virtues have a definite affinity with the project of creating and nurturing a civil society protected by open, publicly accountable government.

One such virtue was the propensity for playing the role of what Raymond Aron once called the 'engaged observer'. The Erasmians tried hard to be objective in Max Weber's sense. They openly declared their normative commitments in order better to describe, analyse and judge ideas, events and institutions, always with a strong measure of distance and with due regard to clashes between means and ends, between strategies and goals and among goals themselves. The engaged observers refused to be silenced: they spoke out and they wrote, and spoke out and wrote again, but they refused on principle to identify themselves with particular movements or organizations or to join political organizations. They followed the stricture of Erasmus of Rotterdam: 'I love freedom and I will not and cannot serve any party.' In this sense, the Erasmians were not characters suspended on a string of quiescent scepticism. Their opposition to totalitarianism was based on a second virtue: what Dahrendorf calls (deliberately using an oxymoron) 'the passion of reason'. The Erasmus intellectuals tried hard to combine their principled self-distancing from power with an unswerving, quietly passionate commitment to cool-headed disputation, counter-intuitive conjectures and an openness to intellectual disagreement and dissent.

The Erasmian friends of civil society were prepared to pay the price for their commitment to passionate reason and distanced observation, Dahrendorf observes. That they were willing and able to do so stemmed from their two other virtues. According to Dahrendorf, the friends of civil society displayed courage in isolation: the courage to stand up and be counted for the cause of freedom, even when it was clear that such courage would result in their solitary confinement in a life of marginal or miserable existence. The Erasmian friends of civil society not only risked irrelevance. Here a fourth virtue came into play: the intellectual opponents of totalitarianism also put their hands up for the principle of living with problems, dilemmas and contradictions. They were not just pluralists, philosophically and politically speaking. They cherished the civil coexistence of the incompatible, which is why, Dahrendorf concludes, their strong spirit of irony, combined with their commitments to objectivity, passionate reason and courage in isolation, remains publicly relevant in today's world – a world prone to longings to belong, to the lure of fundamentalist dogmas, like the worship of 'free markets' or the belief that one particular God is the Way, the Truth, and the Life.

Many people gave generously of their time and energy to this project, which has been prepared under the auspices of the European Commission-funded research project, European Civil Society Network (CiSoNet). Generous assistance with translation and editorial matters has been provided by several institutions, especially the Wissenschaftszentrum Berlin für Sozialforschung (WZB) and the Centre for the Study of Democracy (CSD), at the University of Westminster, London. At the WZB, special thanks are due to its Director, Professor Jürgen Kocka; Dr Georg Thurn, its Research Director; Allison Brown, for her translation of several contributions; and the administrative support and/or scholarly advice provided by Agnes Arndt, Nicola Fielk, Dieter Gosewinkel, Dieter Rucht and Susanne-Sophia Spiliotis. At CSD, special thanks are due to Dr Patrick Burke for his meticulous editorial work and advice on each contribution; and for the research assistance and administration provided by Joanna Llorente and especially Maria Fotou. I am also grateful for the support of many other researchers within CiSoNet; special thanks to Claus Offe, Vukašin Pavlović, Victor Pérez-Díaz, Milan Podunavac, Dragica Vujadinović, Peter Wagner and Björn Wittrock.

John Keane
London/Berlin
May 2005

References

Aron, Raymond. 1978. 'The Dawn of Universal History'. In *Politics and History. Selected Essays by Raymond Aron*, ed. Miriam Conant: 212–33. New York and London.

Blockmans, Wim. 1997. *A History of Power in Europe. People, Markets, States.* Antwerp.

Böckenforde, Ernst Wolfgang. 1976. *Staat, Gesellschaft, Freiheit. Studien zur Staatstheorie und zum Verfassungsrecht.* Frankfurt am Main.

Braudel, Fernand. 1981 *Civilization and Capitalism. 15th–18th Century.* Volume 1. London.

Chatterjee, Partha. 1990. 'A Response to Taylor's "Modes of Civil Society"'. *Public Culture* 3, 1 (Fall).

Colas, Dominique. 1992 *Le Glaive et le fléau: Généalogie du fanatisme et de la société civile.* Paris.

Collinson, Patrick. 2004. *The Reformation. A History.* New York.

Curtin, Phillip D. 2000. *The World and the West. The European Challenge and the Overseas Response in the Age of Empire.* Cambridge and New York.

De Vries, Jan. 1984. *European Urbanization, 1500–1800*. Cambridge, Mass.

Frevert, Ute. 2001. *Der kasernierte Nation. Militärdienst und Zivilgesellschaft in Deutschland*. Munich.

Gellner, Ernest. 1994. *Conditions of Liberty. Civil Society and Its Rivals*. London.

Gerteis, Klaus. 1986. *Die deutsche Städte in der Frühen Neuzeit: Zur Vorgeschichte der 'bürgerlichen Welt'*. Darmstadt.

Hegel, G.W.F. 1821 (1976). *Grundlinien der Philosophie des Rechts*. Frankfurt am Main.

———. 1831. *Über die englische Reformbill*. Berlin.

Hodgson, Marshall. 1974. *The Venture of Islam. Conscience and History in a World Civilization*. Chicago and London.

Hohenberg, Paul M. and Lees, Lynn Hollen. 1985. *The Making of Urban Europe, 1000–1950*. Cambridge, Mass.

Jardin, André. 1988. *Tocqueville: A Biography*. New York.

Keane, John. 1988 (reprinted 1998). 'Despotism and Democracy: The Origins and Development of the Distinction Between Civil Society and the State 1750–1850'. In *Civil Society and the State: New European Perspectives*, ed. John Keane: 25–72. London and New York.

———. 1998. *Democracy and Civil Society*. London.

———. 2003. *Global Civil Society?* Cambridge and New York.

Kocka, Jürgen. 1979. '1945: Neubeginn oder Restauration?' In *Wendepunkte deutscher Geschichte 1848–1945*, ed. Carola Stern and Heinrich August Winkler: 141–68. Frankfurt.

———. 1997. 'The Difficult Rise of a Civil Society: Societal History of Modern Germany'. In *German History since 1800*, ed. Mary Fulbrook: 493–511. London and New York.

Mackeney, Richard. 1989. *The City State, 1500–1700*. Atlantic Highlands, N.J.

Mamdani, Mahmood. 1996. *Citizen and Subject: Contemporary Africa and the Legacy of Late Colonialism*. Princeton.

Marx, Karl and Engels, Frederick. 1953. 'The Foreign Policy of Russian Czarism'. In *The Russian Menace in Europe*. London.

Mill, James. 1817. *The History of British India*. London.

Mundy, John H. and Riesenberg, Peter. 1958. *The Medieval Town*. Princeton NJ.

Offe, Claus. 1996. 'Moderne "Barbarei": Der Naturzustand im Kleinformat'. In *Modernität und Barbarei. Soziologische Zeitdiagnose am Ende des 20. Jahrhunderts*, ed. Max Miller and Hans-Georg Soeffner. Frankfurt am Main.

Peterson, M.J. 1992. 'Transnational Activity, International Society and World Politics'. *Millenium* 21, 3.

Simmel, Georg. 1903. 'Die Grosstadt und das Geistesleben'. In *Die Grosstadt. Jahrbuch der Gehe-Stiftung* 9.

———. 1918. *Lebensanschauung*. Munich and Leipzig.

———. 1965. 'The Nature of Philosophy'. In Georg Simmel, *Essays on Sociology, Philosophy and Aesthetics*. New York.

Tocqueville, Alexis de. 1951. *Oeuvres complètes*, ed. J.P. Mayer. Volume 9. Paris.

Weber, Max. 1978. 'The City (Non-Legitimate Domination)'. In Max Weber, *Economy and Society*. Berkeley, Los Angeles and London.

Wehler, Hans-Ulrich. 2001. 'Deutsches Bürgertum nach 1945: Exitus oder Phönix aus der Asche?' *Geschichte und Gesellschaft* 27: 617–34.

1

CIVIL SOCIETY IN HISTORICAL PERSPECTIVE

Jürgen Kocka

Scholarly terms, like journalistic terms, run their course. They emerge, spread sometimes like epidemics and are on everyone's lips before being pushed back to the margins and becoming outdated. In their heyday the terms fulfil many functions. In the sciences they are used to describe and analyse. In public discussion, like banners, they identify affiliations and their followers gather behind them and march into battle. The scholarly and journalistic functions of a term sometimes obstruct one another.

'Civil society', which has gained great popularity in the last fifteen years and is still used frequently, is one such term. What we call 'civil society' in English is *spoleczenstwo obywatelskie* in Polish, *shimin shakai* in Japanese and *Zivilgesellschaft* or *Bürgergesellschaft* in German. The meanings of these phrases are not identical in the different languages. And even the concept itself oscillates. It has been compared with a pudding that is impossible to nail to a wall.[1]

In order to be able to use the term for scholarly purposes, it is necessary to recall its history and retrace the configurations that have made it both ambiguous and attractive. I do this first. I then define the term; examine the relationship between, on the one hand, civil society and the market and, on the other, civil society and the state; and then discuss the actors in and the resources of civil society. My concluding comments deal with civil society in the nation state and in a transnational context. I do all this primarily with regard to central Europe, including Germany, but I also make comparisons with western and eastern Europe, from England to Russia.

Begriffsgeschichte (History of the Concept)

The term 'civil society' has a long history: it can be traced back to *societas civilis* in the Aristotelian tradition. For centuries it has been a central concept in European thought about politics and society. Its connotations have varied, but it has almost always dealt with social and political life beyond the domestic sphere of home and family. It has usually referred to issues of community beyond the purely particular: that is, to the general and the political. It is often normative and emphatic in nature.

The term *civil society, société civile, Zivilgesellschaft* or *Bürgergesellschaft* assumed its modern meaning in the seventeenth and eighteenth centuries, largely in the works of Enlightenment writers: John Locke, Adam Ferguson, Rousseau, Montesquieu, the Encyclopedists, Thomas Paine, Immanuel Kant, and many others.

'Civil society' had a positive connotation in the Enlightenment. The term stood for what at the time was a utopian project for a future civilization in which people would live together in peace as politically mature, responsible citizens: as private individuals in their families and as citizens in public. They would be independent and free, cooperating under the rule of law without being spoon-fed or repressed by an authoritarian state. There would be tolerance of cultural, religious and ethnic diversity but without great social inequality, and certainly without the traditional corporative (*ständische*) inequality on an ascriptive basis. 'Civil society' came to be defined in contrast to the state; at the time this largely meant the absolutist state. In other words, the idea of civil society was anti-absolutist. At the core of this anti-absolutist , anti-corporative 'plan' for a future society, culture and politics was the notion of social self-organization by individuals and groups. It was critical of tradition, utopian and way ahead of its time.

Under the influence of capitalism and industrialization, the definition changed in the first half of the nineteenth century – for example, in works by Hegel and Marx. 'Civil society' became even more clearly distinguished from the state. It became understood as a system of needs and work, of the market and particular interests, in the sense more of the 'middle-class (*bürgerliche*) society' of the bourgeoisie than of a 'civil society' made up of citizens (*Bürger*). In German the terms *Zivilgesellschaft* and *Bürgergesellschaft*, which traditionally had had a positive connotation, were superseded by the term *bürgerliche Gesellschaft*, which was used into the late twentieth century mostly in a critical and polemical way. The traditional, positive meaning was retained longer in English and French, for example by Tocqueville. On the whole, however, the term 'civil society' receded into the background in other languages as well, playing only a marginal role until roughly 1980 – with some exceptions, Gramsci among them.

Around 1980 the term 'civil society' experienced a dazzling comeback. It became a central concept in anti-dictatorial critique, especially in Central Eastern Europe – in Prague, Warsaw and Budapest, where dissidents such as Václav Havel, Bronisław Geremek, György Konrád and Iván Szelényi used the term to speak out against one-party dictatorships, Soviet hegemony and totalitarianism, and for freedom, pluralism and social autonomy. Corresponding movements could also be observed, in some cases even earlier, in Latin America and South Africa. The term is now used around the world – always with a positive connotation – in various political contexts, by political centrists and on the left, by liberals, communitarians and anti-globalization activists, as well as by social scientists such as John Keane, Ralf Dahrendorf, Charles Taylor and Jürgen Habermas. 'Civil society' has been translated back into German as *Zivilgesellschaft* in an attempt to avoid the critical, polemical meaning of 'bourgeois' that was associated with *'bürgerliche Gesellschaft'*.[2] Eighteenth-century ideas had evidently assumed new relevance at the close of the twentieth century. 'Civil society' became attractive again in the victorious struggle against dictatorships, the most egregious negation of civil society in the twentieth century.

But even in the non-dictatorial Western world, the term fits – then as now – into the general political, intellectual climate. First of all, it emphasizes social self-organization and individual responsibility, and thus reflects the widespread scepticism towards being spoon-fed by the state. Many believe that the interventionist welfare state, by regulating too much and thus becoming overburdened, is approaching its limits. Secondly, 'civil society,' as its use by today's anti-globalization movements demonstrates, promises an alternative to the unbridled capitalism developing successfully around the world. The term thus reflects a new kind of critique of capitalism, since the logic of civil society, characterized by discourse, conflict and agreement, promises different solutions from those of the logic of the market, which is based on competition, exchange and the optimization of individual benefits.

Finally, civic involvement and efforts to achieve common goals are an integral part of behaviour in civil society, no matter how differently the goals may be defined. In the highly individualized and partially fragmented societies of the late and post-industrial periods, 'civil society' promises an answer to the pressing question of what, if anything, holds these societies together. Like Anglo-American discourse on the 'third way', the debate about *Zivilgesellschaft* in Germany is about the need to redefine the relationships between politics, society and the market, and about the moral foundations of politics and the community.

This explains why the term is so attractive and highly charged in many public discussions today.

Two more points arise from this short historical survey of the term. First, from the outset the term 'civil society' has always simultaneously had normative and descriptive (or analytical) layers of meaning. This represents more of an opportunity than a burden. Secondly, the 'main opponents' of the term have changed over the course of time; or, rather, new opponents have appeared and their relative significance is constantly shifting; with these changes have come changes in the scope and nuances of the term's meaning. In the eighteenth century it would not have made much sense for Adam Smith and Adam Ferguson to weaken the prominence of the anti-absolutist and anti-corporative connotation of the term by strongly distinguishing civil society from the market economy, since the market was still establishing its position. On the contrary, the market, competition, capitalism, citizens by virtue of their participation in economic life: these were all allies. Consequently 'civil society' was not marked off from the economy conceptually (although Ferguson already distinguished between the two). Today, things are different. In view of the successful expansion of the capitalist market economy to the most remote regions of the world and into the most intimate corners of our private lives, the type of action specific to civil society is opposed not only to the all-controlling state but also to the all-permeating market. Accordingly, 'civil society' is now mostly distinguished and clearly set apart from the economy. In addition, the postmodern experience of extreme individualization and fragmentation is widespread today, whereas it was still rather marginal in the 1960s and 1970s. In reaction, the communitarian, cohesive and social aspects of civil society are stressed with new emphasis.

Definition

Against this backgroun, 'civil society' can be defined in three related ways: first, as a type of social action; secondly, as an area or sphere connected to but separate from economy, state and the private sphere; and, thirdly, as the core of a draft or project that still has some utopian features.

First, 'civil society' refers to a specific type of social action in contrast to others,[3] that is, to struggle and war, to exchange and market, to rule and obedience, and to the peculiarities of face-to-face relations dominant in private life. As a specific type of social action, 'civil society' is characterized by the fact that it (1) is oriented towards conflict, discourse, compromise, and understanding in public: civil society is realized in the public sphere; (2) stresses individual independence and collective self-organization; (3) recognizes plurality, difference and tension as legitimate; (4) operates non-violently; and (5) is related to general issues: it is frequently oriented towards something like the 'common good', even if different actors and groups usually have very different opinions about what constitutes the common good.

Civil society-type social action, defined in this way, is not totally absent from government administration and politics, and commercial businesses and their relationships with each other; nor is it completely absent from family and kinship relations either. To the extent that state organs and their officials, businesses and their personnel, and families and kinship relations take advantage of this type of social action, they should be seen as part of civil society. But other types (and logics) of social action predominate in these areas, namely, those of, respectively, political rule, the market and private life.

Civil society-type social action is truly dominant in a social area or space that can be distinguished in modern, differentiated societies from government, business and the private sphere – that is, the public space occupied by clubs, associations, social movements, networks and initiatives. This is why 'civil society' also refers to a *social sphere* that encompasses 'a complex and dynamic ensemble of legally protected non-governmental institutions that tend to be non-violent, self-organizing, self-reflexive, and permanently in tension with each other', a *social space* related to but distinguished from government, business and the private sphere.[4]

Finally, it is important to keep in mind that historical experience has shown that civil society as a type of social action as well as a sphere of social self-organization can be established lastingly only in a framework of changing economic, social, political and cultural conditions; these, in turn, will be reinforced by civil society. This is evident in the fact that civil society can often only be created in critical response to existing or impending conditions – an overly dominant or repressive state, or traditional forms of ascriptive inequality (see above); in resistance to being overwhelmed by the success of capitalism; and in reaction to the fragmentation of and lack of solidarity in society. This shows that civil society is *part of a comprehensive project* with features that, since the Enlightenment, have not been fully implemented. To that extent, civil society remains a *utopia*, a promise that has yet to be entirely fulfilled, even if Europe today corresponds much more closely to this project, this utopia, than it did in the past.

This also means that civil society has never been identical to real, existing societies. Instead (and I use 'civil society' in this way), the term refers to a cluster of structural elements in these societies – societies that also include other elements: state, market, private life, as well as violence, fanaticism and chaos. Societies can be distinguished according to the degree to and the manner in which they have implemented the principles of civil society. There is a large task here for comparative historical and social science studies to tackle.

Civil Society, Capitalism and the State

I have separated the logic of civil society from the logic of the market, and distinguished between civil society and capitalism. This is a necessary task, but a modification must be made.

There is not only tension between the market economy and civil society; there is also an affinity. The emergence and success of market economies are at least facilitated, if not actually made initially possible, by the structures of civil society. A market economy presupposes a certain social cohesion; it requires some level of trust and social capital: and these are resources offered by civil society. Conversely, civil society also needs the market. If the decentralization of economic decisions and economic power – typical of functioning market economies – is absent, the chances of civil society emerging are slim. In centralized administrative economies, civil society will not thrive, as exemplified by the social systems that existed in Central Eastern and Eastern Europe until 1989–90. In a cross-national historical comparison, many parallels can be observed between the rise of a market economy and the extension of civil society.

This parallelism is illustrated by the fact that merchants and manufacturers in nineteenth-century urban Europe were frequently among the primary actors in civil society, not only in their private lives, but precisely as entrepreneurs. Present-day discussion of 'corporate culture' and the engagement in civil society of today's large concerns and their foundations also come to mind. Not every form of patronage by wealthy individuals should be celebrated as engagement in civil society. But, conversely, it would be just as false to dismiss every case of 'corporate citizenship' as a mere manifestation of purely individual interests veiled by ideology.

On the other hand, there are variants of capitalism, types of capitalists, and forms of capitalist entrepreneurship that do not lend themselves at all to engagement in civil society; they eat away at social cohesion instead of strengthening it. This negative relationship between entrepreneurship and civil society can be found in forms of earlier and contemporary enterprises that are mobile, spatially flexible and socially barely embedded – for example, in yesterday's New Economy and in today's international finance capitalism. Some forms of capitalism are parasitic on civil society.

The relationship between civil society and the state, too, is complex and ambivalent. Earlier, the logic of civil society and that of administration and rule were analytically separated; that is, civil society was distinguished from the state. This distinction remains valid, but here, as well, a modification must be made.

First of all, it must be kept in mind that the relationship between civil society and the state should be viewed differently depending on whether we are looking at the pre-democratic absolutism of the eighteenth century, at the anti-democratic dictatorships of the twentieth century, or at today's more or less democratic, constitutional states under the rule of law. Civil society emerged as a critical idea and oppositional force in the age of absolutism. In the struggle against dictatorship in the twentieth century it assumed new attractiveness. Its relationship to the state under liberal and democratic conditions must be determined in a different fashion: ideally as a relationship of critical partnership and mutual reinforcement. Liberal, communitarian and social democratic concepts of civil society vary in how they determine the relationship between civil society and the state. A social democratic perspective stresses that a strong civil society needs a strong state, and vice versa. (See Merkel and Puhle 1999: 166–74; Bermeo and Nord 2000; Meyer and Weil 2002).

On the one hand, in order for civil society to develop fully and be maintained in the long term it needs political institutions that satisfy the criteria of a constitutional state and the rule of law, permit democratic participation, make effective decisions on fundamental principles, set legal conditions, and intervene to protect, foster and reconcile its citizens. An inherently diverse civil society finds the unity it needs only in a democratic state under the rule of law. Civil society cannot thrive without a political framework of this kind. Nowhere do non-governmental organizations (NGOs) constitute a substitute for a democratic state. But under pre-democratic conditions, under absolutist, autocratic or dictatorial rule, civil society initiatives can pave the way for and promote democratization (as long as the dictatorship is not so radical that all civil-social movements are prevented from emerging, or are destroyed, as was the case under Hitler and Stalin). On the other hand, it is civil society that influences the constitutional state under the rule of law, fills it with life, makes it dynamic and forces it to be accountable. The dynamic part of civil society supplies the polity with the necessary energy and mobility. The *access* of civil initiatives, social movements and organizations *to the political system* is therefore a central condition of the functioning of civil society.[5]

Strengthening civil society strengthens the state. But current interest in civil society, at least in the West, comes in part from the experience that the state can become overextended in its role as an interventionist welfare state, and that it provides for and spoon-feeds its citizens more than it needs to. The state also weakens itself if it regulates, or attempts to regulate, excessively. We have reached a stage of development in which the division of labour between state and society must be rethought. A strong state is one that limits what it does and leaves much to civil society.

However, this leaves some open questions. For one thing, how and according to what criteria are tasks to be divided between the state and civil society? And how far can the principle of subsidiarity be taken? Furthermore, civil society, if left alone, can show signs of egoism and stagnation, of fundamentalism and resentment, of erosion and fragmentation. Strengthening civil society by having the state practise restraint can thus be politically double-edged and risky. It is important that the reinforcement of civil society does not lead the democratic state to shirk its central tasks. There are great differences in this respect from country to country as a result of their different histories.

Civil Society: Actors and Resources

Who are the potential driving forces of civil society? Who provides its support? What resources are a prerequisite for a civil society? I would like to discuss this historically, using the example of Germany. Let me begin with the relationship between civil society and the middle class.[6]

In the late eighteenth and early nineteenth centuries in German-speaking central Europe, the terms *Bürgertum* and *bürgerlich* referred, on the one hand, to the small urban social formation of businesspeople, industrialists, bankers and directors, and, on the other, to academically educated officials, professors, secondary school teachers, lawyers, physicians, clerics and journalists. As part of the middle class, these people were distinct from the nobility, the common masses and the rural population. They were held together primarily by a common culture – that is, a middle-class culture (*bürgerliche Kultur*) that encompassed general education, values such as self-reliance, a specific model of the family and certain forms of communication. On the other hand, *bürgerliche Gesellschaft*, or *Bürgergesellschaft*, also referred to the model of society that today is called civil society. This ambiguity – *Bürger* means *bourgeois* as well as *citoyen* – is not a semantic coincidence. It can be shown that, at the time, the project of a future civil society was popular in and particularly supported by the lodges, clubs and networks, the correspondence and communication circles, the movements and political parties, and the atmosphere and culture of the urban middle classes (which included some members of the nobility and petite bourgeoisie). Other social strata and classes, in contrast, dissociated themselves more from this project. In fact, they were often virtually excluded from it, they profited very little from it and it meant very little to them.

This early affinity and alliance between middle-class culture and the project of civil society loosened in the late nineteenth and early twentieth centuries. Parts of the middle class became conservative and defensive, turning away from essential aspects of civil society. On the other hand, the civil society project gained new sympathizers, advocates and supporters in social strata and classes that previously had had nothing to do with it, especially skilled workers and the social democratic labour movement. Social democracy became a decisive driving force in the further development of civil society. The history of the bourgeois middle class and that of civil society started going their separate ways.

Even today, remnants of the former affinity between middle-class culture and civic engagement can be observed: civil society activities in the form of clubs, citizens' initiatives and NGOs are mainly supported by people from educated, urban, middle-class milieux. This is the case, at least, in Germany. Nevertheless, today the project of civil society and civic involvement finds strong support in many social strata, not just the middle class (the character of which has anyway become so blurred that it is questionable if it can be clearly identified).

A cross-national comparison reveals that this close connection between the middle class and civil society did not exist everywhere, even in the nineteenth century. In Poland, parts of the gentry took the place of the poorly developed, sometimes ethnically foreign, middle class. In England and France, the middle class and the nobility became much more closely intertwined, creating a broader social basis for the developing civil society. In Russia before the First World War, civil-social tendencies were weak; they existed particularly among the urban middle classes, but also in parts of the petite and intermediate bourgeoisie, particularly in local politics.

In any case, in the past as in the present, certain social groups are more active in civil society than others. The capacity for civil society is distributed disproportionately, depending on time, availability, adequacy of resources, available communication networks, education and other unequally distributed resources. Civil society certainly does not presuppose social equality. But it emerged as a project opposing corporative inequality and it has sometimes been obstructed and damaged by excessive economic and social inequality. Upon examining the mechanisms of civic involvement, it is possible to discover the significant role played by individual civil-social 'entrepreneurs'. The role of religion and religiosity in the development or obstruction of civil society is very different in different situations. Community church life in Nonconformist religious congregations, such as the English and American Quakers, was and is at the root of civic involvement. On the other hand, the principles and practices of the major state religions usually stand in some tension to the self-determination of civil society. It is decisive whether religions and churches appear in the plural or the singular. Another resource is, ultimately, trust: civic engagement requires a certain degree of trust – in oneself, in others, in the future. 'Trust is good, but control is better': Lenin's motto is not a slogan that supports civil society. All of this clearly shows that civil society can be neither decreed nor simply invented. It is dependent on historical prerequisites. It is always a product of history. It can be obstructed or fostered, but not decreed or constructed.

Civil Society and the Family

It is common to categorize civil society and family separately; to view them as occupying different spheres. My earlier argumentation roughly followed these lines. Here as well, though, modifications are necessary. Recent studies, above all in gender history, show that what had always applied (in another way) to families of peasants and workers was also true of the middle classes: namely, that the nineteenth- and early twentieth-century family was definitely not only a private matter. It also had public aspects. Consequently, the categorical separation of 'public' and 'private' must be qualified. To this end, Gunilla-Friederike Budde recently depicted the nineteenth-century middle-class family as a central institution of civil society. Even those who do not wish to go this far cannot deny that part of the lives of middle-class families – at least of the larger ones – took place in civil society, and that they had a profound influence on it, both enabling and strengthening it. Just think of these families' diverse educational achievements – and, within the families, especially those of women – which promoted self-reliance and civic involvement; of the semi-public living spaces of middle-class families (especially in earlier periods), when strangers were invited into homes for socializing, and individuals and families represented themselves to others by displaying, partly in ritualized ways, themselves, their wealth, their taste – in short, their importance; of the civic engagement, especially in cultural, charitable and social fields, of many middle-class women, who maintained their roles in the home and did not break away from the family.

The constitution of family and kinship, at least in western and central Europe, supplied important conditions for the rise of civil society in yet another way. Here, family bonds did not absorb the loyalty and involvement of their members to a degree that was so absolute and without gaps as to leave no room for civic engagement. Not every kind of family and kinship has been equally suited for civil society. This is clearly shown by a comparison of western and central Europe with the ethnic kinship and clan groups in south-eastern and southern Europe, not to mention those in other parts of the world.[7]

Civil Society, Nation and Europe

It is sometimes claimed that civil society and the nation state are twins, that they are inextricably linked. But historical evidence shows that the matter is far more complex.

When comparing European countries in the nineteenth century, we can observe, for example in western Europe, civil-social endeavours and associations – clubs, theatre groups, citizens' movements and other social organizations – that developed within the framework of established territorial sovereignties and nation states. We also see attempts to create entities though no accepted state framework existed, or even in opposition to the given state form, for example in east central and south-eastern Europe. The findings are not uniform. Sometimes, as in Poland, civil-social initiatives in the absence of a nation-state framework were particularly strong. Sometimes the lack of state support was an obstacle to the emergence of such initiatives. There were strong civil society initiatives before and without the nation state.

On the other hand, in late-nineteenth and early-twentieth-century Europe, many civil society movements, networks and NGOs emerged that extended beyond national borders. These included the abolitionist movement, the struggle for women's suffrage, the international labour movement, campaigns against prostitution or alcoholism, and then – continuing to the present – the struggle for disarmament and peace. Above all, recently there have been waves of transnationalization. Civil society has now crossed national borders with unprecedented vehemence and in new political spheres – just think of environmental issues, human rights and anti-globalization movements. New decentralized forms and new means of communication are available for these ends.

Nevertheless, even today civil society has remained largely within a nation-state framework. We are still a far cry from a European – not to mention a global – civil society. There are many reasons for this; I will mention just one. Civil society is closely linked with the public sphere. The public sphere involves communication, and communication requires a common language. Multilingual Europe thus has a difficult hurdle to overcome before a European civil society can emerge. Or should the European civil society of the future speak English?

The idea of civil society was born during the Enlightenment. It is thus a product of the West. But its principles claim universal validity. Within Europe the idea has shifted eastward, but it has changed in the process. In the eastern part of the continent, inspiration came from Western ideas, but that which was, and is being, adopted is not merely an imitation. A selective adaptation to new conditions has usually taken place. Civil society has emerged along different paths and in different variants. In different places it may be stronger or weaker, it may come earlier or later, but always, if it emerges at all, it is different, despite the fact that actors and writers in different countries pay attention to each other's opinions and actions with regard to civil society, despite there being mutual influences at work,and despite civil society's impact extending beyond borders. What happens in one country cannot simply be the model for developments in another country. But comparison serves an important purpose, in scholarly discourse as in social and political life.

Notes

A preliminary version of this chapter appeared in *European Review* 12, 2004: 65–79.

1. For a good introduction see Keane 1998: 12–31.
2. For a more detailed discussion of the history of the concept see Kocka 2000.
3. For a substantively similar analysis, though using different terms, see Lauth 1999 and Rucht 2002.
4. The quotation is from Keane 1998: 6. Sometimes the term 'civil society' is closely related to terms such as the 'third sector' or 'non-profit sector'. See Anheier 1999; Salamon et al. 1999: esp. xvii; Anheier et al. 2000. According to the definition proposed in this chapter, organizations, initiatives and networks of the third sector should be considered part of 'civil society' only if and to the extent that they correspond to the aforementioned type of social action. Consequently, violent or fanatical, intolerant organizations, movements and initiatives may belong to the 'third sector' but do not qualify as belonging to civil society. The distinction, however, is difficult to make in individual cases.
5. The criterion of access to politics is strongly emphasized in Eisenstadt 2002.
6. For greater detail on this see Kocka 1993.
7. For a more in-depth discussion of the nineteenth century see Budde 2003.

References

Anheier, Helmut K. 1999. 'Der Dritte Sektor im internationalen Vergleich. Ökonomische und zivilgesellschaftliche Dimensionen von Nonprofit-Organisationen'. *Berliner Journal für Soziologie* 9: 197–212.

Anheier, Helmut K., Priller, Eckhard and Zimmer, Annette. 2000. 'Zur zivilgesellschaftlichen Dimension des Dritten Sektors'. In *Zur Zukunft der Demokratie. Herausforderungen im Zeitalter der Globalisierung*, ed. Hans-Dieter Klingemann and Friedhelm Neidhardt: 71–98. WZB-Jahrbuch. Berlin.

Bauerkämper, Arnd and Borutta, Manuel, eds. 2003. *Die Praxis der Zivilgesellschaft. Akteuere, Handeln und Strukturen im internationalen Vergleich*. Frankfurt am Main.

Bermeo, Nancy and Nord, Philip, eds. 2000. *Civil Society before Democracy: Lessons from Nineteenth-century Europe*. Lanham.

Budde, Gunilla-F. 2003. 'Das Öffentliche des Privaten. Die Familie als zivilgesellschaftliche Kerninstitution'. In *Die Praxis der Zivilgesellschaft. Akteure, Handeln und Strukturen im internationalen Vergleich*, ed. Arnd Bauerkämper and Manuel Borutta. Frankfurt am Main.

Cohen, Jean L. and Arato, Andrew. 1992. *Civil Society and Political Theory*. Cambridge, Mass.

Eisenstadt, Shmuel N. 2002. 'Civil Society and the Transformation of the Political in the Contemporary Era', Opening Lecture, Conference on European Civil Society (unpublished manuscript). WZB. Berlin.

Foley, Michael and Edwards, Bob. 1996. 'The Paradox of Civil Society'. *Journal of Democracy* 7, 3: 38–52.

Gosewinkel, D. et al., eds. 2004. *Zivilgesellschaft – national und transnational*. WZB-Jahrbuch 2003. Berlin.

Habermas, Jürgen, 1996. 'Civil Society and the Political Public Sphere'. In Jürgen Habermas, *Between Facts and Norms: Contributions to a Discourse Theory of Law and Democracy*, trans. William Rehg: 329–87. Cambridge, Mass.

Hann, Chris and Dunn, Elizabeth, eds. 1996. *Civil Society: Challenging Western Models*. London.

Hein, Dieter and Schulz, Andreas, eds. 1996. *Bürgerkultur im 19. Jahrhundert. Bildung, Kunst und Lebenswelt*. Munich.

Hildermeier, Manfred, Kocka, Jürgen, and Conrad, Christoph, eds. 2000. *Europäische Zivilgesellschaft in Ost und West. Begriff, Geschichte, Chancen*. Frankfurt am Main.

Keane, John. 1998. *Civil Society: Old Images, New Visions*. Cambridge.

Klein, Ansgar. 2001. *Der Diskurs der Zivilgesellschaft. Politische Kontexte und demokratietheoretische Bezüge der neueren Begriffsverwendung*. Opladen.

Kocka, Jürgen. 1993. 'The European Pattern and the German Case'. In *Bourgeois Society in Nineteenth-Century Europe*, ed. Jürgen Kocka and Allen Mitchell: 3–39. Oxford.

———. 2000. 'Zivilgesellschaft als historisches Problem und Versprechen'. In *Europäische Zivilgesellschaft in Ost und West. Begriff, Geschichte, Chancen*, ed. Manfred Hildermeier, Jürgen Kocka, Christoph Conrad: 14–20. Frankfurt am Main.

———. ed. 1995. *Bürgertum im 19. Jahrhundert*, 3 vols. Göttingen. (An abridged edition was published in English as *Bourgeois Society in Nineteenth-Century Europe*: see Kocka 1993.)

Kocka, Jürgen et al. 2001. *Neues über Zivilgesellschaft. Aus historisch-sozialwissenschaftlichem Blickwinkel*. WZB-Paper P 01–801. Berlin.

Krzysztof, Michalski, ed. 1991. *Europa und die Civil Society. Castelgandolfo-Gespräche 1989*. Stuttgart.

Lauth, Hans-Joachim. 1999. 'Strategische, reflexive und ambivalente Zivilgesellschaften. Ein Vorschlag zur Typologie von Zivilgesellschaften im Systemwechsel'. In *Unvollendete Demokratisierung in Nichtmarktökonomien. Die Blackbox zwischen Staat und Wirtschaft in den Transitionsländern des Südens und Ostens*, ed. Heidrun Zinecker: 95–120. Amsterdam.

Lundgreen, Peter, ed. 2000. *Sozial- und Kulturgeschichte des Bürgertums. Eine Bilanz des Bielefelder Sonderforschungsbereichs (1986–1997)*. Göttingen.

Merkel, Wolfgang, and Puhle, Hans-Jürgen. 1999. *Von der Diktatur zur Demokratie. Transformationen, Erfolgsbedingungen, Entwicklungspfade*. Opladen.

Meyer, Thomas and Weil, Reinhard, eds. 2002. *Die Bürgergesellschaft. Perspektiven für Bürgerbeteiligung und Bürgerkommunikation*. Bonn.

Müller, Michael G. 2000. 'Die Historisierung des bürgerlichen Projekts. Europa, Osteuropa und die Kategorie der Rückständigkeit'. *Tel Aviver Jahrbuch für deutsche Geschichte* 29: 163–70.

Rucht, Dieter. 2002. 'Zivilgesellschaft als Forschungsgegenstand. Systematische, historische und forschungspraktische Annäherungen', manuscript. WZB. Berlin.

Salamon, Lester M. et al., eds. 1999. *Global Civil Society: Dimensions of the Nonprofit Sector*. Baltimore.

Trentmann, Frank, ed. 2000. *Paradoxes of Civil Society: New Perspectives on Modern German and British History*. New York.

Van den Daele, Wolfgang. 2002. 'The Not-so-sunny Sides of Civil Society Mobilization'. In *Progressive Governance for the XXIst Century*, ed. Gerhard Schröder: 87–89. Munich.

Walzer, Michael, ed. 1995. *Toward a Global Civil Society*. Providence.

2

CORPORATE RESPONSIBILITY AND HISTORICAL INJUSTICE

Susanne-Sophia Spiliotis

(Society) ... is a partnership between those who are living,
those who are dead, and those who are to be born.
Edmund Burke (1961 [1790])

Taking upon ourselves the consequences for things we are
entirely innocent of is the price we pay for the fact that we live
our lives not by ourselves but ... within a human community.
Hannah Arendt (1969: 50)

The central question of this chapter concerns the relationship between civil society and multinational corporations and how this relationship is normatively and practically reconstituted at a time when past, large-scale, human rights violations are assuming increasing topical significance. This question is pivotal in clarifying a role for business as an actor in civil society that goes beyond what is generally discussed under the headings of corporate social responsibility, corporate governance, corporate citizenship or just philanthropy. The way corporate actors look at history tells one more about their 'civicness' than do these forms of civic involvement. This is why we need to focus on how evil legacies and the questions of repair were dealt with as the twentieth century drew to a close. I shall argue that in this respect we have witnessed a paradigmatic change that has reframed collective responsibility and its categories.

There is accumulating evidence that history plays an ever greater role in public life; part of this trend is the 'setting history straight' phenomenon. It focuses on historical injustice, i.e. on past injustices inflicted on a great number of people under regimes that claimed to act legally, or even legitimately, but which, from today's perspective, were already illegal, intolerable and unjust at the time the injustices were committed (Minow 1999; Meyer 2003; Elster 2004; for a concise introduction to the issue see Waldron 1992). Obviously, such historical injustice and the question of who should bear its consequences has always been an important issue in philosophy, especially in theoretical and applied ethics (May and Hoffman 1991). Over the past twenty years, however, the topic has emerged from the academic trenches, became topical and even developed into a proper 'business of repair'.[1] It is mostly non-governmental organizations (NGOs), i.e. civil society groups, that have engaged in restoring the rights and interests of wronged and presumably neglected groups of people. At the dawn of the new century, civil society has assumed the onerous and honourable task of calculating the bill for the last century's efforts to extirpate civil society. The repeated calls for official apologies, reparations and remembrance seem like a 'pervasive attempt to construct collective passage' (Teitel 2000: 229) from a gloomy past to a brighter future based on universalized civic values.

Transitional Justice

The quest for setting history straight concentrated in the first place on periods of political transition in the second half of the twentieth century, namely the periods after regime changes. The great diversity of legal and moral reactions to past wrongdoing and suffering resulting from these political transitions has even given rise to a new realm of research: transitional justice. This conceptualizes the rule of law in times of political flux as symbolic of the liberalizing dynamics of (Western-style) democratic transition; and it explicitly incorporates a positive normative component in its understanding of transition from less to more democratic regimes (Teitel 2000: 5f.). According to the theory of transitional justice, the law in periods of political transformation derives its specific nature from the fact that it integrates opposing features that ensue from tackling historical injustice: retrospectivenesss and looking forward, the individual and the collective.

Even though the focus of 'transitional justice' is strictly on the state, the theory suggests that the successful search for justice after political change is predicated on the support of civil society. It also seems to be true that establishing and strengthening civil society depends on coming to terms with history. The way a country copes with its past of repression or genocidal violence partly determines the stability of the transition to a participatory political order. Obviously, taking an attitude towards a common past is an essential ingredient not only in achieving true reconciliation but also in maintaining the links between generations: arriving at a common narrative of a painful past serves as a promise of respect for moral standards among contemporaries. 'Memory' and 'remembrance' reconstruct history in a way that anticipates the bonds with successor generations.

Retroactive Justice

The rectification of past wrongs, however, is not confined to times of political flux. Even in stable and thriving democracies, and in spite of thick layers of history covering past human rights abuses, political, moral and economic justifications are marshalled in the service of 'retroactive justice'. This approach is often contrary to prevailing intuitions about the 'supersession' of historical injustice, as changed circumstances promote the withering away of claims and entitlements over time (Waldron 2003). The insistence on settling open accounts after a long time has passed – 'retroactive justice' – might be seen as an implied confession of a moral deficit. When unaddressed, the resolution of historical injustices sometimes becomes even more imperative. Coping with evil legacies thus often appears to be deferrable.[2]

The quest for 'retroactive justice' uses a language resounding with moral reflections that mirror present values and the extent to which they are embedded in political, social and economic change. The quest also has ramifications for the question of who should bear the consequences of historical injustice. Central to retroactive and transitional justice alike is not only the question 'What merits redress?' but also the question 'Who should assume collective moral and historical responsibility?'

As with transitional justice, the retroactive justice phenomenon is characterized by a striking state bias. The state is held responsible for past injustices, and it is the state that is expected to right past wrongs. At least, this is what is discussed in much of the literature.[3]

Setting History Straight: Examples

Some examples may demonstrate the state bias typical in attempts to tackle historical injustice. First, there are the so-called 'truth commissions' concerned with achieving societal reconciliation in the transition to democracy in South Africa and Latin America.[4] The common goals of these commissions, which have been established partly by governments or international organizations like the United Nations and partly by NGOs, are to compile and present records of victims, and of the means and the scope of human rights violations. It is their drawing of a line between past and present that creates an authoritative – not imposed – history as part of a new order establishing 'historical justice'. However, the success of truth commissions depends on the presence of a civil society. Comparative studies show that, where civil societies are weak, truth commissions, official or informal, do not work (Crocker, 2000: the author concentrates on Guatemala).

Secondly, we see demands for official apologies and compensation to victims of colonialism and racism in the form of filing lawsuits in US civil courts and promoting public awareness.[5] The legal foundation for the lawsuits relies on a long forgotten but nevertheless increasingly important law called the Alien Tort Claims Act (ATCA), which was adopted by the first American Congress in 1789. It provides that US federal courts 'shall have original jurisdiction of any civil action by an alien for a tort only, committed in violation of the law of nations or a treaty of the United States'.[6] The statute lay dormant for almost two centuries. Only since the 1990s has it become increasingly relevant as American courts have started adjudicating civil liability for crimes and torts wherever they occurred in the world. Growing numbers of victims of historical injustice – descendants of African slaves, former forced labourers under the Nazi regime, and other Holocaust survivors – are referring to the ATCA in their lawsuits to defend their rights under international law. Ordinary jurisdictional parameters are circumvented, and the fact that 'foreign' is rendered 'domestic' considerably complicates diplomatic relations when defendants in these cases are governments and multinational corporations.

The third example concerns the reparation claims for damages caused during the Second World War; these are still high on the agenda.[7]

Obviously, as these examples suggest, the core understanding of collective responsibility and redress is framed by an inherent orientation to the state: 'succession to old obligations demonstrates how the assumption of collective responsibility constitutes a state's political identity over time' (Teitel 2000: 140f.). The vehicle of social and intergenerational accountability for historical injustice is the state. This is partly due to the modern Western concept that the (legitimate) control of political power by the state goes hand in hand with the (democratic) representation of a pluralistic society, and that public concerns are widely delegated to the authority of the state. It is when the destructive potential endemic in modern societies has spawned gross abuses of human rights that instances of states' unredressed wrongs abound, putting the problem of historical injustice on a state's agenda.

Missing: The Private Side

However, what goes almost unnoticed or is at least scarcely discussed in this state-dominated line of thinking are the private entities that supported, took part in and profited from these gross abuses of human rights, and their assumption of collective responsibility. Here, the analytical divide between state and society does not mirror the intricate and overlapping relations between public and private actors, which together implemented the inhuman policy that the mass torts flow from. Despite these tangled threads of guilt and accountability, it would at first appear that there is no institution, body or entity other than the state that can take on collective responsibility. Or is there?[8]

In the 1990s, something changed. Private enterprise stepped forward to deal with historical injustice. Not only were major corporations in Europe, Asia and America taken to court in the United States because they were involved in regimes that today are regarded as 'rogue states'.[9] They responded to those charges in a way that promoted an alternative – private – form of collective responsibility. The protective skirts of the state no longer provided sufficient cover.

Given the fact that repair marks discontinuity with past injustice, the 'private turn' in coping with evil legacies gives rise to the question: what 'tradition' was broken as corporate actors collectively assumed moral obligations for repairing past wrongs caused by state action?

What does historical injustice have to do with the civic identity of multinational corporations? At what point does the existence of 'historical and moral responsibility' affect the identity of global market players? Does the 'private turn' in the assumption of collective responsibility for human rights violations reflect a more general reconfiguration in the governance of (transitional and retroactive) justice?

The most telling instance of this 'private turn' is the case of the German Business Foundation Initiative for the compensation of forced labourers under the Nazi regime.[10] The very idea of this initiative documents a remarkable change in the corporate attitude towards responsibility arising from past actions. At the same time, this change in attitude suggests a practical, normative shift in the relationship between the marketplace and civil society. Finally, it advances an understanding that regards business as an integral feature of civil society rather than assigning to each mutually exclusive *raisons d'être*: the former being driven by the logic of competition and profit, the latter by ethical accountability and civic involvement. The understanding advanced here defies the profoundly dichotomized conception prevailing in contemporary thought; it sees this analytical distinction as an artificial divorce of what otherwise inseparably belongs together.

This case clearly shows that, by sharing collective, retroactive responsibility, major corporations might be regarded as *part of* rather than as mere *actors in* civil society. One might even speak of the German Business Foundation Initiative as a trendsetter for what we could tentatively call *corporate civil society*. A look at its specifics revisits and complements the view that conceives of the state as a monopolistic instance of collective responsibility over time; it sheds light on corporate citizens in their capacity to assume collective responsibility even when the cause of action dates back generations. A brief description of the case and its political, legal and historical setting will suffice to show the traits of an emerging corporate civil society.

Collective Responsibility 'Reshaped'

Generally, German business made a point of declining any direct responsibility for involvement in the forced labour programme of the Nazi regime.[11] Some individual industrial companies did reach global agreements with the Conference on Jewish Material Claims Against Germany (Claims Conference)[12] during the 1950s and 1960s on compensation for Jewish concentration camp inmates who had been forced to work for the companies during the war.[13] Some of these agreements were reached in the course of a judicial settlement and some as a result of out-of-court negotiations. In return, the Claims Conference explicitly waived any further forced labour claims on behalf of Jewish concentration camp inmates. If some companies in this period steadfastly denied that they were liable in any legal sense, others even had difficulty acknowledging that they were morally responsible.

In the 1980s and 1990s, companies began providing funds for humanitarian assistance programmes for Nazi victims from Eastern Europe, especially forced labourers. Unlike the earlier cases, these recipients need not have worked for the donor companies.[14] It was an examination of their own histories during the Nazi period that prompted some companies to make global payments. The studies brought home how much individual victims had suffered from a cruel and inhumane policy, and many large and medium-sized companies gave material assistance in individual cases on their own initiative.

By the mid-1990s, however, individual compensation payments by companies were no longer the rule. The problem went far beyond the bounds of the individual. As legal claims from former forced labourers piled up in the second half of the decade, it was felt that if there was going to be a solution, it had to be one that dealt equally with all surviving forced labourers. It was also decided that the argument that the labourers had, for the most part, been paid according to what was then the legal wage scale would not be raised. It was felt that such an approach was beneath the companies' historical and moral responsibility, and, moreover, would not be persuasive in the face of public pressure.

The corporate solution that finally emerged was innovative: the *sui generis* 'German Business Foundation Initiative'. It was set up in 1999 by a handful of major German companies,[15] most of them global players, who were the targets of class action suits in the United States for having profited from slave labour: the Nazi regime's forced mobilization of over 12 million civilians from occupied Europe to work for the German war economy.[16] These corporations' prospects of emerging unscathed from the legal battle were excellent, since, under prevailing American civil procedure doctrine, the consequences of a war are political questions that civil courts cannot adjudicate. At least this was how they saw it. According to the German ambassador in Washington, however, they thoroughly underestimated the legal and political *problématique* that lay ahead, to the detriment of German-American relations.[17] And, in fact, all of the cases were eventually dismissed. What did prompt the companies to act was the threat of an imminent public relations disaster. To put it simply: their credibility as corporate citizens was at stake.

The main thrust of the initiative was to secure legal closure for German business without court procedures. What the companies wanted was an all-embracing and enduring legal peace for all German business, not just for themselves. What they offered was something completely new: instead of each single company compensating only those former forced labourers who had worked for them, they suggested pooling financial means in order to compensate *all* surviving forced labourers, thus lending support to those victims who, because of the processes of economic reconstruction, no longer had a company to sue after Second World War.

For this collective approach to work, they needed political support, and they found it in Berlin and Washington. The German government regarded the corporate initiative as complementing the extensive German restitution and compensation programme for victims of the Nazi era that had been in operation for four decades. The Clinton administration had set itself the goal of 'setting history straight', and was pursuing a policy of 'turning old facts into new realities'.[18] In the mid-1990s, US policy accorded highest priority to Holocaust-related issues of compensation, research and education. It focused on the role of neutral states in prolonging the German war effort by purchasing Nazi 'plundered gold', and especially on the case of Switzerland. Another concrete US interest was directed at effecting the return of property that had been confiscated from Nazi victims after the Second World War, and then nationalized, in the communist states of Central and Eastern Europe. That property was now to be re-privatized; first in line were private and communal Jewish holdings. The US government pushed these discussions forward by initiating comprehensive studies. In 1995 President Bill Clinton appointed Undersecretary of Commerce Stuart E. Eizenstat Special Envoy for Property Claims in Central and Eastern Europe, and later, in 1999, Special Representative for Holocaust Issues.[19] At the end of the millennium, the US government had become the driving force of retroactive justice with regard to events that had occurred in Europe decades before.

It took two years to bring this idea of a collective fund to fruition. These were years of intense negotiations among the governments concerned – those of Germany, Israel and the United States – as well as the governments of five Central and Eastern European countries (Belarus, Russia, Ukraine, Poland, Czech Republic), plaintiffs' lawyers, NGOs representing victims (e.g. the Jewish Claims Conference) and German companies. Finally, the Foundation 'Responsibility, Remembrance and the Future' was set up, endowed with 10 billion Deutschmarks (about 5 million euros),[20] with half the sum being paid by German companies and the other half by the German taxpayer. The Foundation was embedded in a baroque architecture of international agreements (signed in Berlin on 17 July 2000) to secure the legal closure envisaged (Wolffe and Authers 2002a: 324). These 'Berlin Agreements' consisted of a Joint Statement of all the parties to the negotiations and a German-American Intergovernmental Agreement, which, together with the German Foundation Law, provided the framework for making the Foundation operative.[21]

While the German companies denied all legal responsibility, they claimed they were living up to their moral and historical responsibility.[22] Was this just a cunning rhetorical ruse by guilt-ridden German companies to dissociate themselves from 'real responsibility' (Zumbansen and Adler 2002)? Was the self-ascribed humanitarian attitude authentic or camouflage? It certainly was part of a clever public relations strategy in order to avoid any notion of (individual) guilt. It goes without saying that the companies had a massive image problem and wanted to get rid of it. The issue of historical injustice with which corporate actors were confronted was framed as a problem of voluntary voice, only in part assuageable through monetary damages.

However, there is another point worth looking at. The companies, which saw the claims for compensation as inadmissible in court, could have been let off the hook more cheaply! According to the logic of the market, they should have chosen a cheaper way to achieve legal closure instead of acting as socially responsible corporations that would have to pay more. This is true even if one takes into account the fact that the initiative's founding companies initially reckoned to solve their problem by pooling a lump sum of DM 1–2 billion, and not, as it later turned out in the course of the negotiations, DM 5 billion. They could have simply set up individual company foundations – paying just for 'their own' victims – with the same result: legal closure for themselves. But they did not, as if it was in their interest not to pursue the less costly variant. They chose the more expensive 'humanitarian gesture'. And they did so not because of mere 'contrition chic' (Brooks 1999: 3). What led them to make this choice?

To answer this we have to emphasize another aspect of the companies' behaviour. The companies presented themselves as a collective actor, speaking for the German business community as a whole, as a moral entity with an onerous past[23] and – an aspect that is frequently overlooked – with a promising future: in addition to providing humanitarian payments for more than 1.5 million former forced labourers, they helped create a so-called Future Fund under the auspices of the humanitarian Foundation. The Fund, it was envisaged, would support projects concerned with human rights, international understanding and democratic thinking; the companies endowed this fund with 700 million Deutschmarks (around 350 million euros).[24] They explicitly wanted to show that German business had learned from past failure; or they at least felt that this was a way to trigger the participation in the Foundation Initiative of German companies that were utterly 'innocent' because they had been founded only after the Second World War. They hoped they would thereby broaden the basis for the Foundation Initiative.

Underlying this line of thinking was the path-breaking concept of private business as a continuous, long-standing and inter-generational association with moral duties – in other words, as part of a *koinonia politiki* – as a group with its own culture of remembrance, relating itself to the passage of time. Constructing continuity by emphasizing the discontinuity with a morally compromised past and – instead of silencing or brushing off any concerns with retroactive justice and accountability – claiming responsibility for historical injustice: this is hardly what we imagine when we think of multinationals as a corporate aggregate of market-driven, historically blind private actors. Rather, it is better described as the epitome of *corporate civil society*.

The leading corporations managed to win over more than 6,500 German companies to their initiative, half of which were founded only after the Second World War.[25] These corporations chose to assume responsibility for who they are today by showing their attitude toward past injustice, regardless of the role they played individually. A considerably widened concept of moral responsibility was applied that dissociated moral responsibility from the 'dirty hands' with which it is traditionally connected. Their agenda of retroactive justice was not exclusively justified by conventional corrective aims, especially since a great number of the victims of forced and slave labour had already passed away. Consequently, it was not moral guilt that made the companies feel morally responsible, but, rather, a feeling of 'how one chooses to regard oneself' (May 1991: 247). Describing their motives in their initial statement, the founding companies spoke of 'solidarity and self-respect'.[26]

Of course, we have to mention the fact that the overwhelming majority of German business – 200,000 corporations were solicited – did not to take part in the initiative. The corporate critics argued that the only body that could take on collective historical responsibility was the state, to which the companies already contributed through their taxes. If there was to be a Foundation, they believed it should be funded by taxes and not by direct corporate contributions.

Conclusion

We are used to speaking about the state as embodying collective responsibility. This is part of the political inheritance of modern Europe. The quest for retroactive justice in cases of past state wrongs is conceptually bound to the collective action represented and taken by state authorities.

However, with the devolution of state power in the global realm, this paradigm is changing. Hybrid forms of governance are emerging in which public and private actors alike are concerned with public affairs. Private entities are assuming their share of public responsibility, acting on their own, although more or less related to but no longer exclusively mediated by state institutions. In our example, these private actors have been German corporations, ranging from multinationals to medium-sized and small companies. They have taken moral responsibility for Nazi crimes without necessarily having been directly involved. Claiming to represent German business's general moral and historical responsibility, the German Business Foundation Initiative has sparked a 'private turn' in the retroactive justice trend.

However, what these practices convey about the conceptual change of retroactive justice and collective responsibility can only be in part grasped by referring to the factual basis. Neither the political exigencies arising from the topical significance of Holocaust-related claims in the United States nor the urgent desire of German business to secure legal closure without resorting to court procedures suffice to explain why German companies chose the collective, and more expensive, path.

Far more elucidating in trying to clarify the parameters of this *sui generis* corporate civic involvement are two related conjectures, delineated below. They may be regarded as tentative answers to the question why and in what context the private approach – which broke the classic state monopoly over collective responsibility – occurred.

The *sui generis* corporate involvement is first of all geared to the critical role civil lawsuits in American tribunals play, in other words to the judicialization of historical injustice. Specific forms of litigation, such as class action suits, can have far-reaching consequences, especially if the defendants are foreign governments or multinational corporations.[27] In such cases, the legal and attendant public pressures are brought to bear on an area long supposed to be outside the jurisdiction of domestic civil courts: foreign policy. This sort of judicialization gives rise to 'plaintiff's diplomacy', which considerably complicates foreign relations. It also enlarges the 'growing chorus of non-traditional actors who have acquired a voice in foreign affairs' (Slaughter and Bosco 2000: 104). German business as such, speaking with one voice as the German Business Foundation Initiative, was thus party to the international negotiations with other private associations and civil society groups that led to the establishment of the Foundation 'Remembrance, Responsibility and the Future'. Nevertheless, in another instance of the 'hybrid' character of the case, the business community was additionally represented by a 'Representative of the Chancellor for German companies'.[28]

Such transnational civil lawsuits are indicative of the rising influence of both civic groups and multinational corporations in world affairs. Hauling corporate actors into court for their role in mass torts may be seen as part of the larger political process. To the extent that such actors are sued for their role in historical catastrophes such as the Holocaust or slavery, legal and public pressure may function as a reminder of their civic identity. Like a refracting prism, transnational civil lawsuits arising from human rights violations invade the civic enclosure of multinational corporations to focus on the manifold facets of their civic failure.

The second conjecture is that the private approach in the governance of retroactive justice reflects the revival of the topic of civil society over the past twenty years.[29] This revival has not only enhanced all sorts of civic involvement by companies; good corporate citizenship, corporate social responsibility and corporate culture in general have become buzzwords. The revival has also helped reshape our mindsets with regard to who is involved in public issues, even retroactively. It has sharpened our awareness of public-private entanglements as a reaction to the shortcomings of welfare states and to the challenges posed by a global (political) economy struggling with legitimacy deficits.

However, what transcends the 'normal' range of business's civic involvement in this particular case is the paradoxical construction of continuity through discontinuity. The companies dissociated themselves from historical injustice, and, in doing so, based themselves on the firm moral ground that attributed failures to the *collective* past of overall business, not necessarily to each company's individual past. This runs contrary to the prevailing liberal tradition that links individual action and responsibility tightly together and leaves 'abstract' collective responsibility to that old warhorse, the state. The companies explicitly broke with this tradition and constructed their own collective, trans-individual continuity.

This is what renders the German Business Foundation Initiative an epitome of corporate civil society. To some critics the disregarding of individual components of past injustice was evidence of an insidious plan by the accused companies to wash their hands of this past. But this critique misses the point. The construction of an 'extra-state', collective continuity relates history to civil society, no matter to which part of it.

One might argue against this interpretation by saying that the moral side of the Foundation Initiative's collective action has been overemphasized, and the 'hard fact' of legal closure as the decisive motive behind their action underestimated. These objections would probably win the support of most of the corporate protagonists. They see the confluence of a number of special circumstances as being decisive: the approaching death of former victims, who at the end of their days sought some measure of justice; American policy aiming at setting history straight, especially in Holocaust-related cases; and, finally, greedy lawyers who engaged in extortionist practices, covering up their money-focused engagement in the 'victims' market' as civic selflessness.

To a great extent, this down-to-earth point of view reflects a deep fear of setting a precedent. 'Real' business would never indulge in any practice that went beyond the realm of manufacturing, investment and returns. Nevertheless, the Foundation Initiative did happen. What remains to be seen is whether and to what extent this collective action will be remembered as such and be emulated: whether private business will define itself as a moral entity over time.

In any case, big companies, the so-called global players, have to factor in a new kind of risk: past human rights violations, which call for *historic risk management*.[30] And the past is continuously growing: the wings of history's angel are tied to an inter-generational chain of morality. No statutes of limitations, no other legal obstacles, no insurance policies will untie them.

Notes

1. *Pars pro toto*: Roger Daniels (1999) provides a telling example of this 'practical shift' with regard to the case of the relocation of Japanese Americans from conference level to the sparking of a mass movement for redress with the support of an organ of the US government. See also Kukathas 2002; Thompson 2002; Minow and Rosenblum 2003.
2. As opposed to Ruti G. Teitel, I prefer to distinguish transitional justice from what I call retroactive justice. I think that the notion 'transitional justice' should be reserved for immediate transitional periods and should not be extended to situations where transition has been completed. Solutions to historical injustice after decades of stable democratic rule have social and political implications that are different from those in transformative periods.

3. See Ruti G. Teitel's brilliant study (2000) for further references. She explores states' legal responses to their illiberal legacies and discusses the nature and function of law in transformative periods.
4. Kritz 1995. These volumes emerged from a longstanding project of the United States Institute of Peace. They provide a comprehensive comparative review of how the legacy of political repression is dealt with in twenty-one countries in Southern Africa, Central and Eastern Europe and Latin America that moved from being repressive regimes to democratic societies in the twentieth century. (There are country studies of Albania, Argentina, Belgium, Brazil, Bulgaria, Chile, Czechoslovakia, Denmark, France, Germany [after Nazism and after Communism], Greece, Hungary, Italy, Lithuania, Portugal, Russia, South Korea, Spain, Uganda, Uruguay (vol. II). Moreover, there are analyses of: the legal basis for the commissions of inquiry; the accessibility of documents of the former secret police apparatus, prosecution; amnesty; 'purges'; screenings; and compensation and rehabilitation questions in a much larger number of cases (vol. III). The studies highlight the way past injustices are treated and how this treatment affects the stability of the transition to a participatory political order. They show that this transition is partly determined by the way a country copes with its repressive past.
5. For a general orientation see Stephens and Ratner 1996; Shapiro and Stone Sweet 2002. A recent example is the lawsuit filed before the Superior Court of the District of Columbia on 18 September 2001 by the Herero People's Reparation Corporation against Deutsche Bank, Terex Corporation and DAL-Lines Columbia (Case No. 01-0004447). The companies were accused of profiting from the colonial exploitation and annihilation of the Herero people in the period 1890–1915. Another case is that of the Khulumani Victim Support Group, which has brought a lawsuit on behalf of a group of victims of past political violence in South Africa in the New York Eastern District Court against twenty-one multinational corporations and leading international banks for helping sustain the apartheid state. For constantly updated news on 'apartheid' litigation in general see the home page of the law firm Cohen, Milstein, Hausfeld and Toll, http://www.cmht.com/casewatch/humanrights/apartheid.html18.

   For an almost classic work on the claims of descendants of slaves in the United States, see Robinson 2002. On the reparation claims of Aboriginal and Torres Strait Islander Australians, see Healey 2000. For an overview of the range of reconciliation activities being undertaken across Australia, see http://www.reconciliationaustralia.org/. The promotion of a continuing national focus for reconciliation was started in 1990 by the Council for Aboriginal Reconciliation (CAR), followed by Reconciliation Australia, an independent, non-government and not-for-profit foundation funded through corporate and government partnerships and individual tax-deductible donations. It aims to promote ongoing wider community education about and engagement with the notion of a formal agreement or treaty between indigenous Australians and the wider community. For corresponding activities of the Australian government and parliament, see http://www.aph.gov.au/senate/committee/legcon_ctte/completed_inquiries/2002-04/re conciliation.
6. Alien Tort Claims Act (ATCA) 1789, 28 U.S.C. §1350.
7. On 10 September 2004 the Polish parliament confirmed reparation claims against Germany. For a discussion on the official political level see: http://www.europa-web.de/europa/03euinf/04AUS_BU/deporepe.htm.

   US officials believe that 'the generations of Germans born after the war should not be saddled with questions that imply their guilt for the policies of Nazi Germany'. The US Congress has expressed its position on the reparations question thus: 'The United States believes that reparations from World War II are no longer an issue on the agenda between Bonn and Washington'. (Congressional Research Service Library of Congress 1990: 26). From a legal point of view, however, the United States still regards the issue as open. For an encompassing overview of restitution claims arising from the Holocaust, see Bazyler 2003. The author gives an account of the Holocaust restitution campaign in the 1990s in the United States. He interprets the settlements that were reached as proof of the accountability of companies for historical injustice and credits human rights advocacy with the extension of universal jurisdiction by the US legal system to corporate actors.

8. One remarkable exception is May 1991. He applies the question of moral responsibility for the wrongs of unjust regimes to communities that have a central decision-making structure and culture in common. He uses the example of universities and their divestment in South African companies. See also Thompson 2002. However, Thompson does not fully explain her claim that corporations can be agents of retroactive justice.

9. For an excellent and well-written first-hand insight into the complicated international negotiations and their political contexts leading up to the settlements of Holocaust claims against European companies in the 1990s see Wolffe and Authers 2002a. Former US Undersecretary of Commerce Stuart E. Eizenstat, who represented the US government in the negotiations, gave his personal account of these politically delicate negotiations (2003). With regard to Asian cases see Bazyler 2003b. In 1999 and 2000, former US, Australian, New Zealand and British prisoners of war (POWs), as well as Korean, Philippine and Chinese civilians, filed over two dozen class action suits against the Japanese companies that had employed forced labour during the Second World War. The suits brought by former POWs were dismissed on 21 September 2000 on the basis of the US-Japanese mutual waiver of reparations claims in the peace treaty of 8 September 1951. (In re World War II Era Japanese Forced Labour Litigation, 114 F. Supp. 2d 939 (N.D.Cal.2000). The civilian cases were dismissed as time-barred. In summary, Bazyler (2004) comments that, as of summer 2003, the restitution movement against Japanese companies and Japan had not been as successful as the movement launched against European corporations and governments for their wartime conduct.

10. For a detailed analysis of the case, see Spiliotis 2005a [forthcoming] (German edition 2003). It is often overlooked that the Foundation Initiative and the Foundation itself were not only concerned with forced and slave labour but also with property claims arising from Nazi persecution. For reasons of brevity, however, in this article I shall concentrate on the forced labour issue, which dominated the public discussion. For a collection of contributions to the discussion about historical responsibility in the case of forced labour during the Nazi period, see Zumbansen and Adler 2002.

11. The question of subjective guilt and collective responsibility in the German context after the war was first explored by Karl Jaspers 1961 [1946].

12. Twenty-three Jewish diaspora groups founded the Claims Conference in 1951 as an umbrella organization to represent the interests of Jewish victims of Nazi persecution living outside Israel in restitution and compensation negotiations with the Federal Republic. For a history of the Claims Conference, see Zweig 2001.

13. I.G.Farben in Liquidation (IV/1958): DM 30 million; Fried. Krupp (XII/1959): DM 10 million; AEG/Telefunken (VIII/1960): DM 4 million; Siemens und Halske (V/1962; XI/1966): DM 5 million; DM 2 million; Rheinmetall (1966): DM 2.4 million; Feldmühle Nobel AG/Deutsche Bank (1986): DM 5 million.

14. Thus, DaimlerChrysler AG made DM 10 million available to the Claims Conference and a further DM 5 million apiece to the Red Cross and the Maximilian-Kolbe-Werk, which serves survivors of concentration camps in Central and Eastern Europe. In 1991, Volkswagen AG gave DM 12 million to organizations that sponsored projects that benefited young people, the elderly and the handicapped in Belarus, Poland and Ukraine. The Electricitäts-Werke of Hamburg gave a sizeable sum to the German-Polish Reconciliation Foundation in Warsaw to assist former Polish concentration camp inmates

and forced labourers. Deutsche Bank donated about DM 2.8 million to the World Jewish Restitution Organization, a sister organization of the Claims Conference founded in 1992. This represented half the proceeds of the sale of gold reserves that might have been looted by the Nazis. The other half went to the 'March of the Living' Foundation.

15. The twelve companies starting the initiative in Febuary 1999 were Allianz, BASF, Bayer, BMW, DaimlerChrysler, Deutsche Bank, Degussa-Hüls, Dresdner Bank, Fried. Krupp Hoesch-Krupp, Hoechst, Siemens and Volkswagen. In May 1999 Commerzbank, Deutz, RAG and Veba joined, and, in November 1999, Robert Bosch.

16. For a historical introduction to the issue of forced and slave labour, see Herbert 1999.

17. Author's interview with Jürgen Chrobog, former German ambassador in Washington (14 April 2005).

18. In the words of Stuart E. Eizenstat. www.law.harvard.edu/alumni/bulletin/backissues/summer99/article4.htlm (Spiliotis 2003: 31).

19. See the 'Eizenstat-Reports' (Eizenstat 1997; Eizenstat 1998).

20. The euro was introduced in Germany on 1 January 2002.

21. *Joint Statement on Occasion of the Final Plenary Meeting Concluding International Talks on the Preparation of the Foundation 'Remembrance, Responsibility and the Future'*, Berlin, 17 July 2000. The Joint Statement provided for any disbursement of Foundation Funds to the beneficiaries to be contingent on legal closure. However, from the moment Foundation payments began in summer 2000, new lawsuits against individual German companies claiming forced labour and property damage, as well as interest claims against the Foundation Initiative and its founders, provided ample opportunity to put the effectiveness of the Berlin Agreements to the test.

    Agreement between the Government of the Federal Republic of Germany and the Government of the United States of America concerning the Foundation 'Remembrance, Responsibility and the Future', Berlin, 17 July 2000, is an intergovernmental accord in the form of an 'executive agreement'. It basically combines two goals: first, the parties agree that the Foundation 'Remembrance, Responsibility and the Future' will be the exclusive remedy and forum for the resolution of all claims that have been or may be asserted against German companies arising from the National Socialist era and the Second World War. Secondly, the United States informs its courts through a Statement of Interest that the Foundation-to-be will be the exclusive remedy and forum for resolving such claims and that dismissal of such cases will be in the foreign policy interest of the United States. The Law Establishing the Foundation 'Remembrance, Responsibility and the Future' entered into force on 12 August 12 2000 (BGBl, 2000 I, 1263). All three documents are available under www.stiftung-evz.de.

22. For a discussion of the legal aspects of corporate accountability with regard to forced and slave labour, see Barwig et al. 1998; Zumbansen and Adler 2002b.

23. For a controversial philosophical discussion about the applicability of the notion of collective responsibility to business see French 1991; Velasquez 1991.

24. For the conceptualization and goals of the Future Fund, see the related entries under www.stiftung-evz.de.

25. For a detailed statistical and structural account of the participating companies, see Spiliotis 2003: 182–92. The participating companies are listed under www.stiftungsinitiative.de.

26. 'Foundation Initiative of German Enterprises: Remembrance, Responsibility and Future' 1999. Joint Statement on the Occasion of the Meeting of Representatives of 12 German Enterprises with Federal Chancellor Gerhard Schröder, 16 February, Bonn. (See www.stiftungsinitiative.de)

27. In class action suits, the individually named plaintiffs sue as representatives of an entire class that has been similarly affected by an injury-causing event. Whereas only the named plaintiffs are formally parties to the case, the legal effect of a decision and the binding effect of a settlement extend in principle to the entire class. Class actions have certain procedural requirements: the claims being asserted must be typical of the class

(typicality); the potential members of the class must be informed of the proceeding (notice); and they can exclude themselves from the class by notifying the court (opt out). The named plaintiffs and their lawyers are under an obligation to represent the class fairly and adequately. At the beginning, the court must determine whether the requirements for a class action have been met, and, where appropriate, it will issue a special certification of the group as a class (class certification). No case against the German companies was ever so certified. Class action suits generally end in a court hearing where the fairness of a proposed settlement is considered (fairness hearing) and a formal procedure for notifying the class of the settlement plan is approved. The procedural rules currently in force for class actions (contained in Rule 23 of the Federal Rules of Civil Procedure), are closely bound up with the US civil rights movement of the 1960s. As amended, they were intended to support the Civil Rights Act of 1964 by promoting the collective interests of groups suffering from discrimination. In the 1980s and 1990s, this device, which is designed to provide for legal redress in mass tort actions, was applied in a series of sensational proceedings, such as the Agent Orange and Bhopal cases. It was not originally intended for use in environmental, consumer and product liability cases, but enterprising lawyers who specialize in this kind of risky but extremely profitable proceeding pushed to expand its applicability. Their goal as a rule was not to win on the merits of the case, but to seek an out-of-court settlement based on a contingency fee agreed on beforehand, usually a sizeable percentage. Under certain circumstances, it is not uncommon for large law firms to compete for judicial 'approval' of their respective classes. Class action suits also function as a means of resolving problems with which the legislature is reluctant to deal.

28. German Chancellor Gerhard Schröder appointed Otto Graf Lambsdorff, a well-known senior politician, to this difficult position.

29. For a thorough account of the political and social effects of the language of civil society see Keane 1998, 2003.

30. For a discussion of the different pressures on the German companies, see Spiliotis 2005a [forthcoming].

References

Agreement between the Government of the Federal Republic of Germany and the Government of the United States of America concerning the Foundation 'Remembrance, Responsibility and the Future', Berlin, 17 July 2000.

Arendt, Hannah. 1969. *Collective Responsibility.* Montreal.

Barwig, Klaus, Saathoff, Günter and Weyde, Nicole, eds. 1998. *Entschädigung für NS-Zwangsarbeit. Rechtliche, historische und politische Aspekte* [Compensation for National Socialist Forced Labour. Legal, Historical, Political Aspects]. Baden-Baden.

Bazyler, Michael. 2003. *Holocaust Justice. The Battle for Restitution in America's Courts.* New York.

———. 2004. 'Holocaust Restitution in the United States and Other Claims for Historical Wrongs – An Update'. American Civil Liberties Union, *International Civil Liberties Report.* http://www.aclu.org/International/International.cfm?ID=17187&c=36

Brooks, Roy L. 1999. 'The Age of Apology'. In *When Sorry Isn't Enough. The Controversy over Apologies and Reparations for Human Injustice*, ed. Roy L. Brooks: 3–12. New York.

Burke, Edmund 1961 [1790]. *Reflections on the Revolution in France.* London.
Congressional Research Service Library of Congress. 1990. *Legal Issues Relating to the Future Status of Germany.* Prepared for the Committee on Foreign Relations, United States Senate. Washington.
Crocker, David. 2000. 'Truth Commissions, Transitional Justice and Civil Society'. In *Truth vs Justice,* ed. Robert Rotberg and Dennis Thompson: 99–121. Princeton.
Daniels, Roger. 1999. 'Relocation, Redress and the Report. A Historical Appraisal'. In *When Sorry Isn't Enough. The Controversy over Apologies and Reparations for Human Injustice,* ed., Roy L. Brooks: 183–204. New York.
Eizenstat, Stuart E. 2003. *Imperfect Justice: Looted Assets, Slave Labour, and the Unfinished Business of World War II.* New York.
———. (Coordinator). 1997. *Preliminary Study on U.S. and Allied Efforts To Recover and Restore Gold and Other Assets Stolen or Hidden by Germany During World War II.* Washington DC. May.
———. (Coordinator). 1998. *U.S. and Allied Wartime and Postwar Relations and Negotiations With Argentina, Portugal, Spain, Sweden, and Turkey on Looted Gold and German External Assets and U.S. Concerns about the Fate of Wartime Utasha Treasury.* Washington DC. June.
Elster, Jon. 2004. *Closing the Books: Transitional Justice in Historical Perspective.* Cambridge.
'Foundation Initiative of German Enterprises: Remembrance, Responsibility and Future'. 1999. Joint Statement on the Occasion of the Meeting of Representatives of 12 German Enterprises with Federal Chancellor Gerhard Schröder, 16 February. Bonn.
French, Peter A. 1991. 'The Corporation as a Moral Person'. In *Collective Responsibility: Five Decades of Debate in Theoretical and Applied Ethics,* ed. Larry May and Stacey Hoffman: 133–49. Maryland.
Healey, Justin. 2000. *Towards Reconciliation.* Thirroul.
Herbert, Ulrich. 1999. *Fremdarbeiter, Politik und Praxis des 'Ausländer-Einsatzes' in der Kriegswirtschaft des Dritten Reiches.* [*Foreign Workers: the Politics and Practice of the 'Use of Foreigners' in the War Economy of the Third Reich*] 3rd edn. Bonn.
Jaspers, Karl. 1961 [1946]. *The Question of German Guilt.* New York.
Joint Statement on Occasion of the Final Plenary Meeting Concluding International Talks on the Preparation of the Foundation 'Remembrance, Responsibility and the Future', Berlin, 17 July 2000.
Keane, John. 1998. *Civil Society: Old Images, New Visions.* Cambridge.
———. 2003. *Global Civil Society?* Cambridge.
Kritz, Neil J. ed. 1995. *Transitional Justice, How Emerging Democracies Reckon with Former Regimes,* 3 vols. Washington.
Kukathas, Chandran. 2002. 'Responsibility for past injustice: how to shift the burden'. *Politics, Philosophy and Economies* 2: 165–90.
May, Larry. 1991. 'Metaphysical Guilt and Moral Taint'. In *Collective Responsibility: Five Decades of Debate in Theoretical and Applied Ethics,* ed. Larry May and Stacey Hoffman: 239–54. Savage. Maryland.
May, Larry, and Hoffman, Stacey, eds. 1991. *Collective Responsibility: Five Decades of Debate in Theoretical and Applied Ethics.* Savage. Maryland.

Meyer, Lukas H., ed. 2003. *Justice in Time. Responding to Historical Injustice.* Baden-Baden.

Minow, Martha. 1999. *Between Vengeance and Forgiveness: Facing History after Genocide and Mass Violence.* Boston.

Minow, Martha and Rosenblum, Nancy L. 2003. *Breaking the Cycles of Hatred: Memory, Law, and Repair.* Princeton.

Robinson, Randall. 2002. *The Debt. What America owes to Blacks.* New York.

Shapiro, Martin and Stone Sweet, Alec. 2002. *On Law, Politics, and Judicialization.* Oxford.

Slaughter, Anne-Marie, and Bosco, David. 2000. 'Plaintiff's Diplomacy'. *Foreign Affairs,* September–October: 102–16.

Spiliotis, Susanne-Sophia. 2003. *Verantwortung und Rechtsfrieden. Die Stiftungsinitiative der deutschen Wirtschaft,* Frankfurt.

———. 2005a [forthcoming]. *Moral Responsibility and Legal Closure. The German Economy Foundation Initiative.* New York.

———. 2005b [forthcoming]. 'Erzwungene Kooperation? Die Stiftungsinitiative der deutschen Wirtschaft'. In *Wirtschaftseliten und Verantwortung,* ed. Dieter Rucht. Paderborn.

Stephens, Beth and Ratner, Michael. 1996. *International Human Rights Litigation in U.S. Courts.* New York.

Teitel, Ruti G. 2000. *Transitional Justice.* Oxford.

Thompson, Janna. 2002. *Taking Responsibility for the Past: Reparation and Historical Injustice.* Cambridge.

Velasquez, Manuel. 1991. 'Why Corporations Are Not Morally Responsible For Anything They Do'. In *Collective Responsibility: Five Decades of Debate in Theoretical and Applied Ethics,* ed. Larry May and Stacey Hoffman: 111–31. Savage. Maryland.

Waldron, Jeremy. 1992. 'Superseding Historic Injustice'. *Ethics* 103: 4–28.

———. 2003. 'Redressing Historic Injustice'. In *Justice in Time. Responding to Historical Injustice,* ed. Lukas Meyer: 55–77. Baden-Baden.

Wolffe, Richard and Authers, John. 2002a. *The Victims' Fortune. Inside the Epic Battle over the Debts of the Holocaust.* New York.

———, eds. 2002b. *NS-Forced Labor: Remembrance and Responsibility. Legal and Historical Observations.* Baden-Baden.

Zumbansen, Peer and Adler, Libby. 2002. 'The Forgetfulness of Noblesse: A Critique of the German Foundation Law Compensating Slave and Forced Laborers of the Third Reich'. *Harvard Journal on Legislation* 39, 1: 1–55.

Zweig, Ronald. 2001. *German Reparations and the Jewish World. A History of the Claims Conference,* 2nd edn. London.

Legal cases

Alien Tort Claims Act (ATCA), 28 U.S.C. §1350.

In re World War II Era Japanese Forced Labour Litigation, 114 F. Supp. 2d 939 (N.D.Cal.2000).

Internet references

www.aclu.org/International/International.cfm?ID=17187&c=36

www.aph.gov.au/senate/committee/legcon_ctte/completed_inquiries/2002–04/
reconciliation

www.cmht.com/casewatch/humanrights/apartheid.html18

www.europa-web.de/europa/03euinf/04AUS_BU/deporepe.htm

www.law.harvard.edu/alumni/bulletin/backissues/summer99/article4.html

www.reconciliationaustralia.org/

www.state.gov/www/regions/eur/holocaustp.html

www.stiftung-evz.de

www.stiftungsinitiative.de

3

THE FACES OF SOCIAL INEQUALITY

Paul Nolte

Civil society is often understood today as a normatively or empirically defined nucleus of the social order, distinct from other institutionalized established social complexes, above all the state, the market economy and the private sphere. The term 'civil society' draws its legitimacy essentially from these distinctions, since it defends certain standards of behaviour and social coexistence that are subjected to a constant and structural external threat through the operational mechanisms of those other sectors.

Justified as this perspective may be, it is problematic for two reasons. First, the state and the market not only threaten civil society; they also promote its relative autonomy, or even enable it to exist in the first place. Secondly, civil society simultaneously exists in a complex and often contradictory network of 'internal' relationships, that is, with respect to its own socio-structural and sociocultural foundations. It can be threatened not only by other, external subsystems, such as the bureaucratic state or the capitalist economy, but also by its own social foundation, that is, by the structures of social stratification and social inequality. What do we mean by this? Jürgen Kocka has revealed the paradoxes that are the product of the ambivalence and ambiguity – both conceptually and historically, since the eighteenth century – of the German term *bürgerliche Gesellschaft*, with its meanings 'civil society', on the one hand, and 'bourgeois society', on the other. Civil society could never be entirely separated from the 'bourgeoisie' in the sense of being connected to a middle class. And yet precisely this bourgeois form, with its exclusive and hierarchical characteristics, worked against the realization of an inclusive and egalitarian civil society. Generalizing these ideas – developed in respect of the middle class – one could say that civil society has something to do with the class stratification of modern society, with this society's system of social inequality and its cultural interpretation and treatment of that system in society itself. How the nature of this relationship between civil society and social inequality can be determined, however, has not been satisfactorily explained – either in terms of social theory or empirically and historically. Recent debates on civil society often have a different theme: they are less concerned with what separates members of a society, but with the question: 'what ultimately holds modern societies together? The often plaintive discourse on civil society is shaped no longer by the experience of social polarization (caused, for example, by class conflict), but by concerns about the loss of social cohesion due to increasing individualization and fragmentation' (Kocka, 2001: 20).

Consequently, I shall now try – in four stages – to clarify and formulate more precisely the fraught relationship between civil society and social inequality. First, an attempt will be made to distinguish some areas of affinity and tension between these poles, in a very fundamental and conceptual sense. The second section – which draws on nineteenth- and twentieth-century German history – will deal with historical experiences of this problem; here the necessarily close connection between historical perspectives and those oriented to the present, as well as between systematic-cum-theoretical and empirical approaches, in research on civil society, will be underlined. In the third part I shall attempt to take up recent debates in the social sciences and social philosophy on the triad of civil society, 'civic spirit' and inequality, and apply them to this issue. I shall then close by briefly suggesting how a research programme in these terms could be developed theoretically and empirically in the future.

Civil Society and Social Inequality: Affinity and Tension

In order to unravel this dense fabric, one can distinguish between a 'positive' and a 'negative' side of the relationship between civil society and social inequality. The two phenomena are tightly intertwined and yet they exist in a certain tension, at times even open conflict, with each other. First of all, the assumption that a functioning civil society requires social inequality (or a certain degree or expression of it) – indeed, that social inequality is a precondition of civil society's potential to exist – can be traced and substantiated on at least three levels. *First*, there is the level of the history of ideas and theories. If – as Jürgen Kocka has done – one investigates the origins of the concept of civil society in the eighteenth century, it is impossible to ignore models of civil society in the Scottish

Enlightenment, for instance in the works of Adam Smith and Adam Ferguson. (Ferguson 1995 [1767]). Here, civil society emerges – at the end point of an idealized process of historical stages – as a bourgeois class society based on the principles of general market trade. It is thus socially differentiated, but at the same time is based on a set of structural principles and behavioural norms that are absolutely essential for the 'civil' – that is, humane, peaceful, liberal – character of a society: the individualism of economic achievement; 'trust' as the social mechanism of an ethics of brotherhood originally generalized in the market;[1] and the related behavioural standards of politeness and moral refinement. In a broader sense, bourgeois class society also facilitates the provision of moral support for those excluded and disadvantaged by it, for example in the form of bourgeois welfare policies and charity (Haskell 1985).

Secondly – as the above implies – there was a parallel empirical and historical development. Civil society developed in parallel with the rise of class society, market society and capitalism – not only in the original conceptions of Enlightenment thinkers, but also in (West and Central) European and North American history in the nineteenth and twentieth centuries. This is true in turn for the further development of the normative project as well as for concrete social institutions, such as clubs or the 'benevolent empire' of civic involvement. In any case, the dissolution of corporative links (and their transformation into market-based social relations) was obviously an important prerequisite for the emergence of civil society. Where corporative traditions were lacking or capitalism's triumphant march began early, as in the United States and England, strong, lasting structures of civil society also appeared relatively early.

Thirdly, one could refer to a counterfactual argument. Where attempts were made to eliminate social inequality through radical means – especially in the major politico-ideological social experiments of the twentieth century – the opportunities for civil society to develop were always extremely poor. The vision of a homogeneous, more or less totally levelled-out society robbed the society of its internal drive and regenerative powers and usually led to conformism and the loss of a civic public.[2] The idea of eliminating class-based inequality was often also closely coupled with the rigid exclusion of the 'other' on racial, religious or other grounds, as was the case with the German *Volksgemeinschaft*. To that extent it appears to be an indispensable precondition of civil society that difference – including different material positions within a class structure – is tolerated and made possible.

Yet it is also possible to make the opposite argument: tension – indeed, open contradiction – can develop between civil society and social inequality; social inequality, at least if it takes certain extreme forms, undermines civil society, both as theoretical concept and as social practice. In order to examine this matter more closely, two forms of social difference and inequality can be distinguished in an initially somewhat abstract fashion: 'dichotomy' and 'hierarchy'. *Dichotomous inequality* refers to the binary coding of affiliation: the inclusion of one and the fundamental exclusion of the other. One example of this is the dichotomy of gender. It is not the difference of gender models (male versus female) per se that runs counter to the basic premises of civil society, but the exclusion, derived from this difference, of the group which the majority culture defines as being less capable. Such a system of inequality need not be strictly bipolar. Where there are cultural or ethnic differences, or a plurality of religions, for example, multipolar gradations are also possible, but they usually still tend to exist in relation to one politically and culturally inclusive entity, such as the language of the ruling elite in a multi-ethnic state. Exclusive inequalities of this kind were an integral part of the history of civil society in the nineteenth and twentieth centuries. 'Wins' could be recorded for civil society while almost all women and, in many countries, ethnically or racially defined groups, were excluded from civil society, sometimes with increasing intensity.[3] This could not be maintained in the long term, however; from a normative point of view civil society demands that such exclusive dichotomies be dissolved. This would not, of course, entail making everyone equal (in the sense of adapting to the previously dominant pattern); rather, 'recognition' is the appropriate remedy in civil society.[4]

In contrast, the principle of *hierarchical inequality* is different; as is its accompanying strategy of inclusion and exclusion. The classical case of hierarchical (one could also say 'graded') inequality is the inequality of socio-economic positions (and the resulting sociocultural opportunities) of individuals or families in the stratification and class system of a society. In terms of the risks for civil society, this means that, if social differences are too great, the 'rungs' of the social 'ladder' will become too far apart (as was often said in Germany from the late nineteenth century); communication over these distances, and thus integration of society, will then no longer be possible. The wealthier or even the middle classes will cease to give charity to the poor (at least to what has traditionally been referred to as the undeserving poor), and the poor will lose sight of any prospects of entering the middle class and thus of participating in society and of taking advantage of opportunities. Consequently, the economic classes withdraw, rather than becoming involved with one another. This pattern appears to be typical for many 'threshold countries', such as those in Latin America. However, there are also countries, such as the United States, in which a strong civil society can evidently withstand a very great degree of socio-economic inequality. The forms and degrees of inequality that can be justified have varied considerably throughout history and from culture to culture.

With respect to hierarchical inequality, the adequate remedy within the context of a civil society is not recognition but 'redistribution'. A politically controlled transfer of income and assets (classically through taxation policies and welfare state transfer) should serve to reduce social differences while at the same time increasing the resources relevant to civil society. This idea can be substantiated by means of an argument based on social theory or social philosophy, such as that developed by John Rawls in his theory of justice.[5] A 'fair' social order requires the just distribution of social and economic goods. Inequality needs to be justified by its also benefiting the less favoured in society. 'Justice' thus becomes a basic category of civil society, one that serves to steer the public management of social inequality. The concept of justice might also be a key to negotiating between the 'positive' and 'negative' correlation of civil society and social inequality (in the sense in which they have been briefly contrasted here).

Germany since the Nineteenth Century

The relationship between civil society and social inequality – not only theoretically, but in reality – needs be described on the basis of empirical case studies. This includes looking at the historical development of this relationship, not only because past experiences can offer an instructive comparison with present-day issues, but, above all, because contemporary structural patterns of social stratification and inequality, civic involvement and the interrelationship of market, state and society are greatly influenced by history. Without an understanding of this history, these patterns cannot be understood nor can they, in political terms, be successfully developed. Even in an age when the nation state has lost considerable significance, and politics and society are being 'de-territorialized', it is hard to exaggerate the importance of national structural patterns and paths of development, especially since the late eighteenth century. Intellectual discourse on Western civil society was already trans- and international during the Enlightenment, but the institutional implementation and cultural standardization of civil society took place largely within the framework of the nation state and national cultures. A classical example of this is the development of social policy and the welfare state in Europe and North America from the second half of the nineteenth century. Although research in this area, too, has recently stressed the significance of the international exchange of ideas and plans (see, for example, Rodgers 1998), the diversity as between nation states of institutional forms is obvious, for example, when comparing Germany and the United States. As can easily be shown in respect of German national insurance, such national solutions are also extremely 'path-dependent'. Early course settings have a continued effect and are difficult to change later on. However, not only institutions have had great impact historically; the 'cultures' of social policy – a complex web of norms, collective expectations, social modes of behaviour, and so on, largely formed within the framework of national societies – also have a history that continues to have an effect into the present.

To illustrate these remarks on the historical dimension of our subject, I shall briefly outline the development of the relationship between civil society and social inequality in Germany since the early nineteenth century. This cannot hope to be a historical reconstruction and 'narrative' in a narrow sense; instead, I shall suggest certain arguments and central terms that might prove helpful for such an analysis. In particular, an attempt must be made to use previous findings and interpretations of history to shed new light on the 'new-old' question of civil society. Even if the concept of civil society up to now has not served as a framework or paradigm for a more comprehensive, historical longitudinal analysis, individual issues contained within it – or in tension with it – have often been dealt with very intensively in historical research. This is true for the aforementioned social policies, as well as for the history of the bourgeoisie and bourgeois society (see Kocka 1987) and of the socially exclusive ideologies of *Volksgemeinschaft* and racism. This also brings out the historical dimension of the two types of inequality that have already been defined as 'dichotomous' and 'hierarchical'. One can thus distinguish four historical stages, using Germany as an example, since the early nineteenth century.

The early and mid-nineteenth century – the *first phase* – was characterized by a fundamental transformation of the functional principles of social inequality, on the one hand, and, on the other, by the successful establishment of patterns of thought and institutions connected with civil society. The corporative order based on birth, descent and honour progressively changed into a class society based on achievement and market opportunities. At the same time – though this process had significant precursors in the eighteenth century – new types of association developed in the form of a diverse network of clubs and associations. This confronted the bureaucratic state of the late absolutist period with the model of a self-controlled, egalitarian civil society; it also – in the form of educational societies and reading circles, of citizens' associations and liberal political clubs – made the demand for 'civility' part of its programme. On the one hand, this 'bourgeois society' – as has often been stressed – broke down corporative boundaries of affiliations (for example between the nobility and the middle class, between public servants and middle-class businessmen); on the other hand, however, in the early nineteenth century it was still limited to a relatively narrow, aristocratic–bourgeois elite and also remained an exclusively male social domain. Above all, from the 1830s the social basis of civil society expanded considerably 'downwards' into to the middle and petit bourgeois classes, sometimes also reaching the rural population.

This trend toward social universalization corresponded in early liberalism to the idea of a 'classless society of citizens': an independent, middle-class society relatively levelled out in a social sense, or which at least avoided the extremes of poverty and wealth (see Gall 1975; Nolte 1994: especially 151–227). Located to a certain extent at the intersection of dissolving corporative inequalities and not yet fully established class structures, the view that political liberality and 'community spirit', as it was already called at the time, could be made to coincide with relative social homogeneity had gained ground. Similar views were held outside Germany in this period, for example, Tocqueville's model of an American democracy supported by the middle classes and their associations. The actual development of social inequality in the period of 'high industrialization' almost always refuted these utopias of a frictionless coexistence of social structure and civil society, but in the 'collective memory' they continue to exist and remain retrievable as socially egalitarian impulses critical of society.

It should not be overlooked that in their time such models already linked aspects of inclusion and equity with those of exclusion. Not only were broad segments of the lower social classes refused access to a politically active, participatory civil society. Women, too, had access at most to marginal areas of civil society constructed according to specific gender models: for example, the responsibility for charity and the family. In addition, early bourgeois civil societies were almost always civil societies in 'ethnically homogeneous environments', to borrow an expression of Joseph Schumpeter (1991). They made their civility and openness available inwardly at the price of ethnic (cultural, religious) homogeneity or outward ethnic exclusion. The primary mechanism of integration was therefore not the recognition of the other, but 'assimilation'. This can be clearly observed in the participation of German Jews in the emerging civil society in the nineteenth century.

A *second phase* in the relationship between civil society and social inequality in Germany encompassed the final third of the nineteenth and the first third of the twentieth centuries: in terms of political regimes, the Second Empire and the Weimar Republic. This was the period of high industrialization and the development of the most clear-cut structures of class society in German history; in this period the liberal 'utopian goal' (Wehler 1988) of the – in social terms – relatively balanced bourgeois society seemed finally to be breaking down in the face of class division between bourgeoisie and proletariat. At the same time the ideas of 1848–49 of a liberal and democratic (nation) state in Central Europe had been defeated. Bismarck's constitution of the German Empire gave power back to authoritarian and bureaucratic traditions; these continued to have a great impact on the political culture after the revolution of 1918–19 and the transition to a republic. This was, at least, the image long portrayed in historiography, above all from the mid-1960s to the mid-1980s. In it civil society and social inequality were, as it were, negatively congruent: inequality and class conflict intensified and the potential for civil society was being constricted by the military and an authoritarian state. In a highly industrial class society with corporative, bureaucratic remnants, as described by Jürgen Kocka (1979), individual segments of society were more and more sealing themselves off from each other. As separate sociocultural 'milieux' hardened (Lepsius 1973), the openness and exchange of civil society could no longer thrive and the civicness of German society decreased.

In the last fifteen years, empirical research in social and cultural history has corrected parts of this image considerably. One must now ask whether one should assume that, in this key phase of modern German history, there was a connection between pronounced social inequality and an apparently 'deficient' civil society. The tension between the two poles was more complex and contradictory than it long appeared to be. Without a doubt the potential for civil society to develop existed within the various 'class cultures' of the German Empire; this was especially true of the labour movement culture with its clubs, educational institutions and self-help facilities and the democratic sociability they fostered. It has become clear that German society – including during the German Empire, and above all at its local roots, the cities – displayed a considerable degree of civicness. It did so not only in a social structural but also in a political sense (see Hettling 1999); it also had a capacity for self-organization and was able to express confidently liberal viewpoints.

But how does one then explain the massive 'loss of civility' that appeared at the latest by 1914 and characterized the European and German phase of war and aggression that lasted until 1945? What role did the culture of 'classical modernity' – much talked about recently – which emerged above all in the major cities around the turn of the century (see Nolte 1996), play in relation to German civil society? With its tendencies towards plurality, openness and tolerance (such as the diverse forms of the 'life reform' movement), on the one hand, and towards sociocultural insecurity, 'nervousness' (Radkau 1998) and a resulting inclination to aggression, on the other, its effects were highly ambivalent. The trend shown by recent research has redirected attention away from problems of the social structure of the German Empire and the Weimar Republic towards the phenomena of culture, mentalities and ideologies.

But, if we have a closer look, the question of social inequality and its political and cultural consequences for civil society is not obsolete: it now simply encompasses the old question of class stratification. This can be observed in detail using two examples. First, there are the distinctions that result from historically changing definitions of citizenship. The naturalization of some meant the exclusion of others; these latter were categorized as nationally, ethnically or 'racially' foreign, as standing outside and beneath political society.[6] Secondly – and related to the first point – in the discourse of the natural sciences from the late nineteenth century, and in its popularization in the social sciences and in public discourse, new patterns of thought about inequality were devised that propagated notions of the biologically based superiority or inferiority of certain groups. In the early twentieth century, these distinctions proved increasingly to be strong obstacles to the further development of civil society in Germany. They overlapped with exclusionary mechanisms – already discussed in earlier research – *vis-à-vis* so-called 'enemies of the Reich' and with the severe conflicts of interest in a highly industrialized class society. In any attempt to understand the relationship between civil society and inequality in this phase of German history, the two must be viewed as interrelated.

This highlights the central problems of the *third phase*, which includes the rise and rule of National Socialism, including the war of extermination and genocide. The 'rupture' of German 'civilization' during the Nazi regime poses in many ways the greatest challenge for a history of civil society in Central Europe. Between the 1960s and the 1980s, the idea prevailed that certain features of the German social structure, especially Germany's late modernization, were responsible for the collapse of civility from 1933.[7] However, this simple nexus between social structure and social inequality, on the one hand, and democracy, liberalness and civil society, on the other, has been often questioned since then, even with regard to explaining the Third Reich. If Nazism is to be understood in part (but not exclusively) as an expression of a specific modernity instead of merely as a manifestation of atavism, what is the relationship of specific German structures of inequality to the chasm between 'civilization and barbarism' (see Bajohr et al. 1991)? The question could be formulated more sharply: in view of recent Holocaust research, which in the 1990s has fundamentally changed the image of the Nazi regime, are not all categories of a classical analysis of social structures useless? So-called 'perpetrator research' has shown that both academic elites (Herbert 1996) and 'ordinary men' (Browning 1993) could plan and carry out murderous policies. This research has emphasized not only external conditions – the way war and occupation policies caused people to lose inhibitions to commit violence – but also, above all, the philosophical and ideological foundations of such actions, in particular extreme but everyday forms of racism.

Yet newer approaches in research can provide stimuli for a revised version of the connection between social inequality and (the lack of) civil society during the Nazi period. For one thing, it remains indisputable that the broad attractiveness of Nazism was essentially due the fact that it promised to ensure social peace and to level out society. The suffering caused by heightened class tensions in the Weimar Republic and the mutual separation of the different 'corporative estates' made the apparently levelled-out *Volksgemeinschaft* seem a very promising goal; to further society's internal homogeneity people were even prepared to accept the exclusion of those whom it was deemed impossible to integrate (Nolte 2000: esp. 77–107, 159–207). In historical terms this development recalls civil society's fundamental dilemma: that it is threatened not only by an excess of social inequality that can no longer be legitimized, but also by extreme utopias – characteristic of twentieth-century totalitarian ideologies – of social levelling and conformism. On the other hand, such ideas of social homogenization can be understood as variants of a more general pattern of a 'radical doctrine of order' (see Bauman 1989; Raphael 2001) that marked the perceptions and actions of the political elite, especially scholars – in the natural and social sciences – in the first half of the twentieth century. The ideological goal of measuring, categorizing, planning and ordering society in a radically new way was always based in part on certain models of inequality: there were always superior and subordinate classes, races and nations, those who belonged and those who were excluded. This also highlights a fundamental political dilemma confronting civil society: without social goals and utopias, it cannot easily progress, yet too much highly ideological utopianism and too strong a desire for order can also threaten, undermine and destroy civil society.

Finally, the *fourth phase* includes the history of both the Federal Republic of Germany and the German Democratic Republic (GDR) after 1945. Historiographers have – particularly with regard to the GDR – only recently begun to reveal the fraught nature of civil society in this period (a feature that was the result of the existence of two states). It will be important to refrain from oversimplifying the West as a success story and the East as a failure. The absence of the structures of civil society in the GDR was linked in a complex fashion to the social structures in East Germany, but it was fundamentally shaped by the fact that society was under excessive political control. The far more pronounced social levelling out of society, as compared with West Germany, in terms of a petit-bourgeois–proletarian ideal, brought with it a loss of social and cultural civicness; this was true with regard to everyday standards of behaviour as well as to political views and civic involvement (see Engler 2000). On the other hand, the renaissance of 'civil society' is a product of the dictatorships in Central and Eastern Europe. This applies less to the GDR than to Czechoslovakia and Poland; but this finding nevertheless directs attention to the social milieux and conditions in which niches of civil society could emerge within the culture of the opposition – for example, in the Protestant Church.

In the Federal Republic, too, there was not a simple, linear link between the development of civil society and the social structures of West Germany. In any case, a Western model of civil society did not exist in 1945 or 1949; it had to be arduously established in numerous stages, and with successive political and social crises: see, for example, the 1961 '*Spiegel* affair' [when the editorial offices of the West German news magazine *Der Spiegel* were searched by police and its editor-in-chief, Rudolf Augstein, was arrested on charges of high treason because *Der Spiegel* had published an article critical of the West German defence ministry – trans.] With regard to social inequality, the establishment of West German democracy presumably profited – as was argued early on – from the dismantling of older hierarchies; this dismantling was a result of the 'loss', above all, of aristocratic, agrarian elites in what had been the eastern provinces of the German Empire. Ideas on the social 'pacification' of West German society in what sociologist Helmut Schelsky referred to in 1953 as the 'levelled-out middle-class society' (Schelsky 1965) also apply in this context, as does the argument that the rise in living standards in the context of the 'economic miracle', and the triumph of mass consumerism, greatly strengthened the legitimacy not only of the West German political system, but also of the system's political, cultural 'rules' of tolerance and plurality.

In fact, however, the 'levelling out' of society only partly took place (for example, in the form of the disappearance of the older proletariat). It can thus conversely be argued that the social structures of the nineteenth and early twentieth centuries, as well as the formation of 'bourgeois society', continued with amazing persistence in West Germany (see Wehler 2001). The success of civil society would then be closely connected not with the disappearance but precisely with the continuation of class structures – including their socio-cultural and political milieux and behavioural norms. Or has civil society, as could in turn be countered, been threatened again, at the latest since the 1980s, by new structures of inequality, epitomized by long-term unemployment, demands on social welfare and 'new poverty'? And have not new forms of ethnic, cultural segregation – in socio-economic terms also usually at the 'lower margins' of society – developed in southern European and Turkish immigrant communities? The 'multiculturalism' of these milieux promises to benefit civil society, but their separation and exclusion harbours just as great a potential danger. The history of the relationship between civil society and social inequality is not yet at an end.

Civil Society Today:
between 'Civic Spirit' and Growing Inequality

There is a strong argument that we are at the beginning of a new debate on the social foundations of civil society. This debate is currently being conducted with two main focuses, both of which receive insufficient consideration (including in their respective historical dimensions). On the one hand, the issue is the cohesion of society, 'community spirit', 'social capital' and 'civic involvement'; on the other, it is the dividing lines in society, about poverty, exclusion and social inequality (see Nolte 2001: 92–96). In order to characterize this situation more precisely, we can begin with the 'dilemma of individualism'. This resembles the ambivalence in the relationship between civil society and social inequality as characterized in section I above. Individualism and (progressing) individualization are indispensable prerequisites for a successful civil society. This is apparent in the dissolution of corporative ties from the eighteenth century: experience has shown that civil society functions better on a foundation of free, autonomous subjects, and not as well in corporative, clientelistic or similar structures. The much-discussed increase in individualization in Western societies in the 1970s and 1980s is thus a prerequisite for the concepts of civil society discussed since, concepts which aim to reinforce civic forces, through, for example, a reduction in the powers of the state.[8] Sociological reflection on these changes (which have not yet been recorded by historiographers) have given rise to theories on individualization and the dissolution of classes, on lifestyles and on how an individual creates his own biography in the course of his life.[9] These reflections viewed radical individualization overwhelmingly as a positive development – indeed, emphatically welcomed it. They also welcomed the disintegration of conventional modern relationships that (it was assumed) accompany such individualization: both the parent-child nuclear family and the social class, with its organizational culture (such as the trade union), which originated in the nineteenth century.

However, individualization not only encourages and promotes civil society; if it radically dissolves the affective cohesion of society and threatens fundamental social mechanisms essential for the functioning of a civil society – 'trust', 'justice' and 'responsibility', for example – then it can pose a threat to civil society. It is no coincidence that these three terms play an important role in current debates across a broad spectrum of social theory and social philosophy, from economic theory to communitarianism. These relationships need to be examined more thoroughly; briefly, however, it can be said that civil society faces clear risks whenever individualism entails primarily egoism and the hedonistic consumer culture. This has been increasingly acknowledged in recent years in a kind of counter movement to the radical individualism of the 1980s. Consequently, the significance of civic spirit and community is again being stressed, as are social bonding forces or 'ligatures' (Ralf Dahrendorf),[10] for societies of post-classical or the 'second' modernity. It might also be of importance here that the Western path of development, which has relied profoundly on the project of individualization, can meanwhile be seen partly as contingent, while other, more community-supported social forms in non-Western countries are becoming attractive as models. The swing of the pendulum is apparent in the new interest in voluntary work, whether in traditional clubs and associations or in new (sometimes generation-dependent) forms.[11] Civil society is increasingly viewed – for example, in the influential work of the US political scientist Robert Putnam – with an eye to the 'social capital' earned through civic involvement or even merely through informal social contacts (see Putnam 1999). From a historical viewpoint, this still does not explain which increases in community orientation and individualism shaped developments in different countries in the last two centuries, or what the respective relationships of these increases were with the progress or retreat of civil society.

This entire complex is opposed by a second pole in social science discourse, which is again linked to the problem of individualism and civil society: namely, a new debate on social inequality in Western societies. This debate directs our attention back to long-neglected issues of material privilege and the lack thereof, of wealth and poverty, and of social hierarchy and class stratification. The empirical background of this debate is the phenomenon, repeatedly identified in numerous studies, of an inequality on the increase (again) or which has appeared in new forms since the 1970s or at the latest the 1980s. The issue here is not even the widening of the affluence gap in the form of global and 'globalized' inequality; it is primarily 'only' social inequality within Western societies. This inequality is particularly marked in the United States (and was discussed early on): segmentation of the labour market, polarization of income, new poverty and 'underclasses' are the relevant catchphrases. The empirical findings in Germany, where there are different traditions and a very different system of welfare and social security, are less clear (there has not yet been a thorough stocktaking of research conducted to date). However, in individual sectors, inequality is evident and has become firmly established or reinforced. In this context the key issues are, above all, mass unemployment and the need for welfare support (on the part of single mothers and multi-children families); the social structural effects of the 'generation of heirs' [the generation in their forties and fifties in Germany whose parents did not lose their assets through either inflation or war, as was largely the case in the early twentieth century – trans.] and the formation of new underclasses by immigrants and refugees, though these two matters have been less a focus of attention; and, finally, the broad area of inequality between east and west Germany since 1989–90. The first wealth and poverty report of the German federal government has meant that the unequal distribution of material resources in German society has recently received considerable political attention.[12]

The corresponding empirical findings have been partly known for two decades as a result of studies on social structure, the welfare state and poverty. However, they have only recently been linked to two trends in the social sciences and the public sphere, trends that will ensure they have a new impact. First, the approach dominating German social sciences for a period – which viewed the individualization of social situations and social fates as the main feature of societal development in the late twentieth century – has apparently run its course.[13] On the one hand, this might have too rashly generalized the experiences of certain groups of the educated middle classes; on the other hand, it might have confused socio-cultural observations about the multiplication of cultural status symbols (for example, in consumer behaviour) with the dissolution of social fates. The view of social groups and collective situations and experiences is once again becoming unobstructed. Secondly, not only in empirical research, but also in social theory, and perhaps in social history too, the claim of the exclusive validity of the culturalist view of society that has been predominant since the 1980s is being questioned. As great as the benefits were of understanding society through the lens not only of 'social inequality' but also of 'cultural difference' (for example, of ethnic communities), the demand is being clearly made, even on the political left, for a return to the categories of economic position and social inequality: 'It should be axiomatic', Nancy Fraser has written, 'that no defensible successor project to socialism can simply jettison the commitment to social equality in favor of cultural difference' (1997: 14).

This dual orientation towards 'community spirit' and 'inequality' is significant in our context because it opens up new approaches in the discussion of civil society and its nexus with social inequality. Research on social inequality has been shaped largely by quantitative, empirical social research. This offers a way for it to be linked – conceptually and in other ways – with the more qualitative, hermeneutic, historical and social-theoretical research on civil society, civicness and community formation. Two recent examples can illustrate this. The aforementioned study by Robert Putnam on civic engagement and social capital in the United States still assigned conspicuously little significance to 'social inequality' and 'class', as if the distribution of social capital were dependent on a large number of individual aspects of social behaviour (the consumption of television, employment and so on), without one being able to aggregate these in some way to class-specific patterns of behaviour.

However, a more recent study on international comparisons, edited by Putnam, adopts a very different tone, and Putnam himself concludes: 'The concerns about inequalities, especially the growing inequalities in the area of social capital, represent perhaps the most important common thread that carries through the national studies in this book' (2001: 787).

However, the authors found that distribution of social capital is substantially dependent on 'classical' mechanisms of distribution – on the (unequal, or even increasingly unequal) distribution of material resources such as assets and income, and not least also on education. The ability to develop bonds, to be engaged in and for the community, that is, to promote and strengthen 'civil society', is thus essentially coupled to one's position in the system of inequality or, one could even say, to one's class position. How did this empirical correlation between class position and social capital develop historically? Peter Hall has shown, with regard to Britain, that the differences between the middle class and the working class in respect of social capital and political engagement have not only not decreased since the 1950s: they have grown: 'The two groups left out of civil society and increasingly marginalized from it are the working class and the young'(1999: 96). Theda Skocpol has observed a shift in the United States towards more 'oligarchic' structures in civil society. In this new system, affluent and educated Americans are far more privileged than they were in the traditional civic system of 'cross-class membership associations' (2001: 646ff).

The second example is Anthony Giddens's recent attempt to place the issues of social inequality and civil society in a single social-theoretical framework (2001). Giddens takes up the empirical research (referred to above) on the increase of social inequality in most industrial countries since the 1970s and attempts to give new relevance to welfare state redistribution. But he feels the old, completely state-centred politics of justice is outmoded; civil society is, instead, the central element of his 'third way' politics. Giddens uses the term 'social exclusion' to link the apparently divergent approaches of inequality and community formation. This allows him to diagnose not only a marginalization of the poor, but also an 'exclusion of elites'; these isolate themselves from the rest of society and retreat from civic engagement.

We should now – using individual examples and being empirically more specific – determine how such approaches can give rise to fruitful ideas and research on the relationship between civil society and social inequality. Not least, we should attempt to incorporate (conceptually and empirically) dimensions of inequality beyond the 'class question', particularly gender difference and ethnocultural differentiation. But even in the classical frame of reference – within which inequality has, above all, socio-economic causes – there are individual questions to examine: these include – by way of indication – the bourgeoisie or the middle class. As

Jürgen Kocka has shown, the rise of civil society can be interpreted as a normative project and as a socio-political practice that has a close causal relationship with the rise of the middle class. Expressed in exaggerated terms, civil society since the eighteenth and early nineteenth centuries has, above all, been a project of the middle classes; it was only later – for example, with the classical labour movement – generalized 'downwards'. Anthony Giddens has indicated that even today not so much the rich but the 'merely affluent' at the centre of society, where financial and social capital converge, play a key role regarding 'social concerns' and the functioning of civil society in general (2001: 133).

Conversely, is it possible to conclude that civil society can be created only with a civic-minded and politically involved middle class? This has unexpectedly become an explosive issue in recent decades in all Western countries. The traditional labour movement culture and, with it, the organizations of the lower classes, which had largely adapted themselves to the middle-class model of civil society, are increasingly disbanding or are losing the power to shape society as a whole. New lower classes outside the classical industrial labour force are withdrawing from organizations and tending to display political indifference or apathy, as demonstrated by the class-specific drop in voter turnout. On the other hand, the new forms of civic involvement that have gained importance in recent decades relative to the classical culture of clubs, associations and organizations (for example, citizens' initiatives and protest movements) consist to a considerable degree of a 'post-educated bourgeois' middle class and are often far less capable of cross-class integration than was the case with traditional movements. Such changes need in future to be examined in much more detail than they have been to date, both systematically and historically – that is, from the standpoint of contemporary social history.

Conclusion: towards a Future Research Programme

This points to some possible directions for future research into the connection between civil society and social inequality. It has also, one hopes, been clearly shown that it is worthwhile examining the issue of civil society in terms of social inequality, not merely within the existing framework but, in many respects, in a new, relevant way. In briefly outlining a few possible aspects of a future research programme, it makes sense to distinguish between, on the one hand, issues of fact and content, and, on the other, methodological issues. With regard to *content*, at least two tasks appear rewarding. First, historical social science should reconstruct, comprehensively and comparatively, the development of social inequality in Western societies since the Second World War, and above all since the 1970s and 1980s. There is a wealth of materials available as a point of departure; the task is to synthesize, analyse and, not least, 'historicize' – that is, locate in a framework of the continuity and discontinuity of a history of modernity, of class society and cultural forms, of poverty and the welfare state – these data and findings. Secondly, new approaches – from a longer-term historical standpoint – are desirable: these would allow one to see the relationship between civil society and inequality since the eighteenth and nineteenth centuries differently, in terms other than those of established historical interpretations. A starting point for this could be Nancy Fraser's appeal not to play off 'recognition' and 'redistribution' against each other; this is essentially a suggestion to merge cultural and social history, cultural difference and social inequality, into a common paradigm or 'narrative'.

It is at least as important to pursue new *methodological* paths. Here too this means that fixed boundaries in research need to be overcome. The preceding considerations have shown that we particularly need to establish a new connection between quantitative and qualitative formulations of problems and methods – especially in Germany, where these strands are more obviously separated than elsewhere. This requirement can be divided into three areas. First, there is a need for a closer connection between, on the one hand, empirical social research, and, on the other, social theory (including the 'diagnosis of society' and contemporary criticism from a social theory perspective). Discussions in the English-speaking world seem to be more advanced in this regard. Empirical social research must get over its occasional tendency merely to describe; social theory must resume and intensify its processing of empirical findings instead of 'getting lost in the clouds'. Secondly, even empirical research needs to combine quantitative characteristics more than it has until now with, for example, sociocultural hermeneutics. In describing inequality in present-day societies it is not enough merely to list statistics on poverty. It can also be said that the analysis of material, social structures and the examination of standards of behaviour, cultural standardization of social behaviour and so on are closely related. Thirdly, new methods of combining contemporary analysis and historical contextualization would be helpful. A historical contextualization would not simply consist of the compulsory brief excursion into the age of the Enlightenment or early industrial class society; instead, it would be a thorough historicization and consideration in its chronological context of the contemporary (above all, in the last third of the twentieth century) issue of civil society and social inequality. If that were possible, other areas of historical social science research could profit, too. Moreover, outside the realm of research, this could increase interest in such issues in both public and political spheres.

Notes

1. On this see, for example, studies by Benjamin Nelson.
2. On this problem, using Germany as an example, see Nolte 2000. See also section II below.
3. It is possible to take this a step further and draw a direct correlation: a more rigid exclusion based on dichotomous principles fostered or enabled the generalization of rights and opportunities in the other group. The introduction of general suffrage for white men in the early nineteenth century in the United States was closely linked to the firm exclusion of women and blacks.
4. Here and in the following argument, I take up Nancy Fraser's distinction between 'recognition' and 'redistribution' as two basic, mutually irreducible principles of equality. See Fraser 1997.
5. Rawls 1999 [1971]. For a more precise discussion of the 'justice' category in the relationship between civil society and social inequality, it is necessary to take up other ideas, especially those of Amartya Sen. See, for example, Sen 1983 and 1999.
6. For contributions to the present, intensive discussion of this matter, see Conrad and Kocka 2001; Gosewinkel 2001.
7. See the classic Dahrendorf 1967.
8. See Schmid 1990, and for the debate on the tasks of the state in the 1990s, for example, Grimm 1994.
9. See Beck 1986 (it is not by chance that he interprets classes to an extent as late corporative configurations; on life-course research, see, for example, the works by Karl Ulrich Mayer.
10. See, for example, Dahrendorf 1988. (Initially, of course, Dahrendorf used this term to denote something different, namely, deep cultural ties in modernity that offer individuals some orientation in the 'world of options'.)
11. On this, see the research of the German Bundestag's commission of inquiry into 'the future of civic involvement'. The research on the 'Third Sector' and its implications for civil society – not least, that conducted at the Wissenschaftszentrum Berlin (WZB) – should be mentioned here: see Anheier et al. 1997.
12. Bundesregierung 2001. From the broad range of recent publications on this subject by the Wissenschaftszentrum Berlin, see Böhnke 2001.
13. Some would instead say, and reproachfully, in sociological newspaper features that shaped public opinion. But then it must be asked why empirical research on social structures did not have the same public impact, and if this was the fault of the media alone.

References

Anheier, Helmut K., Priller, Eckhard et al., eds. 1997. *Der Dritte Sektor in Deutschland. Organisationen zwischen Staat und Markt im gesellschaftlichen Wandel.* Berlin.

Bajohr, Frank et al., eds. 1991. *Zivilisation und Barbarei. Die widersprüchlichen Potentiale der Moderne;* in memory of Detlev Peukert. Hamburg.

Bauman, Zygmunt. 1989. *Modernity and the Holocaust.* Ithaca.

Beck, Ulrich. 1986. *Risikogesellschaft. Auf dem Weg in eine andere Moderne.* Frankfurt.

Böhnke, Petra. 2001. *Nothing Left to Lose? Poverty and Social Exclusion in Comparison: Empirical Evidence on Germany.* WZB-Paper FS III 01–402. Berlin.

Browning, Christopher R. 1993. *Ordinary Men: Reserve Police Battalion 101 and the Final Solution in Poland.* New York.

Bundesregierung. 2001. *Lebenslagen in Deutschland. Der erste Armuts- und Reichtumsbericht der Bundesregierung.* Government report. Berlin. http://www.bundesregierung.de/Anlage253224/Armutsbericht.pdf

Conrad, Christoph and Kocka, Jürgen, eds., 2001. *Staatsbürgerschaft in Europa. Historische Erfahrungen und aktuelle Debatten.* Hamburg.

Dahrendorf, Ralf. 1967. *Society and Democracy in Germany.* London.

———. 1988. *The Modern Social Conflict: An Essay on the Politics of Liberty.* New York.

Engler, Wolfgang. 2000. *Die Ostdeutschen. Kunde von einem verlorenen Land.* Berlin.

Ferguson, Adam. 1995 [1767]. *Essay on the History of Civil Society*, ed. Fania Oz-Salzberg. Cambridge.

Fraser, Nancy. 1997. *Justice Interruptus: Critical Reflections on the 'Postsocialist' Condition* New York.

Gall, Lothar. 1975. 'Liberalismus und "bürgerliche Gesellschaft". Zu Charakter und Entwicklung der liberalen Bewegung in Deutschland'. *Historische Zeitschrift* 220: 324–56.

Giddens, Anthony. 2001. *Die Frage der sozialen Ungleichheit.* Frankfurt.

Gosewinkel, Dieter. 2001. *Einbürgern und Ausschließen. Die Nationalisierung der Staatsangehörigkeit vom Deutschen Bund zur Bundesrepublik Deutschland.* Göttingen.

Grimm, Dieter, ed. 1994. *Staatsaufgaben.* Frankfurt.

Hall, Peter. 2001. 'Social Capital in Britain'. *British Journal of Political Science* 29: 417–61.

Haskell, Thomas L. 1985. 'Capitalism and the Origins of Humanitarian Sensibility'. *American Historical Review* 90: 339–61, 437–566.

Herbert, Ulrich. 1996. *Best: Biographische Studien über Radikalismus, Weltanschauung und Vernunft.* Bonn.

Hettling, Manfred. 1999. *Politische Bürgerlichkeit. Der Bürger zwischen Individualität und Vergesellschaftung in Deutschland und der Schweiz von 1860 bis 1918.* Göttingen.

Kocka, Jürgen. 1979. 'Stand – Klasse – Organisation. Strukturen sozialer Ungleichheit in Deutschland vom späten 18. bis zum frühen 20. Jahrhundert im Aufriß'. In *Klassen in der europäischen Sozialgeschichte*, ed. Hans-Ulrich Wehler: 137–65. Göttingen.

———. 2001. 'Zivilgesellschaft als historisches Problem und Versprechen'. In *Europäische Zivilgesellschaft in Ost und West. Begriff, Geschichte, Chancen*, ed. Manfred Hildermeier et al.: 13–39. Frankfurt.

———, ed. 1987. *Bürger und Bürgerlichkeit im 19. Jahrhundert.* Göttingen.

Lepsius, M. Rainer. 1973. 'Parteiensystem und Sozialstruktur: zum Problem der Demokratisierung der deutschen Gesellschaft'. In *Deutsche Parteien vor 1918*, ed. Gerhard A. Ritte: 56–80. Cologne.

Nolte, Paul. 1994. *Gemeindebürgertum und Liberalismus in Baden 1800–1850. Tradition – Radikalismus – Republik.* Göttingen.

———. 1996. '1900: Das Ende des 19. und der Beginn des 20. Jahrhunderts in sozialgeschichtlicher Perspektive'. *Geschichte in Wissenschaft und Unterricht* 47: 281–300.

———. 2000. *Die Ordnung der deutschen Gesellschaft. Selbstentwurf und Selbstbeschreibung im 20. Jahrhundert.* Munich.

———. 2001. '"Klingeln Sie bei Ihrem Nachbarn!" Die Rückkehr der Gesellschaft: Wie bürgerliches Engagement und soziale Gerechtigkeit zusammengedacht werden können'. *Literaturen*, September: 92–96.

Putnam, Robert D. 1999. *Bowling Alone: The Collapse and Revival of American Community.* New York.

———, ed. 2001. *Gesellschaft und Gemeinsinn. Sozialkapital im internationalen Vergleich.* Gütersloh.

Radkau, Joachim. 1998. *Das Zeitalter der Nervosität. Deutschland zwischen Bismarck und Hitler.* Munich.

Raphael, Lutz.. 2001. 'Radikales Ordnungsdenken und die Organisation totalitärer Herrschaft: Weltanschauungseliten und Humanwissenschaftler im NS-Regime'. *Geschichte und Gesellschaft* 27: 5–40.

Rawls, John. 1999 [1971]. *A Theory of Justice,* rev. edn. Cambridge, Mass.

Rodgers, Daniel. 1998. *Atlantic Crossings: Social Politics in a Progressive Age.* Cambridge.

Schelsky, Helmut. 1965. 'Die Bedeutung des Schichtungsbegriffs für die Analyse der gegenwärtigen deutschen Gesellschaft'. In Helmut Schelsky, *Auf der Suche nach Wirklichkeit*: 331–36. Düsseldorf and Cologne.

Schmid, Thomas. 1990. *Staatsbegräbnis. Von ziviler Gesellschaft.* Berlin.

Schumpeter, Joseph A. 1991 [1927]. 'Social Classes in an Ethnically Homogeneous Environment'. Reprinted in *Joseph A. Schumpeter: The Economics and Sociology of Capitalism,* ed. Richard Swedberg: 230–83. Princeton.

Sen, Amartya. 1983. *Poverty and Famines: An Essay on Entitlement and Deprivation.* Oxford.

———. 1999. *Development as Freedom.* Oxford.

Skocpol, Theda. 2001. 'Das bürgergesellschaftliche Amerika – gestern und heute'. In *Gesellschaft und Gemeinsinn,* ed. Robert D. Putnam: 593–654. Gütersloh.

Wehler, Hans-Ulrich. 1988. 'Geschichte und Zielutopie der deutschen "bürgerlichen Gesellschaft"'. In Hans-Ulrich Wehler, *Aus der Geschichte lernen?* Munich: 241–55.

———. 2001. 'Deutsches Bürgertum nach 1945: Exitus oder Phönix aus der Asche?' *Geschichte und Gesellschaft* 27: 617–34.

4

CIVIL SOCIETY:
DESPERATE WISHFUL THINKING?

Herfried Münkler

From the standpoint of political science, one thing is certain: there is rarely so much abuse of a term as when it gets into the hands of politicians or, to be more precise, when it has become an integral part of political language. The sense and meaning of the term is then twisted to fit the need at hand; it is instrumentalized polemically; or else, once the term has become established and is generally accepted, it is expanded and stretched so much that it can cover all manner of things. In short, scholars are not happy when key research terms find their way into political language, as they are then usually irretrievably lost for any further precise scholarly usage. Most social scientists thus avoid terms that are firmly rooted in politics or social discourse, preferring instead to use neologisms reserved for scholarly language. In cases where such socio-political terminology is impossible to avoid, terms are from the outset redefined and made more precise until they are sufficiently polished again to serve scholarly purposes.

I could deal with the term 'civil society' in this spirit. But I prefer not to do this, as the very process of adapting the term for scholarly use would cause me to lose sight of one of its essential aspects, which the concept 'civil society' has only as long as it is part of socio-political language. I am referring to the traces of general use that it contains, as it were, the wearing out of the term through frequent use: this by no means reveals merely terminological loss or deficit, but also the fact that the term is useful for political agenda-setting or for society's attempts to understand itself. In respect of my topic, if the term 'civil society' has undergone such a rapid semantic development in recent decades,[1] then it has obviously satisfied a need for a way to describe a problem and for a particular analytical standpoint – a need that other terms evidently could not be meet in a comparable way.

My impression, first of all, is that the rapid development of the term 'civil society' in recent decades also has to do with the fact that it contains a promise, namely, that tasks can be delegated from the direct competence and responsibility of state actions (that is, politics in a narrow sense) to areas for which politics is at most indirectly competent and thus not directly accountable. In this sense, 'civil society' is perhaps not a formula for peace, but for *removing a burden*: it is used in order to extract something positive from the obvious limits to the state's ability to control and integrate – in other words, in order not to have to categorize this limited ability entirely as weakness, but to grant it at least an air of sophisticated reform policy. The term's trajectory reflects the growing insight into the limits of state action. At the same time it stands for the attempt not to let this insight turn into political resignation, but to use it to pave the way for a new form of participatory civic politics.

Secondly, however, if we have a closer look at what tasks and problem-solving competencies politicians, political intellectuals and even political scientists have proposed for civil society over the last ten years, it becomes apparent that the flourishing of the term also denotes an almost desperate search for conceptual instruments with which to describe and categorize the political and social changes of the last two decades. In this sense the term 'civil society' reflects a great degree of wishful thinking or, indeed, *desperate wishful thinking*. Almost always, when socio-political problems are identified that cannot be mastered with conventional instruments of state regulation or direct intervention, civil society is introduced sooner or later as the solution. Civil society is resorted to more often if doing so makes it more likely that the result will be a reduction in the costs of the services being demanded. Whenever state services threaten to become too costly – and ultimately prohibitively expensive – as is mainly the case with regard to social security systems, then civil society, with the market and its mechanisms, is repeatedly brought into discussion in an effort to avoid social dysfunction in the market allocation of goods and services.

Thirdly, if we look carefully, the trajectory of the term 'civil society' seems to be closely related to the crisis on the political left, at least in Germany. Because of the crisis of state, the left wing has lost the main addressee of its political demands and proposals. As a result, it is precisely from the ranks of the left that dramatic and exaggerated expectations are occasionally projected onto civil society. The political crisis of the left and the semantic trajectory of civil society are two sides of the same coin.

This, then, is 'civil society': it vaguely and confusedly mixes together the notion of removing a burden, wishful thinking and compensatory hopes. How should we begin to clarify the term? I shall now try to do so, first, by sketching out civil society as a field of socio-political order separate from state and market; then, I shall outline the crisis of the welfare state as a challenge for civil society; after which I shall focus on civil society's integrative function. Finally, I shall offer some brief thoughts on the problem of volunteerism and duty.

Civil Society: a Field of Socio-political Order Alongside the State and the Market

The future of civic involvement – that is, the voluntary willingness of citizens to show social solidarity and political engagement – is a central question if we are to achieve a workable understanding of civil society. This can also be expressed as a demand or presumption about citizens' competence: not only must they be shown to belong to the community by means of membership rules (citizenship law), they must also possess the specific competence to exercise their rights and accept their duties. While this certainly assumes that there are state-supported incentive structures that will help develop this competence, it is based mostly on the continuous willingness of the citizens to invest considerable amounts of time and energy to develop it (see von Alemann et al. 1999; Heinze and Olk 2001). Whereas the development of a liberal state under the rule of law since the nineteenth century has been characterized by a progressive formalization of the concept of the citizen and a reduction in the qualifications needed for one to be a citizen, the political concept of a civil society is clearly connected to a 'requalification' of the concept. These qualifications, however, are no longer linked with ownership of property, tax revenue, and educational qualifications, as was the case in the nineteenth and early twentieth centuries; instead, they are linked to one's engagement in the polity to which one belongs by virtue of being a citizen. This is expressed semantically in the way that attributes denoting qualification are increasingly used in association with the concept of the citizen: references to *active* or *competent* citizens are new descriptions of what during classical republicanism was called a *good* citizen.[2] This has clear consequences, which must be kept in mind when using the political concept of civil society: first, that bad citizens also exist and that they make use of, but do not help to create, the benefits and collective goods of the polity.; and, secondly, that there cannot be too many of these bad citizens in a polity or else its future will be jeopardized.

While the term 'civil society' may have become worn out and unclear, it nevertheless has a relevance that can hardly be stressed enough: it essentially associates the specific form of coexistence in a liberal order not with political or economic institutional mechanisms, but, above all, with citizens who – as the socio-political carriers of this order – can bear the burden of normative expectations. The citizen – as distinct from state and market – is neither a subject, nor a holder of rights, neither a calculating, rational maximizer of benefits nor a foresighted independent businessman. The citizen is, instead, someone aware of the value and preconditions of coexistence based on political participation and social solidarity, someone who knows the burdens of self-government and accepts them, fully aware of the long-term negative consequences of refusing to accept them. But these socio-political carriers of civil society are not simply there, waiting to be activated. They must be continuously and repeatedly educated. The political education of a society of citizens cannot be organized on the basis of dividing society into teachers and pupils, because that would make the education susceptible to forms of paternalism that would undermine its basic principles. The political infrastructure of these societies must, rather, be constituted in such a way that the education of citizens (in the sense outlined above) is a self-evident aspect of everyday life; it cannot be based either on the separation of teachers from students or on any sort of certification of performance and achievements. The privileged space in which civic education takes place is civic involvement. This is where experience is acquired, habits are learned and rehearsed and knowledge is obtained – all of which are necessary if a civil society is to last, indeed survive under pressure. In other words, if one wants to discuss civil society, one must also talk about the citizen and civic education.

So what is the state today of civic involvement? One often hears complaints that it is gradually disappearing. First of all, however, while there have been *shifts*, there has certainly not been a general *decline* in civic involvement (see Klages 2000a,b). This reflects changes in social structures and models, that is, the interaction of social change and changes in values. With regard to the issue of civic involvement, the changing role of women in society is one of several significant factors: the disproportionately large contribution that women have made up to now to the production of social capital is decreasing. Very closely related to this is the dissolution of the three-generation family and thus the disappearance of the potential for social security which it embodied (for which, we now know, neither society nor state can compensate).[3] Finally, civic involvement has been affected by the way the nature and extent of involvement in clubs and associations has changed; this is increasingly affecting political parties as well – which are certainly no longer the main beneficiaries of political involvement. Some time ago, Albert Hirschman observed that the willingness of citizens to engage in actions for the common good is not a constant; it is, instead, subject to fluctuations, which

Hirschman described in analogy to Kondratieff waves (Hirschman 1982: 19–23). If the contribution an individual has to make towards the common good is too great – that is, if citizens are asked to display more civic spirit than they feel makes sense, or necessary or feasible within their individual life plans – then the contribution will erode in the same way as if too little is demanded, that is, if citizens have the impression that their actions for the common good are not necessary or that, as a result, they will receive a role with low social recognition (being labelled a 'club freak' or a 'sucker', and so on) (see Münkler and Fischer 2002). In any case, it is necessary to avoid or at least minimize disappointment. If such disappointment does arise, then the citizen – whose preference constantly fluctuates between private benefit and common good – will tend to choose private benefit. The state and market systems are relatively resistant to such fluctuations because their performance is not essentially based on civic involvement but on income orders and incentive systems, which are not linked to motivation curves. Civil society, however, responds to such fluctuations in an extremely sensitive fashion. Thus it makes sense always to consider civil society, and the responsibilities earmarked for it, in combination with state and market, though it is also important to think about ways of flattening out these cyclical fluctuations. This includes the development of incentive structures aimed at making civic involvement less sensitive to social motivation cycles. One way to do this could be to accumulate claims to benefits, which are then satisfied within civil society (see Kaupp et al. 2000).

Although it makes sense to use civic spirit as a resource, one must always be aware of the danger of exhausting it. And, while I doubt the applicability of Ernst Wolfgang Böckenförde's famous theory, which states that civic spirit is one of the pre-political foundations of political order that is consumed within the political process but never reproducible (Böckenförde 1976: 112), there is, nevertheless, a lot to say for fostering a lasting way of dealing with civic involvement. As long as civic involvement is not strengthened or controlled by social or state incentive systems, it displays three different features. In the sense of what has been said with respect to social-cum-moral resources, it is *fragile*. It also tends towards thematic *singularity;* while state organs at least claim to be engaged in complex operations in their environmental and welfare policies, civic engagement usually involves a one-issue movement (for example, opposition to *Startbahn West* [planned expansion of the Frankfurt airport by constructing a new runway through forest land – trans.], demands for more regular school instruction, opposition to xenophobia, demands for improved health care, and so on). Finally, related to this, civic involvement tends to be *particular* (for example, in Germany, campaigning for local day care while being indifferent towards day-care centres being closed in other federal states); this trend is known as the NIMBY ('not in my back yard') phenomenon. This clearly shows the function of civic education in the form of civic activism. If such education is successful, the initial fragility, singularity and particularity of the activism tend to be overcome; the activism becomes enduring and extends to other issues, and active individuals tend to deal increasingly with complex relations between issues. This leads to the acquisition of precisely the competencies on which civil society depends. Moreover, such forms of political and civic education have an immunizing effect against the attractions of populism, which is a constant companion of democratic orders and can be most successfully domesticated within civil society. In other words, civic activism is the best means by which to transform mere voting citizens into citizens with the capacity for political judgement.

The Crisis of the Welfare State as a Challenge to Civil Society

Recent problems in the welfare state in Germany, and elsewhere in Europe, are generally the result of intensified struggles for a piece of the pie, itself a consequence of the fact that since the early 1980s the pie has been shrinking rather than growing. This change is the result of a general flattening out of global economic cycles, a considerable increase in energy costs, and, finally, demographic changes in birth rate (Kaufmann 1997: 83ff.). In Germany the problem has been magnified since the early 1990s by the extreme costs related to unification. Consequently, a broad debate has ensued on whether welfare state arrangements can be replaced by market economy solutions. This basically involves a realignment of the relationship between collective and individual risk prevention and welfare provision. Some advantages of a more individualized market economy are that it provides more flexible security systems, promotes greater personal responsibility and allocates more precisely goods and services. On the other hand – it has been objected – an individualization of risk prevention and of general services will lead, at least in the long term, to a decrease in social solidarity and a deepening of social divisions.

Within the context of these debates, there has been increased interest in the concept of welfare production in civil society to the extent that this concept is linked to the goal of connecting a more specific socio-political allocation of goods and services with protecting, if not strengthening, social integration through collectivized responsibility for the basic social security of members of society (see Nothelle-Wildfeuer 1999: esp. 280ff.). In debates on civil society's welfare arrangement and the benefits expected from them, certainly the *control aspect* is usually focused on. For example, local or neighbourhood forms of welfare production might be preferred to legal or administrative procedures at a national level with the argument that the allocation is more specific and less expensive. Notoriously underestimated in such discussion is the addressed aspect of civic education. Within the framework of a more civil society-oriented form of welfare work, civic education essentially facilitates the transformation of administered solidarity into real, experienced solidarity, and legal regulations into experienced and practised civic spirit.[4] By focusing on this socialization aspect I do not wish to deny the control aspect, but, in terms of both democratic theory and social policy, the maintenance and reinforcement of civic spirit and social solidarity are more important in the long term than the question of control. Civil society-oriented welfare work arrangements *would be preferable* for the sake of the socialization aspect in a number of cases, *even if*, as compared with forms of welfare production based on a budget-dependent welfare state and market economy, they had certain disadvantages in respect of control. If they function properly, welfare schemes based on civil society are generators of a common good orientation and civic spirit, which are necessary to ensure the durability of political orders with liberal constitutions, insofar as they are significant not only from a socio-political perspective, but also from a democratic theory standpoint.[5] Such civil society-oriented welfare arrangements only function, however, if they are not overcommitted and overextended. It is therefore important to combine them intelligently with welfare state arrangements as well as with market economy solutions, in order to link the respective strengths and compensate for the weaknesses. In order to treat the political concept of civil society seriously, this must be taken into consideration.

The Integrative Function of Civil Society

A major criticism of the concept of civil society is that it falls short of the modern level of sophistication and to that extent is not fitting for modern societies. This argument certainly only applies and is sound *if* and *as long as* the civil society is not perceived as a deliberate, politically desirable and correspondingly implemented counterweight to the processes of differentiation and segmentation, specialization and professionalization that characterize modernity. No one should seriously concern themselves with models of civil society if they trust that the modernization process has a *sustained* capacity to solve problems, and see the corresponding solution to the problems in the related development towards increased law codification, institutionalization and professionalization – in the case treated here, also and especially in the area of welfare production. In view of the overextension of the budget-dependent welfare state, they should rely instead on a stronger market economy for risk prevention and general services, as in fact many do. In contrast, many others doubt that the number of individuals coming together solely through legal rules and the market exchange of goods and services could create a stable, lasting society. Consequently, they assume the need for a complementary balancing out of developments summarized under the concept of modernization. It is this group that demonstrates earnest interest in concepts of civil society and should therefore be prepared to reflect on its social and moral implications.[6]

It must be assumed that the comprehensive presumptions of competence, as contained in the concept of the citizenry, are to be defined in their distinctness from specialization and professionalization, that is, their resistance to a differentiation of society into segmented sub-areas under the heading of '*differentiation compensation competence*'.[7] Otherwise all that would remain is the mere indication of a notoriously ineffective dilettantism that continues to disturb the functional modi of social subsystems and which is connected to the participation and involvement of the citizens.[8] More so than output-oriented models of democracy, conceptions of civil society – that is, input-oriented democracy models – are based on the assumption that social differentiation, segmentation and professionalization without strong political forms of compensation have a self-destructive impact in the long term. They thereby contradict all essentially liberal economic conceptions, in which the unleashing of self-acting social development processes by returning the state to minimal functions is viewed as the answer to the gravest of control and integration problems facing modern societies.

Models of civil society certainly do not aim to block or suppress these developments, but they are convinced that a series of corrective and compensatory instruments are necessary to balance out the process of segmentation and differentiation and observe its functional effects, intervening if necessary as a corrective.[9] If the state's compensatory authority is based on the specific professional ethic of its officials and employees, then in the case of civil society authority is rooted in the ethic of the citizens who recognize their comprehensive right as members of society and participants in political life to have a say and a non-specialized capacity to act. The conception of civil society from a perspective of democratic theory is thus the same as complementing *representation* with *participation*. This applies especially to the specific forms of welfare production in which the oligarchy of welfare associations that represents group interests is not replaced but certainly counteracted by direct civic participation. In respect of the welfare state arrangement, civil society also means that welfare production will be at least in part dissociated from gainful employment without it leading to a system that tends to have a reciprocity of paying in and paying out, as is the case with a market economy solution. The common good orientation of a civil society can therefore be defined as the willingness to refrain from having strict, individualized expectations of reciprocity.[10] The common good orientation of the citizens is more than the reasonable sum of their individual interests, just as solidarity is not the same as egoism directed towards the long term. The conception of civil society relies instead on the connection between civic involvement and social recognition, which functions as an indispensable means of integration in societies based on liberal constitutions.[11] At the same time, the notion of civil society assumes that this connection is the decisive prerequisite in educating people to be citizens and making civic involvement available.

Volunteering and Duty

In this context the question must be posed as to the degree of volunteering and obligation of civic involvement in civil society. If this is not to not remain purely ornamental in nature, as opposed to state actions and market mechanisms, and if it is to guarantee the aforementioned certainty of expectations of those who profit from it, it can hardly be assumed that it can be achieved at the level of volunteerism alone. Instead it must be assumed that serious efforts to trim down the state without drastically reducing social security cannot be successful without any duties to become involved in civic matters. A sharp contrast between volunteerism and obligation can certainly describe only the key aspects of the issue; the area 'in between' the two poles, which can possibly be described as 'volunteer self-obligation' or 'self-obligation to volunteerism', is probaby the most interesting aspect for moral philosophy or political theory debates. Normative discussion and empirical analysis of this subject are still in their beginnings and require directed stimulus and questioning from politics and society. It can be assumed that this debate will be intensified when compulsory military service is eliminated in Germany; this will inevitably also mean the end of community service, which was a legal alternative to military service. The outcome of this debate and the resulting political conclusions that are drawn, such as substituting the introduction of a compulsory social service year, for both young men and young women, would mean that civil society in Germany had been set to develop in a distinct way.

Notes

This is a slightly edited version of the opening talk at the conference on 'Bürgergesellschaft und Sozialstaat' (Civil Society and the Welfare State), which took place on 15–16 February 2002, organized by the Heinrich Böll Foundation in Berlin. Dr Karsten Fischer and Dr

Harald Bluhm (both at the Berlin-Brandenburg Academy of Sciences) deserve more thanks for their remarks and ideas than it is possible to express in a footnote. This chapter was translated from the German by Allison Brown.

1. For an instructive overview of this see Klein 2001.
2. For an in-depth consideration of this, see Münkler 2001; especially Münkler and Bluhm 2001; Münkler and Krause 2001 (where additional references are listed).
3. For an excellent overview of this, see Kaufmann 1997. In addition to the problem of the costs to be covered by society, there is also the question whether a society in which assistance and care services tend to be professionalized and monetarized is even worthwhile and desirable. It must be taken into account that up to now social capital within the family was provided primarily, if not exclusively, by women; this happened largely without any social recognition such as in the form of accumulating an independent claim to social benefits. The social changes of recent decades and the related changes in values alone serve to rule out a 'conservative solution' (see also Bertram 1997). One of the major challenges facing civil society, however, is what to do if welfare state compensation arrangements cannot be financed and care through private insurance policies leads to dramatic social divisions.
4. For an in-depth consideration of this issue, see Münkler 2001b: 31–48.
5. This aspect of societies with democratic constitutions has been largely ignored in modern democratic theories, which have been greatly influenced by rational choice models; on this, see Münkler 1999.
6. The position suggested here is based on profound doubt that the unintended consequences and side effects of the modernization process can even begin to be mastered or even compensated for by increasing the reflexivity of its control mechanisms. In addition to the heightened reflexivity – suggested by a number of sociologists (see Beck et al. 1994; Beck and Bonß 2001)) – it counts on society's capacity to mobilize social and moral resources, which are conceived of not as a controlling and corrective force, but as a balancing counterweight to the modernization process,. These matters are discussed – with trust placed in reflexive control – in Schmalz-Bruns 1995: esp. 189ff.
7. Certain echoes of neologisms used by Odo Marquard (incompetence, compensatory competence) are by no means accidental; see Marquard 1989, 1991.
8. Whereas the modern concept of dilettantism has taken on an extremely pejorative connotation, this was not the case regarding pre-modern societies – from antiquity to early modern times. The beginnings of democracy in classical Athens and its reflection in political theory, especially Aristotle's, relied specifically on non-specialization and non-professionalization in managing political responsibilities. In contrast, in Plato's *Republic (Politeia)*, the harshest counter-plan to democracy ever formulated, the social order and access to positions of rule are regulated by means of specialization and professionalization.
9. In a somewhat condensed and simplified fashion, one could say that the processes of differentiation and segmentation characteristic of modernity lead to maximizing results, but these are not the same as an optimum of social self-control. The observation that maximum and optimum are not the same is the point of departure of environmental criticism of essentially economic indices of progress; on this see Fetscher 1991: 41–97. On the political theory debate on the difference between maximum and optimum, see Röhr 2001.
10. The extent to which individualized expectations of reciprocity can be renounced depends on the kind of incentive systems used to control civic involvement: The more these incentive systems are geared towards the acquisition of entitlements and rights, the stronger the role played by reciprocities of payments in and out. Interest in limiting such expectations of reciprocity is at the same time a powerful argument in favour of

coupling incentive systems to expectations of duties, to the extent that these function largely in isolation of individualized expectations of reciprocity.
11. On this, see Münkler 2001a. Social recognition in the form of civic honours can be viewed as the specific currency of civil society, one with which it seeks to limit the influence of the monetary currency of market society. Such ideas involve theories of justice, discussed in Walzer 1985.

References

Beck, Ulrich and Bonß, Wolfgang, eds. 2001. *Die Modernisierung der Moderne*. Frankfurt am Main.

Beck, Ulrich, Giddens, Anthony and Lash, Scott. 1994. *Reflexive Modernization: Politics, Tradition and Aesthetics in the Modern Social Order*. Cambridge.

Bertram, Hans. 1997. *Familien leben*. *Neue Wege zur flexiblen Gestaltung von Lebenszeit, Arbeitszeit und Familienzeit*. Gütersloh.

Böckenförde, Ernst Wolfgang. 1976. *Staat, Gesellschaft, Freiheit*. *Studien zur Staatstheorie und zum Verfassungsrecht*. Frankfurt am Main.

Fetscher, Iring. 1991. *Überlebensbedingungen der Menschheit. Ist der Fortschritt noch zu retten?* Berlin.

Heinze, Rolf G. and Olk, Thomas, eds. 2001. *Bürgerengagement in Deutschland*. *Bestandsaufnahmen und Perspektiven*. Opladen.

Hirschman, Albert O. 1982. *Shifting Involvements: Private Interest and Public Action*. Princeton.

Kaufmann, Franz-Xaver. 1997. *Herausforderungen des Sozialstaates*. Frankfurt am Main.

Kaupp, Heiner, Kraus, Wolfgang and Straus, Florian. 2000. 'Civic Matters: Motive, Hemmnisse und Fördermöglichkeiten bürgerschaftlichen Engagements'. In *Die Zukunft von Arbeit und Demokratie*, ed. Ulrich Beck: 217–68. Frankfurt am Main.

Klages, Helmut, 2000a. 'Die Deutschen – ein Volk von "Ehrenämtler"? Ergebnisse einer bundesweiten Studie'. *Forschungsjournal Neue Soziale Bewegungen* 13, 2: 33–47.

———. 2000b. 'Engagement und Engagementpotential in Deutschland'. In *Die Zukunft von Arbeit und Demokratie*, ed. Ulrich Beck: 151–70. Frankfurt am Main.

Klein, Ansgar. 2001. *Der Diskurs der Zivilgesellschaft. Politische Hintergründe und demokratietheoretische Folgerungen*. Opladen.

Marquard, Odo. 1989. *Farewell to Matters of Principle*, trans. Robert M. Wallace. New York.

———. 1991. *In Defense of the Accidental: Philosophical Studies*, trans. Robert M. Wallace. New York.

Münkler, Herfried. 1999. 'Republikanische Ethik-Bürgerliche Selbstbindung und politische Mitverantwortung'. In *Unternehmerische Freiheit, Selbstbindung und politische Mitverantwortung. Perspektiven republikanischer Unternehmensethik*, ed. Peter Ulrich, Albert Löhr and Josef Wieland: 9–25. Munich and Mering.

———. 2001a. 'Bürgersinn und Bürgerehre. Warum die Zivilgesellschaft engagierte Bürger braucht'. *Universitas* 56, 666: 1220–33.

———. 2001b. 'Solidarität in modernen Gesellschaften'. In *Sicherheit im Wandel. Neue Solidarität im 21. Jahrhundert*, ed. Franz Müntefering and Matthias Machnig: 31–48. Berlin.

Münkler, Herfried and Bluhm, Harald, eds. 2001. *Gemeinwohl und Gemeinsinn: Historische Semantiken politischer Leitbegriffe*. Berlin.

Münkler, Herfried and Fischer, Karsten. 2002. 'Einleitung: Rhetoriken des Gemeinwohls und Probleme des Gemeinsinns'. In *Gemeinwohl und Gemeinsinn: Rhetoriken und Perspektiven sozial-moralischer Orientierung*, ed. Herfried Münkler and Karsten Fischer: 9–17. Berlin.

Münkler, Herfried, and Krause, Skadi. 2001. 'Der aktive Bürger – eine Gestalt der politischen Theorie im Wandel'. In *Politik im 21. Jahrhundert*, ed. Claus Leggewie and Richard Münch: 299–320. Frankfurt am Main.

Nothelle-Wildfeuer, Ursula. 1999. *Soziale Gerechtigkeit und Zivilgesellschaft* (*Abhandlungen zur Sozialethik* 42). Paderborn.

Röhr, Wolfgang, ed. 2001. *Herausforderung an die hegemonische Denkweise des Politischen*. Hamburg.

Schmalz-Bruns, Rainer. 1995. *Reflexive Demokratie*. Baden-Baden.

von Alemann, Ulrich, Heinze, Rolf G. and Wehrhöfer, Ulrich, eds. 1999. *Bürgergesellschaft und Gemeinwohl. Analyse, Diskussion, Praxis*. Opladen.

Walzer, Michael. 1985. *Spheres of Justice: A Defence of Pluralism and Equality*. Oxford.

5

Transformations of German Civil Society: Milieu Change and Community Spirit

Hans Joas and Frank Adloff

'Public interest' (*Gemeinwohl*) and 'community spirit' (*Gemeinsinn*) are only two of the many concepts that regularly crop up in current discussions on social cohesion and the political capacity for action. Civil society and citizens' society (*Bürgergesellschaft*), communitarianism and revived republicanism, 'social capital' and 'trust', 'Third Way' and the 'modernization of government' – these all belong to the same semantic field. Each of these concepts naturally has its own history, its advantages and disadvantages; some meet with incomprehension in certain circles, or arouse aversion to and suspicion of the motives of the people who use them. Essentially, however, the many coexisting and sometimes competing discourses are all concerned with a common question: what societal forces can ensure that the market and the state as the two dominating mechanisms of modern sociation, are relativized and modified by a third principle? The aim of this principle would be to avoid us having to face just two alternatives: either passively accepting the consequences of unregulated market activity, or – with the attendant risk of societal life falling victim to bureaucratic suffocation – relying exclusively on state intervention to cope with this activity.

Although the various terms point in the same direction, they do not all denote equally well what is meant. 'Civil society' (*Zivilgesellschaft*), for example, although it has a history going back to John Locke, came to the fore only through the anti-communist dissidents of eastern Europe, particularly the Polish Solidarity movement. It clearly expresses the anti-totalitarian effort to seize competence from the state and to create a vital and differentiated society. The Russians have a relevant proverb: 'It is easy to make fish soup out of an aquarium but very hard to make an aquarium out of fish soup.' But, for this very reason, these east European debates on society can provide little stimulus for the West, since they do little to aid understanding of the many types of relationship between state and society in Western countries. However important it is to *strengthen* civil society in the West, it is fortunately no longer necessary to *produce* it. To cite a *bon mot* of Michael Walzer's, the discovery of 'civil society' in the West has always resembled the surprise of Molière's Monsieur Jourdain when he discovered that he had in fact always been speaking prose.

'Communitarianism' arouses fears (primarily in Germany, owing to its association with the semantics of *Gemeinschaft*) of a return to homogeneous collectives or even to a potentially totalitarian 'national community' (*Volksgemeinschaft*) embracing the whole of society – fears that make American communitarians, with their impeccable democratic credentials, just shake their heads. The 'Third Way' slogan has been associated in the past with so many (often esoteric) projects, at least in continental Europe, that its revival by Giddens and Blair has not met with overwhelming enthusiasm. Even its advocates now seem a little uneasy about it. So, because we need a concept, we opt for '*Bürgergesellschaft*' or 'citizens' society'. We have our reservations about this term, too: we do not refer to the 'bourgeoisie' with it; but even the traditional counter-concept of '*citoyen*' sounds more like citizenship or nationality, or a state-centred understanding of participation in the French tradition – and therefore does not quite cover what is meant.

If it is so difficult to find the right word, it is usually because the subject matter is also difficult. Such difficulties are currently evident in the programmatic discussions under way in political parties, with the parties under pressure to rethink the balance between the state, the market and society, and between the individual and the polity. In the process, parties sometimes rediscover neglected strands of their own traditions – like the subsidiarity principle of Catholic social teaching or the cooperative ideas of the labour movement – and address historically new phenomena like widespread individualism. But the same difficulties also permeate popular diagnoses of our age to be found in the media and even professional social science. In the 1990s two attitudes above all disrupted, and indeed were an obstacle to, constructive discussion of the opportunities for greater civic engagement. On the one hand, there was a more 'left-wing' suspicion that all these debates were nothing more than attempts to construct an acceptable façade behind which to dismantle the welfare state; on the other, there was the cultural pessimist theme of the progressive decline of values and community. History has perhaps now left these two attitudes by the wayside; yet, in order to clear the ground for a presentation of our empirical findings, we shall consider them briefly.

The suspicion that talk about *Bürgergesellschaft* expresses an ideology for dismantling the welfare state is based on the false assumption that the relationship between the state and citizens' society is a zero-sum game: the bigger the state, the smaller the citizens' society; the bigger the citizens' society, the smaller the state. The fact that this false assumption is also made at the opposite end of the political spectrum probably indicates that the suspicion may not be completely unjustified. But the assumption itself is false. At first glance, it might seem plausible in the case of the United States, since in the US traditionally relatively weak government appears to go hand in hand with a relatively strong citizens' society.[1] But even in America this is only half the truth. It is false in a *positive* sense because, through self-restraint, and the institutionalization and guarantee of a government-free space, manifested in religious denominations, foundations and the like, government actively participates in establishing the functional conditions for citizens' society. It is false in a *negative* sense, because the weakness of the welfare state in the poor and derelict urban districts, euphemistically termed 'inner cities', does not lead automatically to an increase in civic engagement.

Without seeking to trivialize charitable endeavours and often impressive self-help efforts, it must be said that the phenomena of neglect and exclusion from society, which are so unbearable to European welfare state thinking, would not exist if the situation were so straightforward. Scandinavian welfare societies provide examples that challenge the 'weak government-strong society' thesis. They clearly include governments that accept comprehensive responsibility for the commonweal – but this cannot be said to have destroyed the vitality of the citizens' society. Closer examination shows that the feared destructive effects on society of strong government can, but need not, arise: if, for example, state-run old-age homes are highly centralized, so that their occupants' families live a long way away from them, the frequency of family visits will decrease; where homes are decentralized – usually those run by municipalities – this is not the case (Wolfe 1989). One relevant example from Germany is the controversy that arose with the introduction of long-term care insurance: would such insurance reduce rather than support or promote families' willingness to care for their relatives? A study has shown that, at least in Berlin, there is no general decline in willingness to assume responsibility for care as a result of the new system (Brömme 1999) – although 'perverse effects' can occur in individual cases: that is, as a result of the state treating its guaranteed services primarily in economic terms, care-giving relatives may also think in economic terms.

This suggests that all the intellectual and political discourses referred to above have something to do with the historical situation in which we find ourselves. Today, the extremely successful model of German post-war capitalism, with its high international competitiveness based on quality products and highly skilled labour, which have allowed for high wages and relatively little social inequity compared with other countries, must be adapted in the light of new global economic and demographic conditions – and, of course, of the consequences of German reunification (see Streeck 1999). But doing this is anything but a wilful attempt to abandon the welfare state. Therefore, however unjustified and intellectually inhibiting blanket ideological reservations may be, they do point to the first dilemma of 'community spirit': the tension that exists between it and 'social justice' – that is, whether strengthening civic engagement is always desirable even from the point of view of social equality or equity.

The second burden weighing on debates about community spirit and citizens' society on both sides of the Atlantic has been the constant complaint by cultural pessimists of an alleged decline of the community and of community spirit. The slogans are well known: the 'dog-eat-dog society' and the *Erlebnisgesellschaft* ('experience society') – a society in which people search for enjoyment and powerful inner experiences. These are only two of a wide range of relevant concepts. In the United States, too, some communitarians accompany their demands with appropriate laments. The identification by Robert Putnam of a trend towards 'bowling alone' – that is, the decline of collective recreational sport and of the structures that enable it – is part of a rich tradition (Putnam 1995, 2000). As early as the late seventeenth century, the decline of true Puritan morals was being identified and deplored in North America. Yet, while an understanding of this sort of diagnosis as almost a literary genre should encourage caution, it should not make one refute the diagnosis: such gloomy assessments may have been mistaken in the past, but they may prove accurate in the present. We therefore need a firm empirical basis for our reflections.

The following considerations are based on comprehensive data about and a thorough literature research on the subject.[2] Overall it can be said in advance that, while the first investigation tends to be optimistic with regard to the question of a decline in community spirit, the second confirms radical change in and a far-reaching dissolution of the milieux that support community values. We are particularly interested in the *tension between these two results*. How can it be that the dramatic dissolution and transformation of socio-moral milieux is not reflected in the more dramatic data on civic engagement? Are these data perhaps deceptive? Do they reflect mere nominal membership, so that people's actual community spirit is weaker – and is thus indeed a cause to lament?

Or, on the contrary, do descriptions of individualization and milieu decline overlook something – and therefore need to be corrected – for example, the development or persistence of value-supportive milieux? Can both findings be invalid, which would merely demonstrated that, in this field, too, social research is lost in a fog of societal change? Or are both actually correct, obliging us to recognize that widespread assumptions about the links between milieu and a disposition for engagement are not valid? We argue in favour of the last assumption.

Social Capital and Milieux

Social capital is not in overall decline in Germany, though its nature has changed. The concept of social capital, introduced by Robert Putnam, refers to civil associations like clubs and societies, informal networks, religious communities, self-help groups, social movements, and so on, which are assigned particular value as the substructure of a functioning democracy. Social capital means social elements such as trust, norms and social networks that can make society 'more successful' by enabling action to be coordinated. Social networks produce and reproduce norms of reciprocity; Putnam claims that a society characterized by generalized reciprocity is more effective than a society in which reciprocity exists only in specific sub-groups – the former being based on 'bridging' social capital, the latter on 'bonding' social capital (Putnam 2000: 22ff.). Among the indicators that social research uses for the existence of social capital are data on association membership and on voluntary civic engagement.

Although associations in Germany have changed, they are far from stagnating (Klein 1998: 678). It is estimated that there are between 300,000 and 500,000 clubs and societies in Germany. Whereas in 1960 there were 160 registered associations per 100,000 inhabitants, by 1990 there were almost 500 per 100,000 inhabitants in the old federal states (former West Germany) (Anheier 1997: 33). Most of them – probably between a third and half – are sports clubs. Another third are concerned with animal welfare and breeding, music, and local history and traditions. Finally, there are many charitable and rescue associations, organizations of allotment-holders, horticultural societies and nature and ramblers' associations. Just under 60 per cent of the population in western Germany over the age of 15 belong to one or more associations (Klein 1998: 678). The figure for eastern Germany in 1990 was 25 per cent, and since then the figure has risen close to that for western Germany. In traditional associations, especially sports clubs, men are in the majority in all age groups; women are apparently more attracted by new, commercial courses. In rural areas and small towns, membership rates are higher than in large cities. The upper middle classes with higher educational qualifications are far more strongly represented. Lower income brackets, especially manual workers, are strongly under-represented in associations (Brömme 1998: 7). Between 1956 and 1998 the proportion of manual workers in associations fell by 20 percentage points; among white-collar workers there was a drop of only 4 percentage points. Membership of associations in general has not declined. In contrast, membership of trade unions and political parties has fallen strongly in recent years. Between 1984 and 1993, the trade unions in West Germany lost 6 per cent of their membership and the parties 17 per cent (Brömme 1998: 5). Since the mid-1990s, the annual drop in trade union membership has been about 3.5 per cent. The fall in membership is particularly high among younger people (aged 18–34). In 1998 some 10.5 million gainfully employed people belonged to trade unions. Comparing this figure with the total number of occupied persons, some 33 per cent of the German working population belong to unions.[3] In 1980 the figure was still 39.1 per cent, in 1988 36 per cent (Ebbinghaus and Visser 2000).

The data reveal an (undramatic) increase in public voluntary engagement over the past 30 years. Between about a fifth and a sixth of adults in western Germany engage in voluntary work in some form or other (von Rosenbladt 2000: 18; Offe/Fuchs 2001: 434). Volunteers devote an average of 14.5 hours per month to their activities (von Rosenbladt 2000: 94). A growing field of engagement is the self-help movement and 'new volunteering' (*Neue Ehrenamtlichkeit*). For 1996 it was estimated that 2.6 million people in 67,500 groups were involved in civic and self-help activities (von Rosenbladt 2000: 31). In early 1993, 130,000 people in the new federal states (the former German Democratic Republic (GDR)) were engaged in self-help groups.

East German involvement in voluntary activity differs considerably from that of west Germans. There was a marked fall in participation rates between 1990 and 1992, which did not, however, continue thereafter (Priller 1997: 119). Since East and West German participation was at the same level in 1990, this sudden decline can be attributed to the societal transformation process. In 1994, according to the Socio-Economic Panel surveys, about one-third of the west German population and just under one-fifth of east Germans were involved in volunteering activities (Heinze and Strünck 2001: 237). The Volunteers Survey has recorded an increase in average activism over recent years (von Rosenbladt 2000). Whereas in 1999 34 per cent of the population over the age of 14 were involved in volunteer work, the latest results for 2004 give a figure of 36 per cent.[4] The highest growth was recorded among people aged 56 and older. Engagement in this age group has grown by between 5 and 6 percentage points since 1999. East Germans participate less than west Germans in voluntary work. According to the 1999 Volunteers Survey, 36 per cent of west Germans over 14 were involved in voluntary work, while in the new federal states the figure was 28 per cent in 1999 and 31 per cent in 2004 (see Gensicke 2000: 176).

About half of all unsalaried and voluntary work was performed in the fields of culture and recreation, especially in sports clubs (Anheier 1997: 35). But there is also a high proportion of volunteers in the health-care system, social services, environmental protection groups and civil rights associations. There are fewer in political parties and trade unions: only 4 per cent of all voluntary work takes places in parties, and no more than 2 per cent in trade unions (von Rosenbladt 2000: 19). Volunteering is seen less and less as a long-term commitment and a fulfilment of duties. It is increasingly guided by personal interests and inclinations. The younger generation, in particular, is decreasingly inclined to assume a lasting commitment to the more traditional organizations. In contrast, engagement in 'New Volunteering' – more dependent on particular circumstances and thus not constant and stable, which means volunteers have greater autonomy – is growing strongly (Heinze and Strünck 2001: 236).

In their study of social capital, Claus Offe and Susanne Fuchs examine the factors that determine the level of associative behaviour. They find that associative activities depend on income level (Offe and Fuchs 2001: 443). The higher a person's income is, the more likely he or she is to belong to several organizations. Religious ties also have a positive impact on social capital. The stronger a person's religious commitment, the greater is his or her willingness to engage in voluntary activity (445). This is even more strongly marked among Catholics than among Protestants. The level of education correlates positively with social capital. People with lower formal qualifications are less likely to become involved in civil associations (448). Engagement in associations takes the form of an inverted 'U' in a person's life career. People are members of organizations at the highest rate between the ages of 30 and 59.

As we have mentioned, both the rate of membership of associations and the level of civic engagement in east Germany have been lower than in west Germany since reunification. Offe and Fuchs attribute this 'participation gap' primarily to high unemployment in the new federal states (Offe and Fuchs 2001: 469). The high rate of unemployment, the low number of self-employed business people and the low level of religious affiliation among east Germans make it unlikely that east German associative behaviour will reach west German levels in the next few years. The gap between male and female participation rates has narrowed over the past forty years in Germany, but it has not yet closed (478; see also Beher et al. 2001: 255ff.). Younger generations of women are, however, catching up fast. Higher educational qualifications and a higher labour force participation rate have helped. Women also play a greater role in the new forms of engagement in so-called new social movements.

People in lower income brackets and with a low level of education are under-represented in civil associations, and are thus less well equipped with social capital. These groups were often integrated in the associations of the classical socio-moral milieux: in the organizations of the labour movement or in the organizational milieux of the Catholic Church. These milieux have now largely lost their organizational substructure and security. The formerly integrated lower strata went their own way without transferring to the new associations (clubs and societies, self-help groups, new social movements, and so on). The result for these groups has been social deprivation (Offe and Fuchs 2001: 502). The changed nature of associations goes along with a new, unequal distribution of participation in associations. The new associations demand typically middle-class abilities from members – in contrast, for example, to trade-union and church associations. These abilities entail being a self-reflexive 'consumer', oriented to self-fulfilment, who can organize his or her own, occasional, activism (Brömme and Strasser 2001: 13). Milieu organizations can no longer compensate for abilities that are dependent on education.

In an international comparative study, Putnam, too, admits there is an increasingly unequal distribution of social capital (Putnam 2001). Recent studies on the distribution of engagement and social capital in the American population point in the same direction. Theda Skocpol has recently stressed that American democracy has been characterized since the 1960s by an increase in non-membership political advocacy organizations (Skocpol 1999, 2003). Until the 1960s, almost all nationally active organizations had locally entrenched and active members (Skocpol 1999: 461). Since that period, these organizations have largely been led by highly educated experts and professionals from the upper middle classes. Advocacy groups engage in lobbying and research and seek media publicity, but they have either hardly any members or only members who belong to the same educational milieu. In a cautious assessment of how the social capital of Americans has developed since the 1970s, Robert Wuthnow comes to the same conclusion (Wuthnow 2001). He finds that social capital has not eroded evenly, but has become unequally distributed. Instead of erosion, there has been exclusion. 'The fall in the membership of associations has always been higher among the socio-economically less privileged than among people who are already more privileged' (695).

This brief overview thus gives one no reason to diagnose a general crisis of community spirit in Germany. In the United States, too, recent studies paint a more differentiated picture than that presented by Putnam. There is an empirical change in the motivation for participation and, accordingly, in organizational structures, but, with the exception of certain traditional areas, no dramatic decline. The heated public debate – both in the United States and in Germany – appears thus to be not merely the inevitable expression of empirical processes of change; it is also a struggle for hegemony between differing values, above all a struggle over the claims of radical individualism. However, if such processes of change – up to and including the fundamentally middle-class activism oriented towards self-fulfilment – are taken more seriously as indicators of social developments, then one's assessment will be more sceptical. Is the citizens' society – in terms of social structure – once again becoming a middle-class project, in the sense that only well-established citizens, namely the middle classes, have an inclination for civic engagement? Does this mean that, after a brief period in the mid-twentieth century, in which the project of a cross-class, developed citizens' society expanded to include the lower classes (Nolte 2003: 44), the idea of such a society is at an end?

The contours of value systems and the institutions, cultural traditions and social forces that support them are hardly discernible in the mosaic of survey findings. For this reason, the picture we have so far drawn needs to be relativized by another. In the interest of finding a counterweight to mere individualism, the group around Robert Bellah in Berkeley, using a quite different methodology, has undertaken to investigate the persistence of cultural traditions from which actors can nowadays derive reasons for civic activism (Bellah et al. 1985). They find such counter-forces first in a 'biblical', that is, Christian and Jewish, tradition, and, secondly, in a 'republican' tradition, that is, one that embraces the principle of self-government by free and virtuous citizens. Both traditions have to struggle with individualism in its utilitarian and expressive forms. This clear picture provides a background against which the German situation stands out in stark contrast.

From a historical point of view, these two forms of individualism have played practically no role in Germany, not even in liberal circles. But German community-related traditions also differ strongly from those in the United States. Although there are forms of republicanism comparable to the American traditions in Switzerland, they exist in Germany only in diluted form: in the liberalism of south-west Germany and perhaps among the upper strata of the major Hanseatic cities. Although the biblical tradition has played just as important a part in Germany as in the United States, it has done so in a quite different form: not as a rich and vital pluralism of denominations independent of government, but in the great split between confessions and the clear division of territory between them in accordance with the *cuius regio eiuis religio* principle. This coexistence of religious territorial monopolies was weakened by the territorial reorganization that followed the Napoleonic wars, but it was largely overcome only through industrialization and urbanization and then by the flow of refugees in the aftermath of the Second World War. However, there are other traditions of 'community spirit' in Germany that have not attained the same importance in the United States: a social-democratic/trade union tradition and a conservative-national tradition.

The Concept of Social Milieu

We shall be dealing with these cultural traditions with reference to the concept of 'social milieu'. This requires brief justification. The concept of social milieu spread first of all at the end of the nineteenth century in the context of a naturalistic-cum-deterministic view of society; it was then raised to the status of a sociological concept by the French sociologist Émile Durkheim, who used it to denote social ties in everyday life. In Germany, Rainer Lepsius has used it particularly effectively for a historical sociological study of the links between social structure and party system (Lepsius 1993a). Lepsius uses the term milieu 'to denote social entities that are formed by the coincidence of several structural dimensions like religion, regional tradition, economic situation, cultural orientation, class-specific composition of intermediary groups' (Lepsius 1993b: 38). This made the concept and the corresponding viewpoint attractive for everyone unhappy with unhistorical stratification and class models. The concept then made its way into market and public opinion research, to be revived in the mid-1980s in academic sociology (see Hradil 1987). It was first used to construct typologies of cultural taste, as in Gerhard Schulze's well-known study on the 'experience society' (Schulze 1992).

Particularly important is the creative development of the concept by the research group around Michael Vester. They 'adapt' constructions (with obvious origins in market research) for research the aim of which is – 'in the search for the democratizing subject (classes, collective actors or milieux that will democratize society further)' – to offer political advice to German trade unions and the Social Democratic Party (Vester 1993: 101). This research provides detailed maps of both everyday life and political milieux in Germany. Particularly commendable is the stringency with which these two types of milieu are distinguished. But it is disappointing that the crucial issue, which this very distinction raises, is practically ignored: namely, that of the links 'of whatever type between fundamental socio-political attitudes and associative behaviour orientations' (377). These investigations accordingly come to a halt halfway between market research, in whose 'milieux' no substantial cultural value traditions can be found, and Lepsius's historically saturated sociology. But this indecisiveness itself may well reflect the difficulty of using a more clearly defined notion of milieu in a period when traditional milieux are dissolving. Nonetheless, what we shall be saying draws on Vester's notion of milieu, since this can, at least in principle, cover changes in cultural values and mentality. Unlike Schulze, Vester does not abandon the assumption of vertical stratification. And he posits not the disintegration but the metamorphosis of the old class milieux: they have modernized in the sense of displaying greater self-determination and individualization (Vester 1998).

German Workers

Social Class and Workers' Milieux

Probably no other section of society has been the subject of such intensive social history study as the working class. In *Arbeiterleben in Deutschland*, Josef Mooser has provided an excellent socio-historical review of the often very disparate studies of the history of German labour. He reconstructs changes in the class situation of workers between 1900 and 1970, paying particular attention to the development of labour as a social class (Mooser 1984: 25). In keeping with Max Weber, Mooser considers that the class situation of workers should be described primarily in terms of objective, socio-structural characteristics. If class position embraces common interests and the value attitudes of members, a social class can develop.

The development of income is the most evident phenomenon of discontinuity in the history of labour. The key experience of the West German population is growth in affluence – which workers also enjoyed – at a speed unprecedented in history. Average real wages tripled between the 1880s and 1970 (Mooser 1984: 74). The greatest changes occurred in the post-war decades. In the 15 years between 1950 and 1965 alone, real wages doubled. The growth in affluence was accompanied by a fall in working time and no unemployment.

It was not until the 1950s that working-class families earned enough to escape a mode of life in which most spending was for reproductive purposes. In 1950, 75 per cent of the household budget was still spent on food, clothing and rent. In 1973 these items were covered by only 60 per cent (Mooser 1984: 80). In these years, the whole of the working class attained material prosperity on a scale that only a very small number of well-paid, highly skilled 'labour aristocrats' had known before the 1950s.

The Class Milieu of Workers

A special characteristic of being a proletarian is the fact that one's position in the proletariat is socially 'inherited'. The expansion of white-collar and public service positions above all increased people's chances of escaping their class of origin. Similarly, the opening up of the educational system since the 1960s has increased opportunities for mobility for the sons of workers. Whereas in the early 1950s only 4 per cent of students came from working-class families, by 1969 the figure for first-year students was 11.2 per cent and in 1975 18.8 per cent (Mooser 1984: 116).

Although the expansion of education benefited children from almost all sections of the population, no redistribution of educational opportunities took place in favour of the disadvantaged lower classes. The expansion of secondary modern schools (*Realschulen*) mainly benefited the children of farmers and skilled workers, but not the children of unskilled labourers (Geißler 1996: 260). And the expansion of the *Gymnasium* (secondary school preparing for university entrance) and tertiary education was mostly to the advantage of children from the middle classes. In 1993 7 per cent of manual workers' children went to university – as compared with 27 per cent of white-collar workers' offspring and 47 per cent of public servants' children.

Mobility flows reveal a social class with a relatively stable core, manifested both through the 'inheritance' of occupational positions and in the consistency of individual occupational careers. Social cohesion or distance between societal groups is particularly clearly reflected in marriage behaviour. In 1989, two-thirds of males and three-quarters of females who had completed general secondary school (*Hauptschule*) and occupational training were married to partners who had *Hauptschule* qualifications (Geißler 1996: 170). After farmers, blue-collar workers were thus the most homogeneous social circles of all major societal groups.

Labour and Socio-moral Milieux

The social-democratic milieu of the nineteenth century was the only one to be fundamentally shaped by industrialization and the demand for political democratization. Essentially, the Social Democratic Party (SPD) mobilized the new, modern wage workers unaffiliated to any confessional and regional traditions. These were mainly industrial workers in the cities of Protestant central and northern Germany. But the SPD failed to make any decisive headway among Catholic workers. From the 1890s, there was a differentiated system of social democratic organizations in the major Protestant cities. In 1914 there were 5,000 local party organizations, and the SPD had over a million members (Grebing 1985: 100). A network of party organizations, cooperatives and associations homogenized the social democratic milieu internally and defined it externally.

The destruction of the German labour movement by National Socialism and the changed conditions after 1945 prevented a revitalization of social democratic socio-moral milieux in the Federal

Republic, and the importance of the labour movement as a political camp declined. But this should be seen as a success story: the attainment of many of the goals of the labour movement – for example, the rises in income of the 1950s and 1960s and the increase in the standard of living – individualized, as it were, the political labour movement. The success of the newly developed West German party system is to have integrated all sections of society. Labour and the Catholic population were for the first time fully integrated in politics; the 'pillarization' of German society and the so-called 'negative integration' of labour were thus overcome. The societal significance of class membership waned.

In the Second Empire, the working-class milieu was divided internally into various everyday life-world milieux: those of rural and urban worker milieux, the Protestant and Catholic milieux of the labour aristocrats and unskilled former farm labourers, and so on. By the 1960s, the homogenization process in the class situation of labour, as described by Mooser, had succeeded: differentiation between the various life-world milieux of workers had decreased. The process under way after the 1960s, described by many as individualization, can be cited as evidence of a new internal differentiation of the class milieu.

In the early 1990s, four West German worker milieux could be distinguished. Together they set themselves off against the achievement and status-oriented individualism of middle-class milieux. Two lines of tradition can be distinguished within these four milieux (Vester 1998: 135). The first goes back to the underclass, village and urban milieux of the pre-industrial era, and has been passed down largely within the group of semi-skilled and unskilled workers. This line is embodied in the 'traditionless' worker milieu to which 9 per cent of West Germans could be assigned in 1982 and 12 per cent in 1991. Here, externally driven forms of self-constraint predominate, and cultural points of orientation are standards of security, consumption and broad societal recognition.

The second line of tradition is embodied in the traditional worker milieu. In the course of the 1980s, this shrank from 9 per cent to 5 per cent of the West German population (Vester 1998: 134). Self-discipline, personal responsibility, modesty and diligence play an important role in the personal conduct of members of the traditional worker milieu. The classical skilled worker milieu goes back to the Protestant ethic of the craftsman culture. Vester assumes that more than 25 per cent of the population belonged to this milieu in 1950 (136). Though it has since shrunk, it has produced two offshoots: the 'aspirational' milieu, which, since the 1950s, has grown out of the traditional worker milieu – in the 1980s, its share of the population rose from 20 per cent to 24 per cent; and the 'new worker' milieu, the most recent and rapidly growing descendant of the traditional worker milieu (1982: 0 per cent; 1991: 5 per cent; 1995: 7 per cent). The latter milieu is characterized by its modernized lifestyles, and combines the ethic of good skilled work and a methodical conduct of life with moments of individualization and hedonism.

If we compare parent and child generations (Vester et al. 1993: 24 ff.), we can identify both typical processes of change and continuity. The typical class habitus is retained from generation to generation. Change tends, rather, to take place along the horizontal axis of lifestyle, which ranges from traditionally restrictive basic attitudes to individualized self-fulfilment values. In younger generations, values of achievement and order as well as conventional patterns of behaviour have eroded. Self-determined behaviour and reflexivity are more widespread among young people than among their parents and forefathers.

Class Position and Social Class Formation among GDR Workers

In the post-war period, the GDR, too, experienced a far-reaching deproletarianization of labour. Living and working conditions improved, and standards of education rose. However, the development of the situation for GDR workers lagged behind that in West Germany (Geißler 1996: 174). From the 1960s onwards, women in particular were recruited for the labour market. In 1990, 92 per cent of women between the ages of 25 and 60 (excluding students) were gainfully employed (281), and at this period the GDR achieved a total labour force participation rate (in the population aged 15–64) of about 90 per cent, while in West Germany the employment rate was just under 70 per cent. The most important source of personal income was gainful employment. The GDR was almost without propertied classes, and, because of the centrality of employment, the service classes played a relatively small role.

Socialization within the social structure took place above all in the workplace. Workplace-centred social policy was one of the most significant characteristics of socialist labour society (Kohli 1994). Many functions and services were organized at the level of the workplace. These included facilities such as day-care nurseries, recreational facilities, vocational training schools, as well as medical care and cultural activities.

As far as inter-generational mobility in the GDR was concerned, studies point unanimously to the increasing closure of the opportunity structure as one generation succeeded the next (Engler 1992: 88 ff.; Kohli 1994). To begin with, the so-called reconstruction generation – born in about 1930 – had many good opportunities for social advancement. Until the building of the Berlin Wall in 1961, heavy emigration by highly qualified people contributed further to this process. Later generations – particularly those born after 1960 – had far worse opportunities for upward mobility (Berger 1998: 578). They came up against the increasing closure of channels for advancement and marked self-reproduction by the 'socialist service class'. As early as 1964, there was a change in generation at the top and in the upper middle echelons of society. Eighty per cent of members of the so-called intelligentsia had received their education after 1951 in the new educational system and belonged to the new, socialist generation (Geißler 1996: 240).

Mobility declined in the following decades. From the 1960s, universities increasingly closed their doors to working-class children. Instead, the new socialist intelligentsia, which had emerged from the lower strata, consolidated their position. They secured their children's educational opportunities and shut themselves off against access from below. If one takes the period of the division of Germany as a whole – and not just the founding years of the GDR – West German working-class children had better average opportunities for upward mobility than did workers' children in the GDR (Geißler 1996: 244).

GDR Workers: Everyday Life-World Milieux

A study by the Sinus Institute identified nine social milieux in East Germany in 1990; in part these were quite different from those in West Germany (Vester 1995). West German milieux are concentrated in the horizontal and vertical centre of social space – in the middle-class habitus of the modern centre. GDR society displays three peculiarities at this level: an oversized upper class (32 per cent of the population), a weak middle class (28 per cent) and a large traditional working class: 40 per cent of the population (16). On the horizontal axis, reflecting the degree of individualization, East German society was polarized between a large traditional section and radical, modernized, young milieux. A gap yawned in the middle. Vester accordingly calls these milieux the traditional centre, in contrast with the West German modern centre. It is not only more traditionally oriented but also smaller (27 per cent) than the West German centre (45 per cent) (17).

The class milieu of GDR workers comprised three milieux of the everyday-life-world. The hedonistic worker milieu constituted 5 per cent of the population and was regarded as a modernized milieu (Vester 1995: 48). Members had at least secondary educational qualifications (ten-grade polytechnic high school followed by vocational training), and often became skilled workers, lower-level employees or career public servants. The 'traditionless' worker milieu belonged to the traditional centre and comprised 8 per cent of the population. Here, lower educational qualifications predominated. People in this milieu were industrial workers or lower-level employees in the service sector. The largest everyday life-world milieu in GDR society was the 'worker and peasant' milieu, rooted in tradition: this constituted 27 per cent of the population. It was located at the traditional pole of the horizontal social space axis (50).

Between 1991 and 1993, the research group around Michael Vester conducted a detailed study of worker social milieux and the alternative intellectual milieu in two typical east German regions. They investigated regional developments in the Leipzig area and the industrial city of Brandenburg, where they conducted thorough two-generation interviews (Vester. 1995: 7). Vester's milieu examples revealed enormous inertia in the GDR's worker milieux. Until well into the 1960s, the defence of labour interests relied on the traditional methods of the trade union movement (Hübner 1994: 180). Lacking institutional possibilities for genuine representation, workers had to rely on almost early modern forms of interest articulation on the shop floor. Workplace-centred social policy, the erosion of performance standards, and informal pacts between plant management and workforce habituated industrial workers to the social reality of the GDR and helped conserve egalitarian proletarian value attitudes (181). The cores of everyday life-world labour milieux have re-formed since 1990 – as contexts for communal association and older modes of life.

Religious Milieux in Germany

The Second Empire

In Germany two major Christian Churches dominate religious practice: the Protestant regional churches, united in the Evangelical Church in Germany (EKD), and the Roman Catholic Church. Christian milieux are closely interwoven with the two Churches – as we consider below in detail. Today, some 80 per cent of the population in west Germany and just under 30 per cent of the east German population are Church members.

For Catholics in Germany, the nineteenth century was characterized primarily by feelings of irritation and alienation towards the state and by a sense of cultural inferiority towards Protestantism. In contrast, Protestantism had, since the Reformation, developed into an integral part of the state system in many parts of Germany. The inferior status of Catholicism after the founding of the Empire in 1871 increased Catholic reservations towards the Protestant-dominated state and was a major factor in the development of the Catholic milieu and its political arm, the Centre Party (*Zentrum*). The Protestant side did not perceive itself to be under threat, since it considered itself to be (and indeed was) in the superior position – and thus did not develop a uniform socio-moral milieu.

The legal and political oppression of Catholicism in the *Kulturkampf* mobilized and homogenized the Catholic social milieu (Gauly 1991: 47).

The parallels between the *Kulturkampf* and the Socialist Act are obvious. Both led to the formation of politically active social milieux, which – based on a pre-political network of organizations – were internally cohesive and demarcated externally.

The isolation of Catholics demarcated Protestantism as a whole, but the decisive political cleavages were not between the confessions but within the Protestant section of the population (Oberndörfer et al. 1985b: 23). To begin with, political differences developed between conservatives and middle-class liberals. In the course of industrialization, liberals and social democrats came into conflict. There were thus three political streams and socio-moral milieux within the Protestantism of the Empire: conservatives, liberals, and social democrats. In the Catholic milieu, in contrast, the confessional boundary coincided with the boundary of the milieu.

Mutual support between Catholic voters, the Church, Church organizations and the Centre Party collapsed in 1933. For a while some Catholics wanted to believe that National Socialism would cease its attacks on the Church and Catholicism after the seizure of power. But this hope was soon dashed by Nazi repression. Measures were taken against Church organizations, against the Catholic press, and against denominational schools (see Lönne 1986: 243). Some monastic and Church property was seized. The government sought to thwart any attempt by the Church to exercise influence in society. Organized Catholicism was systematically incapacitated.

The Federal Republic of Germany

In the new German state, Catholics soon made themselves politically at home. The revival of Catholicism also had a great deal to do with the changed demographic situation. The division of Germany brought about numerical parity between Catholics and Protestants in West Germany. Probably the most important contribution to overcoming the confessional split in the party system was the decision not to found a Catholic party (Gotto 1985). The establishment of an interdenominational Christian party (the CDU/CSU) overcame the cleavage in the German party system between a closed Catholic camp and an internally differentiated Protestantism (Oberndörfer et al. 1985b: 24). The Catholic socio-moral milieu, which had been revived after 1945, gradually dissolved in the course of the 1960s.

The dramatic change in religious practice in the 1960s was extremely far-reaching. Church attendance dropped by about one-third between 1968 and 1973 alone. Beginning in 1967/68, there was a radical drop in the number of churchgoers. In 1952 about every second adult Catholic regularly went to mass; in 1963 55 per cent, in 1968 48 per cent, and in 1973 only 35 per cent (Köcher 1988: 145). The trend was similar among Protestants, but at a lower level. In 1952 13 per cent of adult Protestants regularly went to church, in 1965 15 per cent, in 1968 10 per cent; and in 1973 only 7 per cent. By the early 1980s just under 20 per cent of younger Catholics were attending services, but 54 per cent of the over-60s; among Protestants the ratio was 4 per cent to 12 per cent (145). The result has been that old people make up an increasing proportion of churchgoers. The momentous changes in religious practice are also reflected in church membership. In 1973/74, the number of people leaving the church peaked: the Protestant Church lost 202,823 and gained only 20,990 members (Thinnes 1988: 211).

It should be noted first of all that by the 1960s the Catholic socio-moral milieu – in the sense of a *socio-political camp* (Vester) – had largely ceased to exist. There had never been a Protestant socio-political camp in Germany. But this does not yet answer the question of what happened to the Christian milieux at the *everyday life-world* level. After all, it is possible that a Catholic milieu that integrated its members through specific religious practice could have survived at the *everyday life-world* level. The fact that there was no Protestant camp in Germany does not mean that there was and is no Protestant milieu at the everyday life-world level.

One of the few studies that explicitly address the subject of Christian milieux is based on a survey conducted in a district of Cologne (Wolf 1995). It looks at the link between religious socialization and confessional milieux. Confessional milieux are stabilized by a web of confession-specific organizations, as was the case with the Catholic social milieu. The progressive disintegration of confessional milieux after the Second World War has left families more and more to their own devices. They now bear almost sole responsibility for religious socialization and have to combat other influences (346). Under these circumstances both a decline in the success of religious socialization over time and in the practice of choosing a partner with the same religious views would be expected. Wolf's study shows that – in contrast – there has been an increase in religious and confessional homophily.

Wolf discovered (on the basis of 671 interviews) egocentric networks. There is a marked decline in the handing down of religious affiliation from generation to generation within families (Wolf 1995: 351). But, if one considers the differences in the intensity of religious practice, a different picture emerges. While the proportion of people classified as very religious decreases from generation to generation – from 34 per cent in the older generation to 25 per cent in the middle generation to 20 per cent in the younger generation – the successful passing on of intensive religiosity appears to have increased. Although the group of strongly religious persons has become smaller, it has greater success in passing on its religious convictions to younger generations. The role of denominations is also declining. The dividing line appears no longer to run between the confessions but between religious and non-religious people.

This thesis is confirmed at the level of non-family relations between partners. Confessional homophily in relationships is stronger among religious Catholics and Protestants than among non-believing Catholics and Protestants. But non-religious non-church members also prefer people from their own group more frequently than non-church members who believe in God do. The stronger a person's religious or atheistic convictions are, the more likely he or she is to associate with people who share his or her convictions. Declining religiousness and Church affiliation make religious belief less and less a matter of course. According to Wolf, religiousness is becoming an important distinguishing associative criterion.

Naturally, these findings are by no means representative, and their validity is still fUrther limited by their being restricted to a traditionally Catholic area. Nevertheless, the study gives good cause to assume that there are still Christian milieux at the everyday life-world level and/or that they exist in a new form. They now constitute themselves more strongly in terms of being religious/non-religious rather than in confessional terms. It is therefore plausible to posit the existence of a small but vital and perhaps emerging Christian milieu.

The GDR

The situation of the Churches in the GDR was determined primarily by the untiring efforts of the state to expel them from the public sphere of society. Of the 18.3 million inhabitants of the GDR in 1950, 14.8 million were Protestant and 1.37 million Catholic (Gabriel 1998: 376). In 1990, the Protestant Church had only 5.1 million members and the Catholic Church 1.1 million among the then 16 million inhabitants of the GDR. It can, therefore, be assumed that in 1989/90 just under 25 per cent of the East German population were members of the Protestant Church and 4 per cent to 5 per cent belonged to the Catholic Church. The proportion of non-Church members increased from 7 per cent to 70 per cent during the GDR's 40 years (Pollack 1994: 271). Between 1950 and 1990, the Protestant Church experienced a 70 per cent decline in church membership; the Catholic Church a fall of 58 per cent. Within a few decades, the 'catch-all' Protestant Church had become a minority Church – in the heartland of the Reformation. The pressure to homogenize exerted by the state proved stronger than the religious commitment of the Protestant majority.

The drop in Protestant church membership was not a steady process. It proceeded in waves, reaching an absolute climax in the second half of the 1950s. The first – still small – decline occurred in 1953/54. In this period the number of baptisms and church members fell by about one-sixth. The more serious decline took place between 1957 and 1959.

The Churches after Reunification

Since reunification, two religious systems have confronted one another in Germany. Non-church members were a minority of 14 per cent in the west in 1996, whereas in east Germany they constituted almost 70 per cent of the population (Gabriel 1998: 377). On average, Germany is moving towards three-way parity between Protestants, Catholics and non-church members.

Since the end of the 1960s there have been no self-contained Christian socio-moral milieux. By that time, the Catholic camp in West Germany had largely disintegrated. In the Soviet zone of occupation and German Democratic Republic, the repressive policies pursued with regard to all autonomous intermediary organizations in the post-war years meant that no socio-political camps could develop. The situation with regard to Christian milieux is difficult to establish. It is likely that there was an enormous decline – far more drastic in the GDR – in milieux at the everyday life-world level. However, Wolf (1995) draws attention to the intensification of religiousness and higher inter-generational propagation under the conditions pertaining in a secularized society. It can therefore be assumed that there is a core of everyday life-world religious milieux in East Germany, too.

The restriction of the intensive practice of religion to a small, religious core contrasts with the broad acceptance of Christian values and orientations in society. The social policy positions of the Churches, for instance, are broadly accepted, as the reactions to the joint statement in 1997 by the Council of the Evangelical Church in Germany and the (Catholic) German Bishops' Conference indicate. Basic elements of the German welfare state are clearly Christian in origin – the influence of Catholic social teaching, in particular, is evident (Kaufmann 1988: 87).

The Jewish Milieu in Germany

In the 1850s, some 415,000 Jews lived in Germany. Jews developed a relatively self-contained social structure and group identity. After the revolutionary years, a Jewish public sphere developed in the form of a Jewish press. However, German Jewry had no political representation comparable to that of the Catholic Centre Party. The Jewish minority, which constituted just under 1 per cent of the German population, was too weak to achieve any success through its own party. Jewish associative life, although absent from politics, played an important role in the social sector.

The restrictions still imposed on Jews under the Empire were abolished in the Weimar Republic. The constitution stressed that civil and civic rights did not depend on religious confession. But by 1941 the Nazi dictatorship had progressively stripped Jews in Germany of all rights. Until the autumn of that year, Nazi policy was to force Jews to emigrate. After that, however, all Jews under German rule were to be physically exterminated. The Nuremberg Laws of 1935 expelled Jews from society. All sexual intercourse between Jews and 'Aryans' was declared a criminal offence. Numerous individual decrees drove Jews out of all areas of public life. From 1935, Nazi policy increased the pressure on German Jews to emigrate. The November pogrom in 1938 was followed by economic destruction in the form of the official exploitation of Jewish property (Herzig 1997: 227). In the autumn of 1941, the Nazis prohibited emigration. By that time more than half the Jewish population of Germany, 254,000 people, had left the country.

The impact of the Nuremberg Laws is apparent in marriage statistics. At the beginning of the twentieth century, more than 85 per cent of marriages were homogamous. In the years that followed there was a trend towards heterogamy: by 1931 only 64 per cent of marriages were homogamous (Hendrickx et al. 1994: 629). In 1936 the figure was 96.7 per cent. When Himmler issued the emigration ban on 23 October 1941, some 180,000 Jews were living in Germany (Herzig 1997: 250). From the summer of 1941, the Nazis engaged in the systematic murder of European Jews. In summer 1942 the SS carried out the murders, using Cyclon B, in the gas chambers of the extermination camps Majdanek and Auschwitz-Birkenau. From then on the extermination of the Jews was conducted industrially. Between 5,000 and 7,000 German Jews survived the Holocaust in hiding or as spouses in privileged marriages. Of the approximately 134,000 German Jews deported to the extermination camps, only 8,000 were liberated.

After the end of the war, the Jews freed from the concentration camps lived on in camps as 'displaced persons' (DPs). Another 140,000 Jews arrived in the Western zones following pogroms. The number of Jewish DPs rose from 40,000 in 1946 to 182,000 in 1947 (Herzig 1997: 262). People in the camps mostly had to wait years for an opportunity to emigrate to Israel or the United States. The founding of the state of Israel in 1948 meant the end of camp life for them. In 1952 only 12,000 Jewish DPs remained in the Federal Republic. Most of them came from Eastern European countries. These people and an equal number of German Jews who had survived the Holocaust formed the nucleus of Jewish communities that were re-emerging in Germany.

The surviving German Jews and the stranded DPs constituted the new congregations. In 1959 there were eighty communities in the Federal Republic with altogether 21,500 members. Most new communities were in large cities. But most members were scattered across the country. German survivors often had little to do with Judaism in the religious sense; their spouses and children were not infrequently Christian. In 1960 only seven trained rabbis were officiating in West Germany. The Jewish communities were therefore extremely insular in nature.

In 1950 the Central Council of Jews in Germany was established as the national organization of the Jewish communities. By 1990, the Central Council had come to represent about ninety communities with over 30,000 registered members, most of whom were eastern European in origin. The residual German group amounted to only 10 per cent. In the GDR, the number of community members declined steadily over the decades. In 1945 Jewish communities had altogether 3,100 members; in 1990 only 350. Not only the effects of ageing but also the anti-Semitic campaigns of the 1950s certainly contributed to the decline in numbers, inducing many Jews to leave (Herzig 1997: 275). The remaining eight communities in the GDR joined the Central Council of Jews in 1990. In the mid-1990s, Jewish communities had more than 50,000 members (Gabriel 1997: 372). This growth is due to the immigration of Jews from eastern Europe.

The Conservative Milieu in Germany

Protestant Germany was divided between liberals and conservatives. As a rule, the cities, under the leadership of middle-class dignitaries, voted liberal, and the country, under the leadership of often noble landowners, voted conservative. In eastern Prussia, conservatism was based on a social order dominated by the landed nobility, while conservatism in the west, like liberalism, was based on broad communities of like-minded people. Feudal agrarian and nationalist middle-class conservatism were the two variants bracketed together by Protestantism. The bourgeoisie, dependent on the public service, was socialized in the feudal value system and as a class identified with the monarchical state (Lepsius 1993b: 48).

The conservatives shut themselves off in traditional voting regions and constituted a Protestant social milieu that followed agrarian and traditionally paternalistic models. At the turn of the century, the conservative milieu was extraordinarily stable, even though farm workers – the underclass of this milieu – were gradually being detached from the milieu by the social democrats. In the Weimar Republic there was a high degree of elite continuity in all areas of government, the economy and society. There had been no land reform, so that Germany east of the Elbe remained a stronghold of the conservatives. The officer corps in the army survived the revolutionary events unscathed. Like the military, the civil service was taken over almost fully by the new regime, and the judiciary proved to be a bastion of conservatism.

In the summer of 1933 political conservatism had reached its end. The meshing of the conservative elites with the Nazi movement was finally so total that many could not see what they should oppose. The overthrow of the republic had succeeded, the labour movement was shattered, and the new regime missed no opportunity to announce its respect for conservative values. But the National Socialists had set themselves the task not only of destroying the Weimar Republic but also of expanding their power at the cost of their conservative allies. Although political conservatism was shackled, the conservative elites who had dominated the government machinery of the Weimar Republic largely retained their positions under the Nazi dictatorship.

Conservatism in the Federal Republic

For conservatism the turning point after the Second World War was more radical than after the First World War. The estates east of the Elbe – the traditional base of conservatism – were now in the Soviet zone of occupation, Poland or the Soviet Union. Prussia was regarded as the militaristic root of the 'Third Reich' and was abolished by the victorious powers in 1947.

The founding of the Christian Democratic Union (CDU) (in Bavaria the CSU) was the most determined move towards a new approach in political party history (Kleßmann 1991: 142), and was to prove of outstanding importance for the Federal Republic. The CDU soon managed to establish itself as a comprehensive, catch-all party. It integrated the big social groups of employees and farmers, small self-employed craftsmen and tradesmen, people in the small and medium-sized business sector and the owners and managers of big industry (Ritter 1998: 66).

Elites in Germany are recruited to a high degree from the conservative milieu. After the Second World War, the dominant position of the nobility was permanently shattered. In the military leadership and the diplomatic service, the some 60,000 to 70,000 remaining members of the nobility are still disproportionately well represented – though this is decreasingly the case (Geißler 1996: 93). The difficulty of joining the elite rises in proportion to the lowness of a person's group of origin in the stratification hierarchy. The upper middle and upper classes therefore dominate German elites. In industry, in industrial associations and in the administration, there is a particularly strong leaning towards the CDU/CSU. Only trade union elites are predominantly close to the SPD (Hoffmann-Lange and Bürklin 1998: 176).

Conservative Everyday Life-World Milieux in the Federal Republic

The Sinus lifestyle research – on the milieu typology on which Vester's studies are also based – has identified an upper conservative milieu in West Germany. It is localized in social space as a traditionally oriented milieu with an upper-class habitus. Its share of the population fell minimally between 1982 (9 per cent) and 1992 (8 per cent) (Vester et al. 1993: 24). Members of this conservative milieu have an above-average education: they include many academics, executives, civil servants, self-employed persons and members of the professions. They frequently belong to high and extremely high income brackets.

There is strikingly strong agreement between the description by the Sinus Institute and Gerhard Schulze's characterization of the milieu (Schulze 1992: 283 ff.). This seems to indicate that this higher conservative milieu is relatively clearly configured and defined. According to Schulze, the cultured milieu is oriented towards high culture . Members are mostly older, highly educated people, who are primarily oriented towards hierarchy and who have a clear leaning towards the conservative, middle-class camp.

The lower middle-class ('petit bourgeois') milieu – a descendant of the bourgeois liberal milieu – has been integrated to a considerable extent in the conservative socio-moral milieu since about the turn of the century. The lower middle-class milieu traditionally upholds values such as discipline, order, duty and reliability, and has a marked preference for the CDU/CSU. Parts of the milieu lean towards parties left of the CDU/CSU; others are susceptible to the politics of resentment of the right the CDU/CSU.

Conservatism in the GDR

In the Soviet zone of occupation, the replacement of the old ruling classes was much more radical than in West Germany. Expropriation, collectivization and socialization deprived the 'Junkers' and the 'bourgeoisie' of their basis of influence. Moreover, consistent de-nazification was undertaken. Almost everyone who had supported the National Socialist regime was removed from leading positions in politics, administration, the judiciary, industry and the mass media, as well as in the arts. The elites in education, the judiciary, administration and the police were consequently almost entirely replaced (Ritter 1998: 133).

The foundations of the conservative milieu were destroyed at a very early stage in the GDR, at both the political and the everyday life-world levels. Elements of the Protestant Church were almost alone in managing to preserve an autonomous conservative milieu context. And a certain 'peasant conservatism' survived in the GDR, in spite of the changes in living and working conditions (Geißler 1996: 129). Deep local roots combined with above-average reservations about assuming party and trade-union functions.

At both the organizational and personnel levels, the anti-milieu policy of the ruling Socialist Unity Party (SED) was successful: after 1950 there was no discernible conservative political milieu in the GDR. Since the values of conservatism had always had a strong religious colouring, it was only logical that the regime also sought to stamp out religion. As we know, it was not fully successful. Religion always brought a perception of the world that deviated from the official interpretation. It could also provide a refuge for conservative ideas (Matthiesen 2000: 490).

Conservative Everyday Life-World Milieux in the GDR

According to the Sinus milieu study, there were two conservative milieux in east Germany in 1991 which strongly resembled west German conservative milieux (Vester 1993: 14). The middle-class humanistic milieu is a traditional milieu with an upper-class habitus comprising 10 per cent of the east German population. The members of this milieu have a high level of education and earn medium to high incomes; they are mostly executives, public servants or self-employed (Becker et al. 1992: 105). Their orientations are determined by Christian values, by duty, discipline and social engagement. The middle-class humanistic milieu is the successor to the traditional '*Bildungsbürgertum*' or educated middle classes. It appears to have retained Protestant, ascetic and humanistic values in critical opposition to west German consumerism (102). The Protestant Church in the GDR constituted the institutional core of the middle-class humanistic milieu. It was not by chance that Protestant ministers were one of the carrier groups of the milieu.

The lower middle-class materialist milieu is a traditional milieu with a middle-class habitus. In 1991, 23 per cent of east Germans belonged to this milieu (Vester 1993: 14). It is directly comparable to its west German counterpart. Medium educational qualifications and income brackets predominate, and members are often skilled workers as well as lower- and middle-level employees.

Conservatism in Reunified Germany

In west Germany there is a clearly defined everyday-life-world and politically conservative milieu. Although it should be seen as a continuation of the traditional conservative milieu, it is much more liberal and less nationalist than its predecessor before 1945.

For east Germany, the educated middle-class Protestant tradition is particularly important. After the destruction of all conservative structures, conservatism was able to find a home, if not organizationally then at least spiritually, under the auspices of the Church. It is striking that – according to the Sinus studies – a majority of east Germans display elements of a traditional mentality. Precisely the lower middle class contains the highest proportion of potentially conservative persons.

New Social Milieux in Germany

The Federal Republic of Germany (1940s to Reunification)

In the 1960s, the milieu landscape of the post-war period lost its clear definition. Gerhard Schulze stresses – from the standpoint of cultural sociology – how age came to the fore in social perception. Young educated people – *Gymnasium* and university students – turned traditional positions upside down. Age and style became key criteria for group formation (Schulze 1992: 536). The most significant mode of expression for the young generation was the tension schema: action, anti-conventional distinction, narcissism. In a novel combination of the high culture schema and the tension schema, a self-fulfilment milieu developed (538). Members of the entertainment milieu, in contrast, take their orientation solely from the new tension schema. This milieu crystallizes around the concept of 'stimulation'. Since the upheavals of the 1960s and 1970s, Schulze claims that social milieux have increasingly formed in terms of age, education and style. He sees milieu structure as increasingly grounded in taste and experience dispositions.

The self-fulfilment milieu is highly segmented internally. It includes yuppies and adherents of alternative lifestyles, social climbers and dropouts, consumption addicts and new social movements. The milieu is united by an interest in inner reality: all life goals – the wish for an influential occupation and wealth as well as political engagement – are subsumed under the goal of self-fulfilment. The self-fulfilment milieu is the core milieu of the new social movements: the student movement, the women's movement, the alternative movement, the anti-nuclear movement, the peace and ecology movements. People belonging to the entertainment milieu generally have lower educational qualifications. In keeping with the tension schema, direct needs predominate, and experiences with a strong event appeal are valued.

According to the Sinus Institute, the new social milieux of modern self-fulfilment increased their share in the population from 14 per cent to 20 per cent between 1982 and 1992. The modernized milieux include the alternative milieu with an upper-class habitus; over this period this milieu shrank from 4 per cent to 2 per cent. The hedonistic milieu represents a middle-class habitus and grew from 10 per cent to 13 per cent. In the 1980s, the 'new worker milieu' developed with a typical worker habitus. In 1992 it comprised 5 per cent of the West German population.

Vester confirms the passing down of mentality traits from grandparents and parents to members of the new social milieux. From generation to generation, mentality development tends to run in social space towards middle and upper forms of a modernized habitus. The self-realization values of the new social milieux take a range of forms. The habitus of origin shows persistence – which explains the differences between the new milieux. On the other hand, there is a general trend towards a need for free development, towards hedonism, greater self-reflexivity and personal political initiative. These elements always entail growing distance from the habitus of origin.

Individualization in these milieux means more self-determination and is not to be equated with the degradation of social cohesion. Social cohesion does not disintegrate; it is pursued more informally but very actively (Vester 1998: 140). Members of the new social milieux show above-average levels of education, sociability, political participation and willingness to assume personal responsibility.

New Social Milieux in the GDR

There is less literature available on the new social milieux in the GDR. The work by Vester and the Sinus Institute provides less insight than into new West German milieux. Although there are studies that describe the engagement of oppositional groups in the GDR (Wolle 1999), they take no account of the milieu-formation perspective.

According to the Sinus Institute, the modernized milieux in GDR society included 17 per cent of the population, and were hence almost as large as those in West Germany (20 per cent). Their historical origins are probably similar to those of their West German counterparts, which can be traced back to the break in generations after the 1970s. The left-wing intellectual alternative milieu has an upper-class habitus. In 1991 it included 7 per cent of the population (Vester 1995: 48). The subcultural milieu is a middle-class milieu with 5 per cent of the East German population. Members of the hedonistic worker milieu display a working-class habitus. It embraces 5 per cent of the population.

The research group around Michael Vester took a more detailed look at the East German alternative milieu in two case studies in Leipzig and Brandenburg. A structural characteristic common to both milieux is fragmentation. The alternative milieux emerged partly from the educated middle-class milieu and are politically and culturally indebted to it. The Leipzig case study shows that there were indeed alternative milieux showing certain similarities to West German milieux, although they developed differently and later. The East German alternative milieux stand in the tradition of the educated middle-class elite (*Bildungsbürgertum*) with a strong Protestant ethos. The alternative movement spread through the youth and culture scenes.

New Social Milieux after Reunification

The new social milieux are a stable characteristic of Germany. They are well developed at the everyday-life-world level, they are linked with each other and they are aware of their existence as milieux. In west Germany they are associated primarily with the new social movements and the Green Party. In East Germany they provided the resources for oppositional civil rights campaigners.

The new social milieux show very similar orientations in west and east Germany. They share the need for self-fulfilment and self-determination. Disintegration tendencies owing to exaggerated individualization processes are hardly to be expected in the new milieux. The cultural background experience of west and east German milieux brings them closer together: the importance of youth cultures and a new culture scene cannot be overestimated in both cases. The difference between them lies in their milieux of origin. While for new west German social milieux, the worker milieu, social democratic and trade-union background is important, the new milieux in east Germany, at least the higher new milieu, recruit their members largely from the Protestant educated middle class.

Conclusions

How can changes in the socio-moral milieux in Germany be summed up? It can be concluded that the disintegration of the milieux that sustained values over a long period, while considerable, has not been comprehensive. Dissolution is not total, as a glance at the stable Christian milieux, at the conservative milieu and at the residual milieux close to the labour movement shows. The disintegration of the self-contained, Christian socio-moral milieux is to be set against the continued existence of small religious milieux in which religion is intensively practised. The conservative milieu is manifest in west Germany at both the life-world and the political levels. In east Germany, elements of educated middle-class, Protestant mentality and traditions are still in evidence. West German worker milieux have been modernized over succeeding generations; there is no longer a political worker milieu. But a typical milieu habitus can still be identified, even though, in this context as well, associative behaviour has changed considerably. Forces of inertia in worker milieux in east Germany are evident, too. Disintegration is not total in another respect: many people's willingness to be active stems from the solidarity norms of their milieux of origin, for example, industrial labour or peasant life; this is often the case at points when these milieux are no longer clearly defined or the people concerned no longer belong to them. Self-determining behaviour and reflexivity are more widespread among younger generations than among their parents; but young people, too, continue to display a habitus and value ties typical of the milieu. And new milieux are coming into being, as we have indicated with regard to the Green alternative milieu, which is well developed at the life-world level and has strong internal ties. This is by no means the only such milieu: if there is a milieu party in Germany today, it is probably the Party of Democratic Socialism (PDS) with its dependence on an ex-GDR milieu; just as there are stable ethnic milieux of immigrants in present-day Germany.

But, for everyone who regards the transformation and disintegration of these milieux as a loss and a threat to the sources of community spirit, these exceptions to the disintegration diagnosis will be of little comfort. Some remnants of milieux may remain, as may certain patterns of behaviour people have inherited from their origins; and now and again a small, new counter-milieu emerges. But what can this achieve against the disintegrating forces, wherever they are found? Is it not just a question of time before these relics of a value tradition that reaches beyond the individual have lost their hold? But this is precisely the point at which we deliver our empirical 'punch line'. If it is true, as we have asserted, that milieu disintegration is by no means total and that no dramatic loss of community spirit is to be observed, and also that we do not wish to regard the community spirit that does exist as a mere relic (which will soon disintegrate) of the good old days – then there must be forms of generating and reproducing community spirit and values other than those posited by the milieu concept.

The social reality for which the concept of milieu was once so appropriate was that of pillarization, the sealing off of milieux from one another, the defensive stance in 'conscious opposition to third parties'

(Max Weber). When the milieux in the Federal Republic of Germany began to disintegrate, the process was broadly perceived not as deterioration but as positive integration. Escape from the big confessional, socio-regional and class disparities of the Second Empire; the growing participation in education, prosperity and social security; the erosion of polarizing class mentalities; and the coming into being of more modern worker milieux – combined with the tendency of political parties, which had previously integrated limited class milieux, to become milieu-overarching, catch-all parties (Vester 1993: 35) – when all this happened, it was welcomed, not lamented. For Lepsius, the strength of sealed-off milieux explained the specific difficulties facing democratization in Germany. The political systems of the Second Empire and the Weimar Republic were pegged to four social milieux, each sharply differentiated by symbolically dramatic moral positions; as a result conflicts could not be conducted constructively. Hence, there was social integration within milieux, and integration between elite and 'base' within each milieu; but there was no overall societal integration across the various milieux. Social integration took place within milieux – in Putnam's words, social capital was 'bonding', not 'bridging'. Milieux confronted one another and were not linked by any network of trust and cooperation.

This suggests that, although societal disintegration is possible when milieux dissolve, the dissolution of milieux does not amount to the disintegration of society. Who today would really want the old milieux back? Or are we faced with a tragic dilemma: only self-contained milieux can convey community spirit, but the pillarization of society prevents this spirit from pervading the entire body politic? Do we have to choose between an integrated society without community spirit and a pillarized society with community spirit?

Certain important questions thus remain to be answered about the importance and 'performance' of stable milieu contexts. As we have seen, marginalized classes and poorly qualified workers, as well as insecure members of the middle classes, are among those who are most exposed to the danger of inadequate social capital formation. This indicates that social milieux were able to stabilize and sustain motivation and opportunities for participation. Milieu organizations provided a motivational infrastructure lacking in the 'new volunteering', which is based more strongly on personal calculations. At the same time, the classical milieux brought together young and old, teachers and manual workers. Where such milieu structures break down, the intergenerational and cross-class context can also be expected to dissolve. The effective political representation of ideas and interests is then best assured if political actors are socially embedded (see Schubert 2002: 268f.). Integration in a shared milieu context both places the political elite under obligation to the social group they represent and provides shared motives and value orientations. Everyday life-world milieux are usually located within the vertical structure of social space. Political milieux, in contrast, cut across these vertical positions, they can be understood as vertical coalitions between upper and lower milieux (Vester et al. 2001; Adloff 2003). In other words, elites are tied to their social basis by political milieux and vice versa.

Despite the social and political regulatory function of socio-moral milieux, the issue should not be only how milieux can be stabilized or saved, but how values can be generated and passed on. Some values are difficult to pass on, precisely because they are locked in a milieu. The magnificence of the message of the Gospel can quite be lost sight of in milieu Catholicism. And the vitality of social democratic ideals of justice can suffer from cliquism in party and trade-union circles. It is not the values themselves that demand encapsulation in a milieu. Usually it is the milieu elite that gives priority to safeguarding the identity of the milieu, sometimes even in preference to the actual dissemination of values. The question must hence be reversed. The data on the spread of civic engagement are a fact that needs to be explained. For it seems that the existence of stable milieux is not among the obvious conditions for civic engagement. Although values live in these milieux, they do not live *only* in these milieux. We must rather direct our attention to the experience in which commitment to values can develop. Under conditions of cultural diversity, value commitments are generated not through indoctrination and by fending off rival influences, but only through ways of life in which the values themselves can be experienced. Not milieux but opportunities for participation and experience, organizational infrastructures and role models are the factors that lend new vitality to value traditions in each generation. Such value commitments – which reflect cultural plurality in the way in which they are 'embedded' in people – enable a commitment to, not just a reluctant acceptance of, tolerance and pluralism to develop. Value commitments can become more reflexive and more modest without losing any of their intensity.

In a culturally diverse society, one that is not fragmented into stabilized and fixed mentalities and milieux, people may at least become aware of the contingency of their own value commitments; thus they may place themselves deliberately in the value tradition from which their own motivation emanates. However, this will not work unless attempts are made to articulate precisely these values in a contemporary fashion. Sociological research that shies away from the adequate reconstruction of motives and their implementation through the articulation of cultural traditions and that sells the types that emerge in conventional manner from data analysis as real cultural figures cannot do justice to this task. And reconstructions of milieu change and milieu dissolution also remain blind if they do not reflect that they are themselves part of the societal discourse on values.

Notes

1. The expansion of welfare programmes in the years of the Great Society did, however, contribute to the expansion of the non-profit sector in the USA. The voluntary sector benefits from the supplementary financing of social services by government (see Salamon 1995).
2. Brömme 1998 and Adloff 1999. Both studies are the result of cooperation with Hans Joas. See also Joas 2000.
3. Statistisches Bundesamt [Federal Office of Statistics] 2000: 167. These figures are based on union information. Survey findings suggest a far lower level of membership. In 1980 18.6 per cent of people employed stated that they were members of a union; in 1996 the figure was 16 per cent (Offe and Fuchs 2001: 434). What is decisive with regard to both figures is that they confirm the observation that membership is falling.
4. See the first explications from the Federal Ministry for Family Affairs, Senior Citizens, Women and Youth: www.bmfsfj.de

References

Adloff, Frank. 1999. *Die Entwicklung sozialer Milieux in Deutschland nach 1945*. Berlin.

———. 2003. 'Sozialkapital, soziale Milieux und Integration'. *Forschungsjournal Neue Soziale Bewegungen* 16: 109–14.

Anheier, Helmut K. 1997. 'Der Dritte Sektor in Zahlen: Ein sozial-ökonomisches Porträt'. In *Der Dritte Sektor in Deutschland. Organizationen zwischen Staat und Markt im gesellschaftlichen Wandel*, ed. Helmut K. Anheier, Eckhard Priller, Wolfgang Seibel and Annette Zimmer: 29–74. Berlin.

Anheier, Helmut K., Eckhard Priller, Wolfgang Seibel and Annette Zimmer, eds. 1997. *Der Dritte Sektor in Deutschland. Organizationen zwischen Staat und Markt im gesellschaftlichen Wandel*. Berlin.

Becker, U., Becker, H. and Ruhland, W. 1992. *Zwischen Angst und Aufbruch. Das Lebensgefühl der Deutschen in Ost und West nach der Wiedervereinigung*. Düsseldorf.

Beher, Karin, Liebig, Reinhard and Rauschenbach, Thomas. 2001. 'Vom Motivations- zum Strukturwandel – Analysen zum Ehrenamt in einer sich verändernden Umwelt'. In *Bürgerengagement in Deutschland. Bestandsaufnahmen und Perspektiven*, ed. Rolf Heinze and Thomas Olk: 255–81. Opladen.

Bellah, Robert et al. 1985. *Habits of the Heart: Individualism and Commitment in American Life*. New York.

Berger, Peter A. 1998. 'Soziale Mobilität'. In *Handwörterbuch zur Gesellschaft Deutschlands*, ed. Bernhard Schäfers and Wolfgang Zapf: 574–83. Opladen.

Berger, Peter A. and Vester, Michael, eds. 1998. *Alte Ungleichheiten. Neue Spannungen*. Opladen.

Brömme, Norbert. 1998. *Soziales Kapital in Deutschland*. Berlin.

———. 1999. *Eine neue Kultur des Helfens und der mitmenschlichen Zuwendung? Über die sozialen Auswirkungen des Pflegeversicherungsgesetzes*. Bielefeld.

Brömme, Norbert and Strasser, Hermann. 2001. 'Gespaltene Bürgerschaft? Die ungleichen Folgen des Strukturwandels von Engagement und Partizipation'. *Aus Politik und Zeitgeschichte* B25–B26: 6–14.

Ebbinghaus, Bernhard and Visser, Jelle, eds. 2000. *Trade Unions in Western Europe since 1945.* London.

Engler, Wolfgang. 1992. *Die zivilisatorische Lücke. Versuche über den Staatssozialismus.* Frankfurt am Main.

Gabriel, Karl. 1998. 'Kirchen/Religionsgemeinschaften'. In *Handwörterbuch zur Gesellschaft Deutschlands*, ed. Bernhard Schäfers and Wolfgang Zapf: 371–82. Opladen.

Gauly, Thomas M. 1991. 'Konfessionalismus und politische Kultur in Deutschland'. *Aus Politik und Zeitgeschichte*, B20: 45–53.

Geißler, Rainer. 1996. *Die Sozialstruktur Deutschlands. Zur gesellschaftlichen Entwicklung mit einer Zwischenbilanz zur Vereinigung.* Opladen.

Gensicke, Thomas. 2000. 'Freiwilliges Engagement in den neuen Ländern'. In *Freiwilliges Engagement in Deutschland, Bd.1: Gesamtbericht*, ed. Bernhard von Rosenbladt: 176–85. Stuttgart.

Gotto, Klaus. 1985. 'Wandlungen des politischen Katholizismus seit 1945'. In *Wirtschaftlicher Wandel, religiöser Wandel und Wertwandel. Folgen für das politische Verhalten in der Bundesrepublik Deutschland*, ed. Dieter Oberndörfer, Hans Rattinger and Karl Schmitt: 221–35. Berlin.

Grebing, Helga. 1985. *Arbeiterbewegung. Sozialer Protest und kollektive Interessenvertretung bis 1914.* Munich.

Heinze, Rolf G. and Olk, Thomas, eds. 2001. *Bürgerengagement in Deutschland. Bestandsaufnahmen und Perspektiven.* Opladen.

Heinze, Rolf G. and Strünck, Christoph. 2001. 'Freiwilliges soziales Engagement – Potentiale und Fördermöglichkeiten'. In *Bürgerengagement in Deutschland. Bestandsaufnahmen und Perspektiven*, ed. Rolf G. Heinze and Thomas Olk: 233–53. Opladen.

Hendrickx, John, Schreuder, Osmund and Ultee, Wouter. 1994. 'Die konfessionelle Mischehe in Deutschland (1901–1986) und den Niederlanden (1914–1986)'. *Kölner Zeitschrift für Soziologie und Sozialpsychologie* 46: 619–45.

Herzig, Arno. 1997. *Jüdische Geschichte in Deutschland. Von den Anfängen bis zur Gegenwart.* Munich.

Hoffmann-Lange, Ursula and Bürklin, Wilhelm. 1998. 'Eliten, Führungsgruppen'. In *Handwörterbuch zur Gesellschaft Deutschlands*, ed. Bernhard Schäfers and Wolfgang Zapf: 167–78. Opladen.

Hradil, Stefan. 1987. *Sozialstrukturanalyse in einer fortgeschrittenen Gesellschaft. Von Klassen und Schichten zu Lagen und Milieux.* Opladen.

Hübner, Peter. 1994. 'Die Zukunft war gestern: Soziale und mentale Trends in der DDR-Industriearbeiterschaft'. In *Sozialgeschichte der DDR*, ed. Hartmut Kaelble, Jürgen Kocka and Hartmut Zwahr: 171–87. Stuttgart.

Joas, Hans. 2000. *The Genesis of Values.* Cambridge.

Kaelble, Hartmut, Kocka, Jürgen and Zwahr, Hartmut, eds. 1994. *Sozialgeschichte der DDR.* Stuttgart.

Kaufmann, Franz-Xaver. 1988. 'Christentum und Wohlfahrtsstaat'. *Zeitschrift für Sozialreform* 34: 65–88.

Kaufmann, Franz-Xaver and Schäfers, Bernhard, eds. 1988. *Religion, Kirchen und Gesellschaft in Deutschland. Gegenwartskunde*, Sonderheft 5. Opladen.

Klein, Hans Joachim. 1998. 'Vereine'. In *Handwörterbuch zur Gesellschaft Deutschlands*, ed. Bernhard Schäfers and Wolfgang Zapf: 676–87. Opladen.

Kleßmann, Christoph. 1991. *Die doppelte Staatsgründung. Deutsche Geschichte 1945–1955*. Göttingen.

Köcher, Renate. 1988. 'Wandel des religiösen Bewußtseins in der Bundesrepublik Deutschland'. In *Religion, Kirchen und Gesellschaft in Deutschland. Gegenwartskunde*, Sonderheft 5, ed. Franz-Xaver Kaufmann and Bernhard Schäfers: 145–58. Opladen.

Kohli, Martin. 1994. 'Die DDR als Arbeitsgesellschaft? Arbeit, Lebenslauf und soziale Differenzierung'. In *Sozialgeschichte der DDR*, ed. Hartmut Kaelble, Jürgen Kocka and Hartmut Zwahr: 31–61. Stuttgart.

Lepsius, M. Rainer. 1993a. *Demokratie in Deutschland*. Göttingen.

———. 1993b. 'Parteiensystem und Sozialstruktur. Zum Problem der Demokratisierung der deutschen Gesellschaft'. In M. Rainer Lepsius, *Demokratie in Deutschland*: 25–50. Göttingen.

Lönne, Karl-Egon. 1986. *Politischer Katholizismus im 19. und 20. Jahrhundert*. Frankfurt am Main.

Matthiesen, Helge. 2000. *Greifswald in Vorpommern. Konservatives Milieu in Demokratie und Diktatur 1900 bis 1990*. Reihe: *Beiträge zur Geschichte der Parteien und des Parlamentarismus Nr. 120*. Düsseldorf.

Mooser, Josef. 1984. *Arbeiterleben in Deutschland 1900 – 1970. Klassenlagen, Kultur und Politik*. Frankfurt am Main.

Nolte, Paul. 2003. 'Zivilgesellschaft und soziale Ungleichheit'. *Forschungsjournal NSB* 16, 2: 38–45.

Oberndörfer, Dieter, Rattinger, Hans and Schmitt, Karl, eds. 1985a. *Wirtschaftlicher Wandel, religiöser Wandel und Wertwandel. Folgen für das politische Verhalten in der Bundesrepublik Deutschland*. Berlin.

———. 1985b. 'Wirtschaftlicher Wandel, religiöser Wandel und Wertwandel: Eine Einführung'. In *Wirtschaftlicher Wandel, religiöser Wandel und Wertwandel. Folgen für das politische Verhalten in der Bundesrepublik Deutschland*, ed. Dieter Oberndörfer, Hans Rattinger and Karl Schmitt. Berlin.

Offe, Claus and Fuchs, Susanne. 2001. 'Schwund des Sozialkapitals? Der Fall Deutschland'. In *Gesellschaft und Gemeinsinn. Sozialkapital im internationalen Vergleich*, ed. Robert D. Putnam: 417–514. Gütersloh.

Pollack, Detlef. 1994. 'Von der Volkskirche zur Minderheitskirche. Zur Entwicklung von Religiosität und Kirchlichkeit in der DDR'. In *Sozialgeschichte der DDR*, ed. Hartmut Kaelble, Jürgen Kocka and Hartmut Zwahr: 271–94. Stuttgart.

Priller, Eckhard. 1997. 'Der Dritte Sektor in den neuen Bundesländern: Eine sozial-ökonomische Analyse'. In *Der Dritte Sektor in Deutschland. Organizationen zwischen Staat und Markt im gesellschaftlichen Wandel*, ed. Helmut K. Anheier, Eckhard Priller, Wolfgang Seibel and Annette Zimmer: 99–126. Berlin.

Putnam, Robert D. (1995), 'Tuning In, Tuning Out: The Strange Disappearance of Social Capital in America'. *Political Science and Politics*, December: 664–83.

———. 2000. *Bowling Alone: The Collapse and Revival of American Community*. New York.

———, ed. 2001. *Gesellschaft und Gemeinsinn. Sozialkapital im internationalen Vergleich*, Gütersloh.

Ritter, Gerhard A. 1998. *Über Deutschland. Die Bundesrepublik in der deutschen Geschichte*. Munich.

Salamon, Lester M. 1995. *Partners in Public Service. Government-Nonprofit Relations in the Modern Welfare State*. Baltimore.

Schäfers, Bernhard and Zapf, Wolfgang, eds. 1998. *Handwörterbuch zur Gesellschaft Deutschlands*. Opladen.

Schubert, Hans-Joachim. 2002. *Demokratie in der Kleinstadt. Eine empirische Studie zur Motivation lokalpolitischen Handelns*. Opladen.

Schulze, Gerhard. 1992. *Die Erlebnisgesellschaft. Kultursoziologie der Gegenwart*. Frankfurt am Main and New York.

Skocpol, Theda (1999), 'Advocates without Members: The Recent Transformation of American Civic Life'. In *Civic Engagement in American Democracy*, ed. Theda Skocpol and Morris P. Fiorina: 461–509. Washington, DC.

———. 2003. *Diminished Democracy. From Membership to Management in American Civic Life*. Norman.

Skocpol, Theda and Fiorina, Morris P., eds. 1999. *Civic Engagement in American Democracy*. Washington, DC.

Statistisches Bundesamt. 2000. *Datenreport 1999. Zahlen und Fakten über die Bundesrepublik*. Bonn.

Streeck, Wolfgang. 1999. 'Deutscher Kapitalismus: Gibt es ihn? Kann er überleben?' In *Korporatismus in Deutschland*. Frankfurt am Main.

Thinnes, Petra. 1988. 'Sozialstatistik zum kirchlichen und religiösen Leben in der Bundesrepublik Deutschland'. In *Religion, Kirchen und Gesellschaft in Deutschland. Gegenwartskunde*, Sonderheft 5, ed. Franz-Xaver Kaufmann and Bernhard Schäfers: 203–17. Opladen.

Vester, Michael. 1993. 'Das Janusgesicht sozialer Modernisierung. Sozialstrukturwandel und soziale Desintegration in Ost- und Westdeutschland'. *Aus Politik und Zeitgeschichte* B26–B27: 3–19.

———. 1995. 'Milieuwandel und regionaler Strukturwandel in Ostdeutschland'. In *Soziale Milieux in Ostdeutschland. Gesellschaftliche Strukturen zwischen Zerfall und Neubildung*, ed. Michael Vester, Michael Hofmann and Irene Zierke: 7–50. Cologne.

———. 1998. 'Klassengesellschaft ohne Klassen. Auflösung oder Transformation der industriegesellschaftlichen Sozialstruktur?' In *Alte Ungleichheiten. Neue Spannungen*, ed. Peter A. Berger and Michael Vester: 109–47. Opladen.

Vester, Michael et al. 1993. *Soziale Milieux im gesellschaftlichen Strukturwandel. Zwischen Integration und Ausgrenzung*. Cologne.

———. 2001. *Soziale Milieux im gesellschaftlichen Strukturwandel. Zwischen Ausgrenzung und Integration*. Frankfurt am Main.

Von Rosenbladt, Bernhard. 2000. *Freiwilliges Engagement in Deutschland, Bd.1: Gesamtbericht.* Stuttgart.

Walter, Franz. 1999. 'Westerwelles Milieu'. *Blätter für deutsche und internationale Politik* 10: 1165–69.

Wolf, Christof. 1995. 'Religiöse Sozialisation, konfessionelle Milieux und Generation'. *Zeitschrift für Soziologie* 24: 345–57.

Wolfe, Alan. 1989. *Whose Keeper? – Social Science and Moral Obligation.* Berkeley.

Wolle, Stefan. 1999. *Die heile Welt der Diktatur. Alltag und Herrschaft in der DDR 1971–1989.* Berlin.

Wuthnow, Robert. 2001. 'Der Wandel des Sozialkapitals in den USA'. In *Gesellschaft und Gemeinsinn. Sozialkapital im internationalen Vergleich*, ed. Robert D. Putnam: 655–749. Gütersloh.

Internet reference

www.bmfsfj.de

6

CIVILITY, VIOLENCE AND CIVIL SOCIETY

Sven Reichardt

As far as the dream of peace and human
happiness is concerned, the words written over the
portal into the unknown future of human
history are: 'lasciate ogni speranza'
(Max Weber, 1994 [1895])

The modern notion of 'civil society' originates with the thinkers of the Scottish Enlightenment, for whom the term was closely connected with the expressions 'civil' and 'civilizing', on the one hand, and with free, independent and self-reliant individuals, on the other. During the second half of the eighteenth century and at the beginning of the nineteenth century, the concept 'civil society' expressed an attitude critical of the state; it often had an anti-absolutist thrust. It was closely connected with the realm of freedom and expressed the self-confidence of a well-educated and relatively small elite.

During the nineteenth century the circle of people fighting for freedom, education and self-organization was steadily expanding: from political groupings and interest groups in the early nineteenth century to the huge number of leisure clubs and life-style societies in the middle and late nineteenth century. Even before political democracy was fully established, there was a flourishing landscape of voluntary associations.

At about the same time – roughly the last third of the nineteenth century – civil society ceased to be a central concept; it become increasingly connected with the sphere of needs and labour, including the economy but excluding the state. The normative implications it entailed were viewed far more critically, since its talk of universal rights remained oblivious to inequalities in gender, class and race. In the second half of the nineteenth and the first half of the twentieth century, there was a relative calm surrounding the debate on the definition and meaning of 'civil society'.

The renaissance of the concept in the twentieth century began in the 1970s and 1980s in central and eastern Europe and Latin America. Again, as in the eighteenth century, the concept was targeted against the state: it expressed freedom and the wish for self-organization beyond the totalitarian or dictatorial state. Some of the central figures who defined the central and east European understanding of civil society were European dissidents like Václav Havel, György Konrád or Adam Michnik. For Havel, civil society is a call for 'living within the truth' with oneself and for tolerance towards others: a vision of society that is not just independent from the state but actually opposed to it. For Konrád, 'antipolitics' is the 'ethos of civil society, and civil society is the antithesis of military society' (Konrád 1984: 92; Havel 1985; see also Keane 2000). Civil society means self-defence, an island of utopia against a greedy socialist state – and it is more a political than a scientific concept. For Konrád, it is a term that circumscribes a certain style of living and is deeply entangled in the everyday life of the east European dissident. Humanistic anti-statism, a strong emphasis on the social-ethical imperative of action, with this imperative's values of tolerance, pluralism, autonomy, dignity, subtle irony and self-development: these were central features of Eastern Europe's understanding of civil society (Konrád 1984).

In Latin America, too, the term has been used since the early 1970s; here it has been linked with a political struggle against military dictatorships. For the Brazilians, 'sociedade civil' primarily conveyed a non-military world. In the words of Francisco Weffort: 'We want a civil society, we need it to defend ourselves from the monstrous State in front of us' (Weffort 1989: 349). The reception of the concept of civil society in Latin America was based mainly on Antonio Gramsci's model of civil society, in which social movements and/or unions aimed to transform capitalist class conditions. Even today, after the historical period of the military dictatorships in Latin America, the term is still connected with decoupling from the state, with support from the Catholic Church and a critical, investigative journalism (Stepan 1985; Olvera 1999; Leiva and Pagden 2001).

In the 1980s and 1990s the concept also experienced a revival in the post-industrialized and democratic Western societies, with four different and sometimes interrelated conceptual variants becoming established (Kneer 1997; Reichardt 2004a: 43–45; 2004b: 69–75). First, there is a communitarian model that places voluntary associations – with their function of socializing and building solidarity – at the heart of a civil society; the formal legal principles upon which these associations and communities rest are of less interest than the notions of the 'good life' anchored in their life-worlds. According to a second approach, civil society is a concept that promotes reflection in liberal democracies. Civil society is seen as a 'radical democratic concept'; it refers to the project of an autonomous – self-constituting and self-organising – society of citizens, with all its members participating equally in power (Rödel et al. 1989). In contrast to the communitarian model, this view is more interested in political participation than in socializing effects or in the establishment of community structures that promote solidarity.

At the heart of the third, liberal, version of civil society stand liberty and the 'existence of autonomous, that is, not state or otherwise centrally-managed organizations' (Dahrendorf 1991: 262), which safeguard the diversity, autonomy, civil rights and public life of civil society. This version of coexistence in civil society, however, also accentuates individual citizens' reason, their social and moral competence, which, above and beyond the state's coercive integration, independently contributes – even if it is out of pure self-interest – to the underlying conditions for the existence of community (Dahrendorf 1994: 67–73). In Jürgen Habermas's discourse-theory approach – the fourth variant – civil society is the social space in which communicative action takes its most distinct form. Non-coercive discourse and open discussion form the core of Habermas's notion of civil society. A key role is played by associations that arise relatively spontaneously and work within the institutional order of the public sphere. Communicative action and rational argument inside interlinked and competing public spheres generate civil society – a civil society here understood as a pluralist and free community of communication.

This very short overview of the history of the concept shows how this prismatic and polymorphic term reflects a wide variety of historical societies and how the term's meaning is embedded in historical developments. 'Civil society' should be seen not as a static concept but as a concept in flux, with changing meanings, norms, actors and adversaries (Kumar 1993).

From the start, civil society was a normative concept with universalist claims, yet with an exclusionary reality (social, ethnic or gender). To understand the attractiveness of the concept, it is crucial to know against whom or what it was aimed – fanaticism and barbarism, a profit-oriented economy, a clientelistic private sphere, a power-ridden state or a militarized society. Today the term is often connected with political programmes: individualization and atomization (communitarians); international turbo-capitalism (anti-globalization movement); a strong welfare state that provides too much (neoliberals); the petrification of parliamentary organizations (radical democrats); the hypertrophy of the state and uncontrolled market competition (social democrats); the totalitarian state (East European dissidents); or corrupt and military states (parts of east Asia's and Latin America's social movements).

A historical overview reveals how these contra-terms have changed over time and space and how they are embedded in specific historical constellations. For the topic of violence and civil society, this means tracing the historically shifting definitions of 'civil' and 'civility'. The historical nature of civil societies makes it important to keep in mind how much 'civility' was and is embedded in the word 'civil society'.

Civil societies must be able to pursue a variety of interests; furthermore, there is no such thing as a civil society without some conflict and inequality. Here, the logic of consensus and unity is less important than is the willingness on the part of civil society actors to compromise and negotiate and, in so doing, to regulate conflicts. The civil society approach is sensitive to questions of culture and 'civility'. Research on civil society implies a study of those rituals which explain stratification and conflict as well as cultural and social integration. Rituals of interaction and their allocation in time and space are of special importance for our knowledge of civil society.

Energies generated by sheer civic activism do not of necessity feed into a politics of toleration and inclusion; they can just as well be utilized for repressive ends. Civic mobilization is also capable of fragmenting societies into different pillars or milieus – as the example of the Weimar Republic with its extensive intermediate civic infrastructure shows. Although voluntary clubs and associations were able to mobilize more members than ever before in German history, the Weimar Republic was not shaped by the values of civility. Voluntary associations are not necessarily synonymous with the capacity to compromise and with civil integration (Berman 1997; Reichardt 2004c).

Every civil society is grounded in a certain degree of self-government, discipline and communication. Instead of naïvely understanding civil society as a highly normative utopia, it should be seen as a sphere or realm with power relations. Civil society links power, communication and governmental virtues in a certain way – it is where societal norms are formed and cultivated. It is the space within which societal consensus is negotiated and struggled over and in which 'responsible' social beings are constructed. Civil society means governing by community; this is not possible without permanent conditioning, power strategies and informal governance structures (Burchell at al. 1991; Dean 1999; Foucault 2004: 406–30; Gosewinkel and Reichardt 2004).

Part I addresses the question how far 'civility' is an essential part of the definition of civil society. Part II sketches six possible thematic fields of more detailed research into the relationship between violence and civil society. I shall discuss the history of protest and terrorism, and present some thoughts on the links between civil society and, respectively, the state monopoly on violence and war. I ask whether the civility of civil societies can be interpreted as a historical learning process, and raise the question of the hidden violence inside civil societies. I focus mainly on German history of the nineteenth and twentieth centuries. While this reduces the geographical and temporal range of the chapter, my main interest will be the arguments associated with the historical examples, rather than the examples themselves.

Concepts: 'Civility' and Violence

Even semantically, the term civil society connotes 'civility' and the 'civil' as an assumed antithesis to violence. (for definitions of civil society in this sense see Tester 1992: 9; Münkler 1994: 6; Keane 1996: 65–70; Dubiel 2001:138). Indeed, John A. Hall has called for the delimitation from violence to be made part of the term's very definition. Civil society, he writes, 'should be seen not merely as the presence of strong and autonomous social groups able to balance the state but also as a high degree of civility in social relations' (Hall 2000: 48). Likewise, John Keane finds that violence is incompatible with particular ideals of civil society – the rules of solidarity, liberty, equality and tolerance. Other civil society ideals, such as the guarantee of civil and human rights or freedom of communication in the public sphere, also stand in opposition to violence (Dubiel 1994: 94; Keane 1996: 68, 80; 1998: 139; Kocka 2000: 26).

However, the standards and expectations with regard to evaluations of behaviour as civil or violent are not historically invariable. The historically shifting semantics of violence need to be problematized and opened up by scholarship as discursive constructions. The moment when the bodily touch of another person is perceived, classified and evaluated as violence is something that has changed over the course of time (Neidhardt 1986: 121, 135; Bonacker and Imbusch 1999: 94). Even the civil societies of present-day Western Europe legitimate certain uses of violence, whether as part of the right to self-defence and assistance in emergencies or, until recently, in the parental disciplining of children (Milanes 1999). In the course of history the same practice has been perceived at one point as self-defence or an initiation rite, at another as manslaughter or torture.

Zygmunt Bauman has identified three strategies by which violence can be stripped of its violent appearance: first, victims can be devalued and defined as barbarians – their civil society status is negated; secondly, violence can be defined in different conceptual terms, for instance as an educational measure; and, thirdly, violence can be represented as an unpleasant means to a good end – whether this is democracy or indeed civil society itself (Bauman 1997: 226). Such classificatory strategies in the semantics of violence can be traced historically, with special attention being paid to the variability of the classifications. This yields a discursive history of violence for which one can then create a parallel account of actual historical developments. One might thus ask what social developments have corresponded to what strategies of making or removing taboos on violence (Bonacker 2002).

Two dangers are faced by an enquiry into violence that takes civil society as its starting point. One of these is the idealizing tendency criticised by John Keane, who stresses the 'chronic persistence of violence within all extant civil societies'. He reminds us that civil societies are not immune from becoming 'uncivil societies': 'civil society can never become a haven of nonviolent harmony' (Keane 1996: 22, 107; 1998: 119, 136, 141). The concept must thus avoid falling into an optimistic historical teleology that bypasses actual historical actors. Secondly, analysis must address the violence practised on those excluded on national, ethnic, social or gender grounds, in other words on the actors regarded as being outside civil society; attention should also be paid to the repercussions such exclusions have on the spectrum of inclusion within civil society. The discursive history of the concept of civility should work with terms like barbarity, violence or colonization as complementary concepts, since this can help reveal the substance of what has historically been understood by civility. To comprehend the dimensions of what a civil society includes, we need to study what and how it excludes (Colas 1997; Goody 2001; Heins 2002).

The discourses with regard to civility, civic courage or civil disobedience show that civilised behaviours are often thematically enmeshed with the concept of the 'civilising process' (Bauman 1985; Goldschmidt and Mies 1995; Keane 1996: 14–31; Kneer 1997: 235–36; Hall 1998; Trentmann 2000: 3; Dubiel 2001: 138, 140). As early as the eighteenth century, such comments can be found in the work of Adam Ferguson (1767), James Dunbar (1780), John Logan (1781) or Immanuel Kant (1798) (Ferguson 1995: 74–105, 224–64; Dunbar 1780; Logan 1781; Kant 1970: 176–90). Norbert Elias's famous study, above all, helped disseminate the thesis of the differentiation of human affect and control structures. According to Elias's modernization theory, the increasing domestication of people's instinctual nature arose through each individual being subjected to exact rules and laws and through the emergence of a state monopoly on violence. Over time, the increasingly long interactional chains of modern societies made it necessary for citizens to habitually internalize the renunciation of violence (Gleichmann et al. 1982, 1984; Bogner 1989; Kuzmics and Mörth 1991; Elias 1994; Jäger 1995; Rehberg 1996; Schwerhoff 1998; Dubiel 2001: 140, 143).

Compared with modernization theory, the concept of civil society has several advantages. For one thing, where modernization theory is often structuralist in approach, the culturally sensitive concept of civil society takes account of the intervention of particular actors in social confrontations. Their actions, value motivations and interests are of key importance. Secondly, when analysing the emergence and development of civil societies, attention is not restricted to endogenous factors, but also addresses the ways they are embedded in larger international constellations and their integration in transnational exchange. This raises new questions as to how far international constellations and wars relate to processes of cultural disciplining (Joas 2000a: 188–89, 19293). Thirdly, in contrast to Talcott Parsons, who 'represented modern society as genuinely unwarlike' (Gill 2002: 50), the significance of violence and peacefulness for civil societies receives serious attention (Joas 1992: 329–33, Joas 2000b: 49–66, 183–235; Mann 1999, 2000). And, fourthly, the concept of civil society is not associated with any evolutionary teleology. The twentieth century's barbarity can thus be interpreted not as an archaic relic of pre-modern traditions but as 'post-civilized barbarity' (Claus Offe) (Mennel 1990; Offe 1996). Understanding the possible destructive qualities residing in the interplay of instrumental reason and a modern 'gardening state' (Bauman) has provided insight into the quality and necessity of an autonomous civil society. Such a civil society recognizes and tolerates plurality and difference, and publicly and perpetually reflects on life-world categories such as everyday morality, style, decency, moral sensibility, internalized discipline or civilizational inhibitions. Being in civil society means mirroring and contemplating modern social engeneering, morally reflecting on a feasibility-oriented cost-benefit rationality, and subjecting a politics based on technological and administrative measures to norm-oriented scrutiny (Bauman 1989, 1991, 1995; Peukert 1989; Joas 1998).

Problems for Research into Historical Civil Societies

With regard to possible fields of empirical research, it is, first, clear that civil societies have to deal with a multiplicity of conflicts, opposing life plans, diverging interests and contested viewpoints. Often, thinking on civil society overemphazises discursive and associative elements. Instead of unnecessarily stressing those forms of action that are cooperative and oriented towards understanding, we should, rather, see civil society as a conflictual arena. Following Lewis A. Coser, we might want to consider both the integrative and stabilizing effects of conflicts as well as the opportunities for a civilized handling of conflict (Coser 1956; Oberschall 1973; Coser and Larsen 1976; Senghaas 1995; Kneer 1997: 248–49; Rucht 2004). Here, the logic of consensus and unity is less important than the regulation of conflicts through negotiations by actors in civil society. I now present six possible themes for research connected with this issue.

Protest and Civil Societies

It makes sense, in an enquiry into the significance of violence in the space of civil society, to look at social movements and their forms of protest. Associations, along with less formalized types of organization such as networks or non-governmental organizations (NGOs), are, perhaps, almost classic fields of investigation. With regard to the theme of violence, it might be asked whether in the long nineteenth century (the 'rebellious century') we can really – as some authors have claimed (Kocka and Jessen 1990) – observe a trend of declining violence in social protests. The argument runs that the nineteenth century saw a decline in comparatively unregulated subsistence protests and food riots, endemic firewood theft, beer riots and machine-breaking, craftsmen's protests against outrages to the honour of their trade, and protests of the lower classes against bans on public smoking. Gradually, strikes – legal in Germany since the 1860s – took the place of these protests. The strike was more targeted and, because it adapted itself to the dynamics of the market economy, it fulfilled its purpose more rationally. Accordingly, it was more successful and, as a result, the strike as a pattern of conflict increasingly gained ground over violent social protest. Step by step, rational planning and organization became dominant. Violent campaigns seemed dysfunctional since they mobilized the superior repressive apparatus of the state, which was notoriously likely to escalate the violence of the conflict. The situation was reinforced by the trend towards formalized, judicialized and bureaucratized procedures for representing interests and regulating conflicts. As the nineteenth century continued, protests and demonstrations became less violent: a long-term pacification and rationalization of conflict processes had been achieved. This argumentation is based on the view that civil society fosters democratic behaviour and assumes that citizens who are able to arrange their affairs together through democratic institutions will no longer have any need to use violence.

Certainly, the nineteenth century, with its thoroughgoing politicization and its democratization, brought the dream of a peaceable, democratic civil society much closer to reality. On the other hand, the democratic rights to agitate and participate were, if anything, a prerequisite for the rise of the aggressive mass movements which, from the early twentieth century, were becoming increasingly violent. Although the radical movements presented themselves as the adversaries of democratically constituted societies, they operated within the spectrum of participatory expectations and opportunities that had, ironically, been opened up by modern democracy itself. The notions allied with violent action – spontaneity and renewal, charismatic leadership and the power to act – merged into populist concepts of direct representation and fundamentally oppositional forms of politics. It is therefore important not to render exotic and trivialise violence as merely a survival from pre-democratic days; violence, rather, must be understood as a fundamental concomitant of civil society's expanded participatory rights (Rohkrämer 1990; Joas 2000a; Keane 2004). To this extent, the violence of protest did not retreat in a linear fashion from the nineteenth to the early twentieth century. Nevertheless, the hypothesis of declining violence of social protests still needs more precise empirical investigation. (For the rich research on social protests see as overviews: Tilly et al. 1975; Haupt 1977; Hausen 1977; Tenfelde and Volkmann 1981; Mommsen and Hirschfeld 1982; Volkmann and Bergmann 1984; Giesselmann 1987; Schumann 1997: 369–70; Spehr 2000; Aminzade et al. 2001; McAdam et al. 2001.)

With regard to the discursive history of violence and protests, it would be useful to trace the historical roots of the concept 'civil disobedience', which is very important for the history of Western protests from the 1960s to the 1980s. The expression goes back to *On the Duty of Civil Disobedience*, by the American philosopher Henry David Thoreau, published in 1849. The term then experienced a chequered history at the hands of demonstrators – from Leo Tolstoy to Mahatma Gandhi – who drew, in different ways, on the right to a morally grounded violation of the rules. The notion of 'civil disobedience' became influential in central and eastern Europe in the 1970s and 1980s, and was explicitly used as a conceptual counterpoint to the omnipresence and coercive violence of state power. The democratic oppositional movements of Central Eastern Europe expressly rejected 'heroic' uses of violence in the Sorelian style. Of interest here would be how far life under the state-socialist dictatorships – a life marked by state-organized surveillance, imprisonment and fear, the build-up of armaments and ostentatious military parades – helped generate antipathy to the use of violence. In this political context it was not terrorism, kidnapping or assassinations but civil disobedience that became the dominant form of protest. In the new social movements of the West, too, civil disobedience with an eye to publicity – located in a dynamic field of tension between the rule of law and democracy, legality and legitimacy – was an important protest form (from the 1980s, however, violent forms of action were by no means entirely absent from the new social movements) (Thoreau 1963 [1849]; Laker 1986; Rödel et al. 1989: 22–46; Cohen and Arato 1992: 564–604; Rucht 2003).

Terror and Civil Societies

The violence-ridden history of political demonstrations in the Weimar Republic – a time of expanded participation and of booming associational life and socio-political democratization – suggests that a condition of preventing violence is not only the formal opening of the political system but also the sociocultural civility of civil society. To see how fast civility can change into its opposite, one need only look at the First World War. In combination with the subsequent rise of non-state violent organizations, the war was able to brutalize bourgeois society to such an extent that an 'unconscious militarization of the political habitus' took place (Weisbrod 2000: 27). If almost every political articulation took the form of grand promises, panicked threats or violence-laden hatred, this was fundamentally connected with changes in the representation of the symbolic forms of the political. This shift in form during the Weimar Republic cannot be understood without looking at the rise of the mass media and the visualization of political life; it found expression both in the popular press and in the political atrocity propaganda of radical forces. The repertoire of emotionally loaded images of salvation, and the weakening of inhibitions on violence must be seen in the context of the mass media's influence on the style of politics. The deep-reaching sociocultural, political and socio-economic crisis of the Weimar Republic expressed itself in a general loss of security and certainty; as a result, important pillars of the bourgeois value system began to sway (Weisbrod 2000).

The history of fascism shows that a lifestyle defined by violence could be used as propaganda precisely in the social space between the state, the economy and the private sphere. The fast-moving and spontaneous *vivere pericolosamente* could be impressively enacted as a foil to 'ponderous reformism' and to the convolutions of bureaucratic procedures in a mass society struggling for legitimacy against a background of economic crisis. Even in the early phase of fascism, the violence of the paramilitary groups was directed not primarily at efficiently destroying their opponents, but, rather, at capturing the arena of media publicity. Propaganda was not a substitute for violence, but one of its aspects. Fascism drew together mass mobilization, terrorism and the public sphere (Paul 1990; Weisbrod 1992; Reichardt 2001). It is precisely civil society's unprotected and open nature and the liberality of its political culture that make this kind of political violence possible.

With regard to terrorist violence and civil society, W. Lee Eubank and Leonard Weinberg have studied 379 terrorist groups in the period 1945–87. The study shows that, in the 172 states investigated, terrorist groups were found 3.5 times more frequently in democratic civil societies than under authoritarian regimes. Nor is this uncomfortable finding significantly altered if we introduce criteria such as the openness of a state's political culture or the stability of its democracy (Eubank and Weinberg 1994; Waldmann 1998: 126–32). Historical research would do well to examine this purely quantitative finding and ask which varieties of terrorism enjoy opportunities within civil societies and which do not. Might it be the case that terrorism in civil societies receives greater attention as a public problem and is thus more visible, but in fact does not occur more frequently than in authoritarian regimes suffused by state power? If a critical examination confirmed Eubank and Weinberg's findings, the reason for this susceptibility would have to be sought – perhaps it would be the fact that guaranteed basic rights to freedom provide fertile soil for violent political protest. Do liberal-democratic institutions offer opportunities to exercise violence by protecting the private sphere, guaranteeing individual freedom of movement and rights of association? Do press freedom and freedom of opinion create an effective sounding board for acts of terror? Or does the media system even stimulate terror attacks? One might also ask whether it is not precisely the peacefulness of democratic civil societies sensitive to violence that generates the media impact of terrorist attacks (which themselves are communicative appeals). All these issues may have a role to play.

Above and beyond these considerations, there is the question of why Western civil societies do not have more educational success and why Western civic virtues do not produce sustainable cultural integration. The problem here is how to achieve – in a democratically expanded model of civil society – a balance between normative orientations and the greatest possible degree of democratic participation. The danger is that the more that Western, liberal civil society tries to be pedagogical towards, for example, Islamic groups, the more it transgresses the boundaries of individual liberty and independence. The more the discourse of Western virtues has recourse to an imprecise formula of commitment to an unspecified 'common good', the more inevitable will be the call for politics to intervene in individual life plans. The paradoxical nature of liberal and enlightened civil societies is evident in the danger that such societies will tip over into suppressing wishes for freedom and emancipatory needs – just as Robespierre attempted to coerce citizens into virtuous behaviour through a policy of terror.

Civil Society and the State Monopoly on Violence

In Europe, from the eighteenth century, a modern police force came into being whose origins lay in the political field of 'policey', the domestic policy care of the 'common good'. Increasingly, its responsibility was narrowed down to the 'maintenance of public calm, security and order', as the Prussian civil code put it as early as the eighteenth century (Haupt and Narr 1978; Liang, 1992; Knöbl 1998; Reinhard 2000: 363–70). The state monopoly on violence thus focused on the fields of security and order, and was institutionally expanded in the form of the police, the military and the prison system. Over time, institutionalization and the increasingly anonymous possibilities of surveillance open to the 'panoptic state' has meant that the state's physical exercise of violence has become less visible: society has become less aware of it. Civil society contains elements of self-supervision; the extent and form of police violence are thus only one gauge of the liberty and internal integration of a given civil society (McMullan 1998; Pütter 2002).

Jürgen Habermas has argued that the democratic constitutional state, with its 'monopoly of the legitimate use of physical force in the enforcement of its order' (Max Weber), should be viewed as the precondition and guarantee of a civil society that will tend to be open to violence. Only the certainty of being able to establish clubs and societies; protected opportunities for voluntary associations to intervene in the process of the formation of public opinion; and the freedom of the press and its openness to competing opinions – together with the right to vote and to stand for election – can guarantee the autonomy and spontaneity of civil society associations (Weber 1978: 54, 1988: 506; Habermas 1991a: 368; 1991b: 162; Keane 1996: 83). State protection from the application of physical force – beginning with state gun control – should be seen as one of the safeguards of the opportunity to develop in civil society.

Norbert Elias's famous model of a civilizing process consists, at base, in the assertion of a transformation from external control to self-control. Elias identified an ever greater self-control by human beings, an internalization of rules of behaviour and a shift of unacceptable types of behaviour from the public sphere to the space behind the scenes, the private sphere, and associated this with the process of state formation and the state monopolization of violence. The history of public lynching in the United States, or other forms of self-administered justice considered legitimate by civil society actors, shows what can happen – even in modern societies – when the state does not own the monopoly on violence (Tolnay and Beck 1995; Keane 1996: 24–25, 51–57; Brundage 1997; Moses 1997; Ketelsen 2000).

Of course, Elias's teleological view of historical development is anything but uncontested, and it has been pointed out that in some cases the state monopoly on violence has itself bred or exacerbated violence – for example, through the use of prisons or in brutal police operations. Nevertheless, if it is to cultivate successfully its values of civility, unprotected civil society requires security for its actions, and one of the means of achieving this is the constitutional state's sanctioning of violence. At the same time, however, there is a danger that civil liberties will be smothered by rigid security controls (van Krieken 1989; Dinges 1995).

Another relation of tension between civil society and state violence can be seen in the history of the peace and human rights movements. This history demonstrates that civil societies possess the potential to pacify themselves, irrespective of state coercion, and are even in a position to address publicly and restrict state violence, be it torture or capital punishment (Gestrich et al. 1996; Keane 1998: 135; Gesterkamp 1999).[1]

Yet another, and very different, tension vis-à-vis the state emerges in the history of the totalitarian dictatorships in Europe or the military dictatorships in Latin America: these destroyed vigorous civil societies (Dubiel 2001: 141–42).

The state executive organs of the military and police are thus, as Norbert Elias has put it, double-edged inventions. On the one hand, they are necessary, in liberal societies, in order to protect civil society from the violence that grows from civil society itself. On the other, they can abuse their monopoly of violence to destroy an extant civil society. In view of this, historians must seek the point at which the state monopolization of violence ceases to be useful in sustaining civil societies and ask how much – or what kind of – state violence is detrimental to the growth of civil societies.

One way of using concrete examples to conceptualize the historically important relationship of civil society and state violence is offered by Ute Frevert in her history of military conscription in Germany. Other studies related to 'social militarism' – on topics such as the figure of the reserve officer, military parades or veterans' clubs – have also analysed the mutual influence of the civil and military spheres. Such studies can help us to read the marks the military has left on German civil society and to analyse the militarization of the ideals of civic engagement, concepts of social integration and gender-political figurations. After all, the male citizen had been, from the early nineteenth century until at least the First World War, the citizen in uniform, and, in line with the principle of equality in arms, a figure that cut across social classes and religious denominations. Conscription intervened in civic life and, as Frevert notes, 'its history thus opens up fascinating insights into the constitutive conditions and developmental problems of bourgeois societies'. Here, the violence that had been defined out of civil society found its way back: in the military sector, male citizens learned to overcome their inhibition against killing, to use lethal weapons, to obey principles of command and to overcome their fear of death. Conscription bridged 'the structural and habitual gap between the military and civilian worlds' and carried violence back into the civil sphere (Ritter 1954–68; Kehr 1965: 53–63; Rohkrämer 1990; Frevert 1997, 2001: 9–17; Vogel 1997; Lipp 2000: 215–17).

A comparison with countries with a professional army, such as Britain, and with Austro-Hungary and Russia, which introduced military conscription only much later, in the 1860s and 1870s, allows us to measure how far civil societies adopted military practices, orientations and values. Put conversely, how far was civil society able to seal itself off culturally and institutionally from the permeating influence of the military? From this perspective, a whole range of historical questions arise regarding the possible importation into and fusion with, on the one hand, civil society values and styles of behaviour and, on the other, military values such as order, discipline, sacrifice, punctuality, cleanliness, obedience, thrift or notions of masculinity based on self-defence.

Similarly, with regard to the police, one might ask how the experience of police violence shaped the idea of statehood in the imaginations of citizens. In which cases did civil societies fail to find agreement through voluntariness, compromise and discussion, so that the police, as the legitimate monopolist of violence, intervened to secure the contentment, safety and physical protection – as well as the integrity and coherence – of civil societies? Which forms of violence did the police prevent and suppress, and to what extent did this police practice influence the shape a given civil society would take? (For empirical studies see Lüdtke 1977, 190–211; Emsley 1984; Funk 1986; Palmer 1988; Leßmann 1989; Jessen 1991; Waldmann and Schmid 1996; Hachenberg 1997; Dunnage 1997.)

Wars and Civil Societies

The significance of war for social change and the formation of civil society, the cultural processing of war and civil society's adaptability, sensitivity to shock or defencelessness, the role of war in processes of state rationalization and cultural disciplining – all these have hitherto been omitted from many conceptualizations of the notion of civil society. As in modernization theory, the debate has so far remained largely restricted to endogenous factors, while the impact of international constellations on the emergence and continued existence of civil societies has been almost entirely ignored. A study of the relationship between peacefulness and violence in civil societies, in particular, requires far more attention to the relation of internal and external, endogenous and exogenous factors (Joas 2000a: 188–89, 192–93; Greiner 2002). It should also be asked what social repercussions war prompts within civil societies. To what extent have foreign policy interventions and coercive measures influenced civil societies' internal configurations? Might the levels of violence in US society, higher than those in Europe, be associated with the tradition of colonial wars and the slave trade – in other words, violence that was originally directed outside civil society? Britain, France, Denmark, the Netherlands and Latin America also look back on a colonial past and slavery, which in some cases persisted well into the nineteenth century. How far did this influence or determine the forms of inclusion in their civil societies? Put in more general terms, what was the relationship between endogenous peacefulness and exogenous violence? (See Wirz 1985; Klein 1986; Binder 1993; Thomas 1997.)

In *Perpetual Peace*, Immanuel Kant – one of the founding fathers of the concept civil society – outlined the notion of a positive peace as the product of human reason. With the institutionalization of world citizenship, the abolition of standing armies, the guarantee of the freedom of sovereign states and the republican constitution, Kant sets out the central elements of an international order of peace. Alexis de Tocqueville, in turn, claimed that people in different nations organized along civil society lines would become ever more similar as a result of their interaction, merging their interests to such an extent that wars would be perceived as a 'calamity almost as severe to the conqueror as to the conquered'. Does history confirm the claim put forward by Kant in 1795 and Tocqueville in 1840: the claim that it is very difficult to entangle democratically organized civil societies in war (Kant 1927: 19–59; Tocqueville 1994: 264–86, quotation: 281; Habermas 1995)?

It could be argued, quite to the contrary, that the gradual internal pacification of European civil societies was matched by violence and fear at the external, interstate level. Melvin Small and J. David Singer's 1976 study mapping proneness to wars between 1816 and 1965 shows that 58 per cent of interstate wars were initiated by democracies. If one considers only the 'extrasystemic' colonial wars between 1871 and 1965, 65 per cent were started by democracies. Precisely the violence-laden history of colonialism, 'ethnic cleansings' based on organicist ideas and the decolonization of Africa, Asia and Latin America show that democracies cannot be acquitted of a degree of outwardly directed violence. Tocqueville's hopes were in vain: democracies resort to violence against groups and states they perceive as outsiders; the main protagonists here have not been only ideologically driven militarists, but also pragmatically motivated civilians who, in principle, gave preference to civic values (Small and Singer 1976; works critical of Kant's thesis: Mann 1999; Garzke 2001; Müller 2002).

However, two kinds of reservation are clearly necessary here. First, the finding depends very much on definitions. Small and Singer define wars as conflicts that claimed more than a thousand lives, and states are defined as democracies where 10 per cent of the population was enfranchised; where free, multiparty elections were held; and in which a parliament either controlled or strongly participated in the executive. A stricter definition of democracy, working with normative civil society criteria, would probably have yielded different results. Hence, it remains unclear whether, in a given case, warlike behaviour was not fuelled instead by inadequate democratization and deficits in the elements of civil society. A second point has been made by Michael W. Doyle and many others, who show that democracies almost never wage war on each other. Doyle's findings support both Kant's and Tocqueville's stress on the significance of democratic peace. Kant's thesis is substantiated, in particular, for the period after 1945, in which a far-reaching pacification can be observed within the Organisation for Economic Cooperation and

Development sphere. In contrast, there were dramatic increases in violent conflicts, the so-called 'wars on the periphery', mainly within and between states in impoverished and often undemocratized regions of Africa, in the Middle East and in parts of Asia (Doyle 1983; Dülffer 2000; van Creveld 1991; Czempiel 1996; Rohloff and Schindler 2000).

Over and above the quantitative findings, it should be asked what causes underlay the democracies' supposed bellicosity and how they legitimized their aggression. Ultimately, the issue is whether and when the wars of the democracies can be what Michael Walzer calls 'just wars' (1977). Here a wide field awaits the attention of historical research: the task of identifying the factors and variables that have influenced the interaction of nationally constituted civil societies and their foreign-policy peacefulness or bellicosity. Is the influence of civil society actors truncated at an especially early stage in the case of foreign-policy issues, and, if so, why? In this respect, it could be revealing to compare the conditions and achievements of the peace and anti-war movements with those of other social movements.

Norbert Elias pointed out early that a lower level of civilization has been reached in the interaction between states than within states themselves. In civil societies, too, violent acts at the foreign-policy level are more highly valued than those at the level of domestic policy. Elias attributed this circumstance to the weaker monopolization of interstate violence. There is no international army, Elias says, 'that is stronger than the states preparing for violent conflict or entangled in violent actions and that could effectively prevent them from working out their conflicts in a warlike way' (Elias 1981: 102). True enough, the United Nations lacks strong executive organs, and the international courts are relatively weak institutions compared with their nation-state counterparts. They cannot yet induce or compel nation states gradually to internalize and habituate themselves to peaceable attitudes. As yet there is no such thing as a legally guaranteed, global domestic policy – despite the existence of the offences of war crime, crime against humanity and genocide (Bartosch 1998; Habermas 2001). As a result, there has been no movement from external constraint to self-constraint comparable to that identified by Norbert Elias in the case of the civilizing process within states. Where might the causes of this mismatch be sought? Do the inertia and power-consciousness of the institutional order of nation states and national thinking hamper the emergence of an international legal order and executive?

Civility: the Outcome of a Historical Learning Process?

In his famous essay of 1784 on the philosophy of history, 'Idea of a Universal History with a Cosmopolitan Purpose', in which he outlined a process of the optimization of bourgeois world society, Immanuel Kant gave a key role to the history of wars. For, writes Kant, the human desires for 'honour, power and property' drive humanity into wars which, in turn, cause distress, devastation and inner exhaustion. It is then that reason reasserts itself, learning from 'sad experience' to 'abandon a lawless state of savagery and enter a federation of peoples'. Only in a state of peace can a fully fledged civil society develop; but 'as long as states apply all their resources to their vain and violent schemes of expansion, thus incessantly obstructing the slow and laborious efforts of their citizens to cultivate their minds ... no progress in this direction can be expected. For a long, internal process of careful work on the part of each commonwealth is necessary for the education of its citizens' (Reiss 1970: 41–53, quotations 44, 47, 49; Niethammer 1990: 17–30).

Can this type of learning from the catastrophes and wars of history really be observed – do civil societies arise from bloodstained origins? Kant's hypotheses were presented five years before the French Revolution; they may be read in the context of subsequent events, when revolutionary violence and the invention of democracy seemed, to the actors of the day, to be complementary aspects. A fundamental difficulty lay in advancing from the unity of the principles of people and sovereignty to a recognition of pluralism. Political liberties and unlimited sovereignty proved to be worse bedfellows than the use of force and the claim to sovereignty (Baczko 2000: 12–21; Mayer 2000: esp. 171–226).

However, in some cases the establishment of organizations of civil society may be regarded as the immediate products of a learning process. In 1863, on the recommendation of the Swiss writer and philanthropist Henri Dunant, the International Committee for the Relief of the Wounded, later renamed the International Committee of the Red Cross, was founded in Geneva. The future Nobel Peace Prize-winner's initiative was prompted by a violent event, the battle of Solferino in 1859 and the misery of the war-wounded. Similar interrelationships between experiences of violence and charitable foundations can be found in, to name but a few, the children's charity 'terre des hommes', founded in 1959 by Edmond Kaiser in response to the situation in the Algerian internment camps; the 1946 foundation of UNICEF (United Nations International Children's Emergency Fund); the Save the Children Fund; and the 1992 international campaign against landmines: all owe their existence not least to horror at the violence unleashed in the modern world (Libby 1964; Mützenberg 1984; Black 1996; Keane 1996: 159–63; Riesenberger 2002; for human rights, see: Amnesty international 1998; Donnelly 1998: esp. 3–17; Köhne 1998).

The experience of violence in the Second World War and the frightening vision of dictatorial violence fostered and underpinned adherence to civil society models. Sociologists of war in the United States and Britain have put forward the thesis that the mass mobilization necessitated by war was the motor behind important democratic and welfare developments in civil society – from the extension of the franchise, to the development of social insurance, to the improvement of civil rights (Gill 2002: 53). The Universal Declaration of Human Rights by the General Assembly of the United Nations in December 1948 can be seen as an outcome of traumatic experiences with unlimited violence during the Second World War (Joas 2000b).

The constitutional state of the Federal Republic of Germany, too, supported the emergence of a West German civil society by applying the principles of the protection of personal freedom and human and civil rights and reinforcing the trade unions and social pacification. Civic values emerged as a consequence of the experience of extreme violence (see Kocka 1979; Wehler 2001: esp. 627f.). A recognition of the disastrous consequences of what Detlev Peukert has called *Machbarkeitswahn* (the intoxicated sense of the possible) led, in Zygmunt Bauman's view, to a greater tolerance of ambivalence, acknowledgement of society's heterogeneity, acceptance of the strengthening of autonomous intermediate institutions and a plural public sphere and networked thinking and to greater consideration for ethics in science. Abandoning plans for the total malleability of society, the state ceded important formative tasks to a self-organizing, plural and democratic civil society (Bauman 1995; 'Über die Rationalität des Bösen' 1999: 115).

Of course, this is not to say that civic virtues arise 'naturally' from the collapse of violent regimes. Again and again, social movements have been forced to fight to gain a space for civil society and participatory rights. A brief consideration of the First World War shows how important it was for civil society to have an insulating layer of culture. While there was, in general, a brief blossoming of democracy in the first years after the war, the period between 1922 and 1938 saw almost all the new democracies collapse. In 1920, of the sixty-five states worldwide, a total of thirty-five had constitutional, elected governments. At the end of this phase, democracy survived only in Britain and its white dominions, the United States, Czechoslovakia, France, Belgium, Holland, Switzerland and Scandinavia. In most of these states, the roots of civil society were historically longer and stronger than in Germany. Indeed, many of them were advanced civil societies, whose resistance to the lure of dictatorship making itself felt all over Europe should not be undervalued. Be that as it may, in 1944, only twelve democracies remained worldwide (Hobsbawm 1994: 111–13).

Hidden Violence: Civil Society's Blind Spots

Violence within families – violence against children, men's violence against women – has only been a topic of discussion in Western societies for around twenty years, although the phenomena are anything but new. Violence in the family remains widespread, and accounts for a large proportion of violent acts. It is the form of violence least subject to social control and most seriously underestimated. However, it is becoming ever more visible and public and is being re-evaluated (Windaus 1986; Honig 1988; Schneider 1993; for further literature, see: Schönfeld 1993).

In view of the long existence of hidden violence, one might conclude that civil societies are quite able to live with physical violence as long as it is not brought onto the public agenda and delegitimated. Domestic violence, sexual violence within marriage or the corporal punishment of children: none inhibited the formation of Western civil societies before the early 1970s, even though these societies knew and respected the human right to freedom from bodily harm. Alongside the beating of children for educational purposes – long considered legitimate – another form of violence only recently classified as such is physical assault on the elderly and sick in nursing homes and clinics. In contrast, the master craftsman's violence against his journeyman or the employer's or householder's against his servants was problematized as early as the nineteenth century.

In short, the perception and evaluation of violence are subject to change and is embedded in specific contexts. A historical perspective will ask when and why particular actors, their actions and their intentions were judged to be violent at a particular point. Violence is both a discursive construction and a social practice – but at what moment does the assessment of a behaviour as violent occur, and what might be the conditions promoting or impeding such a classification (Lindenberger and Lüdtke 1995; Baecker 1996: 99; Liell 1999: 34–39)?

We need to discover whether the self-reflexive nature of civil societies results in violence being increasingly de-privatized and, in the long term, impossible to keep out of public debate. Was it inevitable that the principle of the right to freedom from bodily harm, once established, could not ultimately be restricted to those who – with whatever ideological intentions – introduced it? Historically, it is of interest to know when and which relations of violence became subject to public interrogation and why this occurred. This question applies not only to violence against women and children, but also to violence against the socially disadvantaged (such as farmhands and apprentices), ethnic minorities (for example, slaves) or the disabled (for example, those affected by institutionalization or the subjects of euthanasia).

In the social space of civil society, civility can only ever be realized in a fragmentary form. With respect to the topic of hidden violence, we must interrogate the status of an autonomous and non-partisan public sphere as the site of responsibility for reflection and learning in civil society. Which tasks of the public sphere – monitoring the socio-political environment, proposing topics, creating platforms or enabling dialogue – are the crucial factors for the development of civic values and mutual respect, including the respect for freedom from bodily harm (Habermas 1991a: 365–66, 368, 373–79; Rödel 1996: 674; Alexander 1998; Dubiel 2001: 149)?

Some Conclusions

Understanding violence as a discursive construction raises the question of the cultural conditions that contributed to the assessment of certain physical actions as constituting either uncivil violence or, simply, measures to enhance education and civilisation. Hence one must deal with processes of the establishment of norms, the legitimation of violence and the historically changing criteria of the definition of violence. This approach also includes the historicization of the normative core of civil sociability as a mode of conflict regulation.

As the historical examples have shown, violence is not only the opposite of civility and civil society; it is also a prerequisite of emerging civil societies. Civil societies developed, first, sometimes from partly violent protests in which historical actors fought for their own autonomy and civil rights. Even more – secondly – some important elements of civil society emerged from wars; the concept of the 'nation in arms' is ambivalent: it promises political participation and societal self-organization, on the one hand, and readiness for violence, on the other. The importance of the monopolization of legitimate violence by the state, thirdly, was reconstructed as a precondition for the emergence and development of civil societies. Sometimes civil societies and civil society organizations have bloodstained origins; they emerge by learning from catastrophes and wars.

It seems paradoxical that, in self-reflexive civil societies that are sensitive to violence and have increasingly problematized forms of bodily harm, terrorist groups are found more frequently than under authoritarian regimes. But, even if civil society is the space in which societal norms have been formed and cultivated through power, communication and governmental virtues, its structures of governmentality are never perfect and the processes of cultural disciplining can never be finished.

The most important historical requirements, conditions and deep political-cultural and sociocultural ties in a non-violent civil society may be summarised as the seven elements of an ideal-typical and multidimensional constellation of civil society. These are: first, the implementation of a state monopoly of violence; secondly, control of that state monopoly guaranteed by the rule of law; thirdly, the control of affects necessary for an interdependent society based on the division of labour; fourthly, a compromise-oriented capacity for conflict and a culture of tolerance; fifthly, the possibility of democratic participation without social or cultural discrimination, so that social conflicts can be handled in a non-violent and regulated way; sixthly, social justice is ensured on the basis of equal opportunities and a guarantee that basic needs will be met; and, finally, the de-privatization of violence with the help of a reflective public sphere (Senghaas 1995; Keane 1998: 154–56).

It would be an interesting task to investigate the mutual influence and interlinking of these elements. A historical analysis of such connections would have to decide whether the individual components in particular historical configurations reinforced each other, and which combinations, or the absence of which elements, tended to nudge the configurations of civil society towards collapse. Ultimately, comparative historical research can help outline a typology of different civil societies.

Note

1. For the 'European Convention for the Prevention of Torture and Inhuman or Degrading Treatment or Punishment', established in 1994, see Morgan and Evans 2001.

References

Alexander, Jeffrey, ed. 1998. *Real Civil Societies. Dilemmas of Institutionalization*. London.

Aminzade, Ronald R., et al. 2001. *Silence and Voice in the Study of Contentious Politics*. Cambridge.

Amnesty International, ed. 1998. *Menschenrechte im Umbruch. 50 Jahre Allgemeine Erklärung der Menschenrechte*. Neuwied.

Baczko, Bronislaw. 2000 'Hat die Französische Revolution den Totalitarismus hervorgebracht?'. In *Wege in die Gewalt. Die modernen politischen Religionen*, ed. Hans Maier: 11–36. Frankfurt.

Baecker, Dirk. 1996. 'Gewalt im System'. *Soziale Welt* 47, 1: 92–109.

Bartosch, Ulrich, ed. 1998. *"Weltinnenpolitik"*. Internationale Tagung anläßlich des 85. Geburtstags von Carl-Friedrich von Weizsäcker in der Evangelischen Akademie Tutzing. Münster.

Bauman, Zygmunt. 1985. 'On the Origins of Civilisation: A Historical Note'. *Theory, Culture and Society* 2, 3: 7–14.

———. 1989. *Modernity and the Holocaust*. Cambridge.

———. 1991. *Modernity and Ambivalence*. Cambridge.

————. 1995. 'Civilizing the Ambivalence – Ambivalence of Civilizing'. *Dialektik* issue 3: 13–34.

————. 1997. *Flaneure, Spieler und Touristen. Essays zu postmodernen Lebensformen.* Hamburg.

Berman, Sheri. 1997. 'Civil Society and the Collapse of the Weimar Republic'. *World Politics* 49, 3: 401–29.

Binder, Wolfgang, ed. 1993. *Slavery and the Americas.* Würzburg.

Black, Maggie. 1996. *Children First. The Story of UNICEF. Past and Present.* Oxford.

Bogner, Artur. 1989. *Zivilisation und Rationalisierung. Die Zivilisationstheorien Max Webers, Norbert Elias' und der Frankfurter Schule im Vergleich.* Opladen.

Bonacker, Thorsten. 2002. 'Zuschreibungen von Gewalt. Zur Sinnförmigkeit interaktiver, organisierter und gesellschaftlicher Gewalt'. *Soziale Welt* 53, 1: 31–48.

Bonacker, Thorsten and Imbusch, Peter. 1999. 'Begriffe der Friedens- und Konfliktforschung. Konflikt, Gewalt, Krieg, Frieden'. In *Friedens- und Konfliktforschung. Eine Einführung mit Quellen,* 2nd edn, ed. Peter Imbusch and Ralf Zoll: 73–116. Opladen.

Brundage, Fitzhugh, ed. 1997. *Under Sentence of Death. Lynching in the South.* Chapel Hill, NC.

Burchell, Graham, Gordon, Colin and Miller, Peter, eds. 1991. *The Foucault Effect: Studies in Governmentality.* Chicago.

Cohen, Jean L. and Arato, Andrew. 1992. *Civil Society and Political Theory.* Cambridge.

Colas, Dominique. 1997. *Civil Society and Fanaticism: Conjoined Histories.* Stanford.

Coser, Lewis A. 1956. *The Functions of Social Conflict.* Glencoe.

Coser, Lewis A. and Larsen, Otto N., eds. 1976. *The Uses of Controversy in Sociology.* New York and London.

Czempiel, Ernst-Otto. 1996. 'Kants Theorem. Oder: Warum sind Demokratien (noch immer) nicht friedlich?' *Zeitschrift für internationale Beziehungen* 3, 1: 79–101.

Dahrendorf, Ralf.1991. 'Die gefährdete Civil Society'. In *Europa und die Civil Society: Castelgandolfo-Gespräche 1989,* ed. Krzysztof Michalski: 247–63. Stuttgart.

————. 1994. *Der moderne soziale Konflikt: Essay zur Politik der Freiheit.* Munich.

Dean, Mitchell. 1999. *Governmentality: Power and Rule in Modern Society.* London.

Dinges, Martin. 1995. 'Gewalt und Zivilisationsprozess'. *Traverse* 1: 70–82.

Donnelly, Jack. 1998. *International Human Rights,* 2nd edn. Oxford.

Doyle, Michael W. 1983. 'Kant, Liberal Legacies and Foreign Affairs'. *Philosophy and Public Affairs* 12, 3: 205–35; 4: 323–53.

Dubiel, Helmut. 1994. *Ungewißheit und Politik.* Frankfurt.

————. 2001. 'Unzivile Gesellschaften'. *Soziale Welt* 52, 2: 133–50.

Dülffer, Jost. 2000. 'Internationale Geschichte und Historische Friedensforschung'. In *Internationale Geschichte. Themen – Ergebnisse – Aussichten,* ed. Wilfried Loth and Jürgen Osterhammel: 247–66. Munich.

Dunbar, James. 1780. *Essays on the History of Mankind in Rude and Cultivated Ages*. London.

Dunnage, Jonathan. 1997. *The Italian Police and the Rise of Fascism. A Case Study of the Province of Bologna, 1897–1925*. Westport, Conn.

Elias, Norbert. 1981. 'Zivilisation und Gewalt. Über das Staatsmonopol der körperlichen Gewalt und seine Durchbrechungen'. In *Lebenswelt und soziale Probleme* (Verhandlungen des 20. Deutschen Soziologentages in Bremen 1980), ed. Joachim Matthes. Frankfurt and New York.

———. 1994 [1939]. *The Civilizing Process. The History of Manners and State Formation and Civilisation*, trans. Edmund Jephott. Oxford and Cambridge.

Emsley, Clive. 1984. *Policing and its Context, 1750–1870*. Basingstoke.

Eubank, W. Lee and Weinberg, Leonard. 1994. 'Does Democracy Encourage Terrorism?' *Terrorism and Political Violence*, 6, 4: 417–43.

Ferguson, Adam. 1995 [1767]. *An Essay on the History of Civil Society*, ed. Fania Oz-Salzberger. Cambridge.

Foucault, Michel. 2004. *Geschichte der Gouvernementalität II: Die Geburt der Biopolitik. Vorlesung am Collège de France 1978–1979*, trans. Jürgen Schröder. Frankfurt.

Frevert, Ute. 2001. *Die kasernierte Nation. Militärdienst und Zivilgesellschaft in Deutschland*. Munich.

———, ed. 1997. *Militär und Gesellschaft im 19. und 20. Jahrhundert*. Stuttgart.

Funk, Albrecht. 1986. *Polizei und Rechtsstaat. Die Entwicklung des staatlichen Gewaltmonopols in Preußen 1848–1918*. Frankfurt.

Garzke, Erik. 2001. 'Democracy and the Preparation for War. Does Regime Type Affect States' Anticipation of Casualties?' *International Studies Quarterly* 45: 467–84.

Gesterkamp, Harald. 1999. 'Amnesty International. Von der Gefangenenorganisation zum Menschenrechtsmulti?' *Forschungsjournal Neue Soziale Bewegungen* 12, 1: 80–83.

Gestrich, Andreas, Niedhart, Gottfried and Ulrich, Bernd, eds. 1996. *Gewaltfreiheit. Pazifistische Konzepte im 19. und 20. Jahrhundert*. Münster.

Giesselmann, Werner. 1987. 'Protest als Gegenstand sozialhistorischer Forschung'. In *Sozialgeschichte in Deutschland. Entwicklung und Perspektiven im internationalen Zusammenhang*. Vol. 3: *Soziales Verhalten und soziale Aktionsformen in der Geschichte*, ed. Wolfgang Schieder and Volker Sellin: 50–77. Göttingen.

Gill, Bernhard. 2002. 'Organisierte Gewalt als ,dunkle Seite' der Modernisierung. Vom nationalen Krieg zum internationalen Terrorismus'. *Soziale Welt* 53, 1: 49–66.

Gleichmann, Peter et al., eds. 1982. *Materialien zu Norbert Elias' Zivilisationstheorie*, 2nd edn. Frankfurt.

———. 1984. *Macht und Zivilisation. Materialien zu Norbert Elias' Zivilisationstheorie 2*. Frankfurt.

Goldschmidt, Werner and Mies, Thomas, eds. 1995. *Zivile Gesellschaft und zivilisatorischer Prozeß*. Hamburg.

Goody, Jack R. 2001. 'Civil Society in an Extra-European Perspective'. In *Civil Society. History and Possibilities*, ed. Sudipta Kaviraj and Sunil Khilnani: 149–64. Cambridge.

Gosewinkel, Dieter and Reichardt, Sven, eds. 2004. *Ambivalenzen der Zivilgesellschaft: Gegenbegriffe, Gewalt und Macht.* WZB discussion paper. Berlin.

Greiner, Bernd. 2002. 'Der Wandel von einer Zivil- in eine Kriegsgesellschaft. Pearl Harbors langer Schatten'. *Mittelweg* 36, 11, 1: 27–42.

Habermas, Jürgen. 1991a. *Between Facts and Norms. Contributions to a Discourse Theory of Law and Democracy*, trans William Regh. Cambridge.

———. 1991b. *Erläuterungen zur Diskursethik.* Frankfurt.

———. 1995. 'Kants Idee des Ewigen Friedens'. *Kritische Justiz* 3: 395–419.

———. 2001. *Zeit der Übergänge.* Frankfurt.

Hachenberg, Karin. 1997. *Die Entwicklung der Polizei in Köln von 1794 bis 1871.* Cologne.

Hall, John A. 1998. 'Genealogies of Civilities'. In *Democratic Civility. The History and Cross-cultural Possibility of a Modern Political Ideal*, ed. Robert W. Hefner: 53–77. New Brunswick and London.

———. 2000. 'Reflections on the Making of Civility in Society'. In *Paradoxes of Civil Society. New Perspectives on Modern German and British History*, ed. Frank Trentmann: 47–57. New York and Oxford.

Haupt, Heinz-Gerhard. 1977. 'Zur historischen Analyse von Gewalt'. *Geschichte und Gesellschaft* 3: 236–56.

Haupt, Heinz-Gerhard and Narr, Wolf-Dieter. 1978. 'Vom Policey-Staat zum Polizeistaat'. *Neue Politische Literatur* 23: 185–218.

Hausen, Karin. 1977. 'Schwierigkeiten mit dem "sozialen Protest". Kritische Anmerkungen zu einem historischen Forschungsansatz'. *Geschichte und Gesellschaft* 3: 257–63.

Havel, Václav. 1985. *The Power of the Powerless: Citizens against the State in Central-Eastern Europe*, ed. John Keane, intro. Steven Lukes. London.

Heins, Volker. 2002. *Das Andere der Zivilgesellschaft. Zur Archäologie eines Begriffs.* Bielefeld.

Hobsbawm, Eric. 1994. *Age of Extremes. The Short Twentieth Century 1914–1989.* London.

Honig, Michael-Sebastian. 1988.'Vom alltäglichen Übel zum Unrecht. Über den Bedeutungswandel familialer Gewalt'. In *Wie geht's der Familie? Ein Handbuch zur Situation der Familien heute*, ed. Deutsches Jugendinstitut: 189–202. Munich.

Jäger, Wolfgang. 1995. '"Menschenwissenschaft" und historische Sozialwissenschaft. Möglichkeiten und Grenzen der Rezeption von Norbert Elias in der Geschichtswissenschaft'. *Archiv für Kulturgeschichte* 77: 85–116.

Jessen, Ralph. 1991. *Polizei im Industrierevier. Modernisierung und Herrschaftspraxis im westphälischen Ruhrgebiet 1848–1914.* Göttingen.

Joas, Hans. 1992. *Die Kreativität des Handelns.* Frankfurt.

———. 1998. 'Bauman in Germany. Modern Violence and the Problems of German Self-Understanding'. *Theory, Culture and Society* 15, 1: 47–55.

———. 2000a. 'Die Modernität des Krieges. Die Modernisierungstheorie und das Problem der Gewalt'. In *Die Gegenwart des Krieges. Staatliche Gewalt in der Moderne*, ed. Wolfgang Knöbl and Gunnar Schmidt: 177–93. Frankfurt.

———. 2000b. *Kriege und Werte. Studien zur Gewaltgeschichte des 20. Jahrhunderts.* Weilerswist.

Kant, Immanuel. 1927 [1795]. *Perpetual Peace. A Philosophical Proposal*, trans. Helen O'Brien. London.

———. 1970 [1798]. 'The Contest of Faculties'. In *Kant's Political Writings*, ed. Hans Reiss, trans. H.B. Nisbet: 176–90. Cambridge.

Keane, John. 1988. *Democracy and Civil Society. On the Predicaments of European Socialism, the Prospects for Democracy, and the Problem of Controlling Social and Political Power*. London and New York.

———. 1996. *Reflections on Violence*. London and New York.

———. 1998. *Civil Society. Old Images, New Visions*. Cambridge.

———. 2000. *Václav Havel: A Political Tragedy in Six Acts*. London.

———. 2004. *Violence and Democracy*. Cambridge.

Kehr, Eckhard. 1965. *Der Primat der Innenpolitik*. Berlin.

Ketelsen, Judith. 2000. *Das unaussprechliche Verbrechen. Die Kriminalisierung der Opfer im Diskurs um Lynching und Vergewaltigung in den Südstaaten der USA nach dem Bürgerkrieg*. Hamburg.

Klein, Ansgar. 2001. *Der Diskurs der Zivilgesellschaft. Politische Kontexte und demokratietheoretische Bezüge der neueren Begriffsverwendung*. Opladen.

Klein, Herbert S. 1986. *African Slavery in Latin America and the Caribbean*. New York.

Kneer, Georg. 1997. 'Zivilgesellschaft'. In *Soziologische Gesellschaftsbegriffe II*, ed. A. Nassehi and M. Schroer: 229–51. Munich.

Knöbl, Wolfgang. 1998. *Polizei und Herrschaft im Modernisierungsprozeß. Staatsbildung und innere Sicherheit in Preußen, England und Amerika 1700–1914*. Frankfurt and New York.

Kocka, Jürgen. 1979. '1945: Neubeginn oder Restauration'. In *Wendepunkte deutscher Geschichte 1848–1945*, ed. Carola Stern and Heinrich August Winkler: 141–68. Frankfurt.

———. 2000. 'Zivilgesellschaft als historisches Problem und Versprechen'. In *Europäische Zivilgesellschaft in Ost und West: Begriff, Geschichte, Chancen*, ed. Manfred Hildermeier, Jürgen Kocka and Christoph Conrad: 13–39. Frankfurt and New York.

Kocka, Jürgen and Jessen, Ralph. 1990. 'Die abnehmende Gewaltsamkeit sozialer Proteste. Vom 18. zum 20. Jahrhundert'. In *Verdeckte Gewalt. Plädoyers für eine "Innere Abrüstung"*, ed. Alexis Albrecht and Otto Backes: 33–57. Frankfurt.

Köhne, Gunnar 1998. *Die Zukunft der Menschenrechte. 50 Jahre UN-Erklärung. Bilanz eines Aufbruches*. Reinbek.

Konrád, György. 1984. *Antipolitics*. New York.

Kumar, Krishan. 1993. 'Civil Society. An Inquiry into the Usefulness of an Historical Term'. *British Journal of Sociology* 44: 375–95.

Kuzmics, Helmut and Mörth, Ingo, eds. 1991. *Der unendliche Prozeß der Zivilisation. Zur Kulturgeschichte der Moderne nach Norbert Elias*. Frankfurt

Laker, Thomas. 1986. *Ziviler Ungehorsam. Geschichte – Begriff – Rechtfertigung* Baden-Baden.

Leiva, L.C. and Pagden, A. 2001. 'Civil Society and the Fate of the Modern Republics of Latin America'. In *Civil Society: History and Possibilities*, ed. Sudipta Kaviraj and Sunil Khilnani: 179–203. Cambridge.

Leßmann, Peter. 1989. *Die preußische Schutzpolizei in der Weimarer Republik. Streifendienst und Straßenkampf.* Düsseldorf.

Liang, Hsi-Huey. 1992. *The Rise of Modern Police and the European State System from Metternich to the Second World War.* Cambridge.

Libby, Violit Kelway. 1964. *Henri Dunant. Prophet of Peace.* New York.

Liell, Christoph. 1999. 'Der Doppelcharakter von Gewalt. Diskursive Konstruktion und soziale Praxis'. In *Ordnungen der Gewalt. Beiträge zu einer politischen Soziologie der Gewalt und des Krieges,* ed. Sighard Neckel and Michael Schwab-Trapp: 33–54. Opladen.

Lindenberger, Thomas and Lüdtke, Alf, eds. 1995. *Physische Gewalt. Studien zur Geschichte der Neuzeit.* Frankfurt.

Lipp, Anne. 2000. 'Diskurs und Praxis. Militärgeschichte als Kulturgeschichte'. In *Was ist Militärgeschichte?,* ed. Thomas Kühne and Benjamin Ziemann: 211–17. Paderborn.

Logan, John. 1781. *Elements of the Philosophy of History.* Woodbridge.

Lüdtke, Alf. 1970. 'Praxis und Funktion staatlicher Repression: Preußen 1815–50'. *Geschichte und Gesellschaft* 3: 190–211.

Mann, Michael, 1999. 'The Dark Side of Democracy. The Modern Tradition of Ethnic and Political Cleansing'. *New Left Review* 235: 18–45.

———. 2000. 'Krieg und Gesellschaftstheorie: Klassen, Nationen und Staaten auf dem Prüfstand'. In *Die Gegenwart des Krieges: Staatliche Gewalt in der Moderne,* ed. Wolfgang Knöbl and Gunnar Schmidt: 25–52. Frankfurt.

Mayer, Arno J. 2000. *The Furies. Violence and Terror in the French and Russian Revolutions.* Princeton, NJ.

McAdam, Doug, Tarrow, Sidney and Tilly, Charles. 2001. *Dynamics of Contention.* Cambridge.

McMullan, John. 1998. 'Social Surveillance and the Rise of the "Police Machine"'. *Theoretical Criminology* 2, 1: 93–117.

Mennel, Stephen. 1990. 'Decivilizing Processes. Theoretical Significance and Some Limits of Research'. *International Sociology* 5: 205–23.

Milanes, Alexander. 1999. 'Notwehr. Zur strategischen Operationalisierung legalisierter Gewalt'. In *Ordnungen der Gewalt. Beiträge zu einer politischen Soziologie der Gewalt und des Krieges,* ed. Sighard Neckel and Michael Schwab-Trapp: 21–32. Opladen.

Mommsen, Wolfgang J. and Hirschfeld, Gerhard, eds. 1982. *Sozialprotest, Gewalt, Terror. Gewaltanwendung durch politische und gesellschaftliche Randgruppen im 19. und 20. Jahrhundert.* Stuttgart.

Morgan, Rod and Evans, Malcolm. 2001. *Combating Torture in Europe. The Work and Standards of the European Committee for the Prevention of Torture.* Strasburg.

Moses, Norton H. 1997. *Lynching and Vigilantism in the United States. An Annotated Bibliography.* Westport.

Müller, Harald. 2002. 'Antinomien des demokratischen Friedens'. *Politische Vierteljahrsschrift,* 43, 1: 46–81.

Münkler, Herfried. 1994. *Zivilgesellschaft und Bürgertugend. Bedürfen demokratisch verfaßte Gemeinwesen einer sozio-moralischen Fundierung?* Public lecture 23 at the Humboldt University, Berlin.

Mützenberg, Gabriel. 1984. *Henri Dunant, le prédestiné.* Geneva.

Neidhardt, Friedhelm. 1986. 'Gewalt. Soziale Bedeutungen und sozialwissenschaftliche Bestimmungen des Begriffs'. In *Was ist Gewalt? Auseinandersetzungen mit einem Begriff*, ed. Bundeskriminalamt. Wiesbaden.

Niethammer, Lutz. 1990. 'Einführung: Bürgerliche Gesellschaft als Projekt. In *Bürgerliche Gesellschaft in Deutschland. Historische Einblicke, Fragen, Perspektiven*, ed. Lutz Niethammer et al.: 17–38. Frankfurt.

Oberschall, Anthony. 1973. *Social Conflict and Social Movements*. Englewood Cliffs.

Offe, Claus. 1996. 'Moderne "Barbarei": Der Naturzustand im Kleinformat?'. In *Modernität und Barbarei. Soziologische Zeitdiagnose am Ende des 20. Jahrhunderts*, ed. Max Miller and Hans-Georg Soeffner: 258–89. Frankfurt.

Olvera, A.J., ed. 1999. *La Sociedad Civil: De la teoría a la realidad*. Mexico City.

Palmer, Stanley H. 1988. *Police and Protest in England and Ireland, 1780–1850*. Cambridge.

Paul, Gerhard. 1990. *Aufstand der Bilder. Die NS-Propaganda vor 1933*. Bonn.

Peukert, Detlev. 1989. 'Die Genesis der "Endlösung" aus dem Geist der Wissenschaft. In Detlev Peukert, *Max Webers Diagnose der Moderne*: Göttingen: 102–21.

Pütter, Norbert. 2002. 'Polizei und Gewalt'. In *Konflikt und Gewalt. Ursachen – Entwicklungstendenzen – Perspektiven*, ed. Wilhelm Kempf: 141–56. Münster.

Rehberg, Karl-Siegbert, ed. 1996. *Norbert Elias und die Menschenwissenschaften. Studien zur Entstehung und Wirkungsgeschichte seines Werkes*. Frankfurt.

Reichardt, Sven. 2001. 'Formen faschistischer Gewalt. Faschistische Kampfbünde in Italien und Deutschland nach dem Ersten Weltkrieg. Eine typologische Deutung ihrer Gewaltpropaganda während der Bewegungsphase des Faschismus', *Sociologus* 51, 1/2: 55–88.

———. 2004a. 'Civil Society – A Concept for Comparative Historical Research'. In *Future of Civil Society. Making Central European Nonprofit-Organizations Work*, ed. Annette Zimmer and Eckhard Priller: 35–55. Wiesbaden.

———. 2004b. 'Gewalt und Zivilität im Wandel. Konzeptionelle Überlegungen zur Zivilgesellschaft aus historischer Sicht'. In *Zivilgesellschaft – national und transnational*, WZB Yearbook 2003, ed. Dieter Gosewinkel, Dieter Rucht, Wolfgang van den Daele and Jürgen Kocka: 61–81. Berlin.

———. 2004c. 'Selbstorganisation und Zivilgesellschaft: Soziale Assoziationen und politische Mobilisierung in der deutschen und italienischen Zwischenkriegszeit'. In *Zivilgesellschaft als Geschichte: Studien zum 19. und 20. Jahrhundert*, ed. Ralph Jessen, Sven Reichardt and Ansgar Klein: 219–38. Wiesbaden.

Reinhard, Wolfgang. 2000. *Geschichte der Staatsgewalt. Eine vergleichende Verfassungsgeschichte Europas von den Anfängen bis zur Gegenwart*, 2nd edn. Munich.

Reiss, Hans, ed. 1970. *Kant's Political Writings*, trans. H.B. Nisbet. Cambridge.

Riesenberger, Dieter. 2002. *Das Deutsche Rote Kreuz. Eine Geschichte 1864–1990*. Paderborn.

Ritter, Gerhard. 1954–68. *Staatskunst und Kriegshandwerk. Das Problem des "Militarismus" in Deutschland*. 4 vols. Munich.

Rödel, Ulrich. 1996. 'Vom Nutzen des Konzeptes der Zivilgesellschaft', *Zeitschrift für Politikwissenschaft* 6, 3: 669–77.

Rödel, Ulrich, Frankenberg, Günter and Dubiel, Helmut. 1989. *Die demokratische Frage*. Frankfurt.

Rohkrämer, Thomas. 1990. *Der Militarismus der "kleinen Leute". Die Kriegervereine im Deutschen Kaiserreich 1871–1914*. Munich.

Rohloff, Christoph and Schindler, Hardi. 2000. 'Politik und Krieg. Die Zivilmacht Europa und ihr Verhältnis zum Krieg'. In *Konflikt und Gewalt. Ursachen – Entwicklungstendenzen – Perspektiven*, ed. Wilhelm Kempf: 239–63. Münster.

Rucht, Dieter. 2003. 'Violence and New Social Movements'. In *International Handbook of Violence Research*, ed. Wilhelm Heitmeyer and John Hagan: 369–82. Dordrecht, Boston and London.

——. 2004. 'Die konstruktive Funktion von Protesten in und für Zivilgesellschaften'. In *Zivilgesellschaft als Geschichte. Studien zum 19. und 20. Jahrhundert*, ed. Ralph Jessen, Sven Reichardt and Ansgar Klein: 135–52. Wiesbaden.

Schneider, Ursula. 1993. 'Gewalt in der Familie. Grundformen, Verbreitung, Auswirkungen, Ursachen, Vorbeugung'. *Der Bürger im Staat* 43: 117–22.

Schönfeld, Gerhard, ed. 1993. *Gewalt in der Gesellschaft. Eine Dokumentation zum Stand der Sozialwissenschaftlichen Forschung seit 1985*. Bonn.

Schumann, Dirk. 1997. 'Gewalt als Grenzüberschreitung. Überlegungen zur Sozialgeschichte der Gewalt im 19. und 20. Jahrhundert'. *Archiv für Sozialgeschichte* 37: 366–86.

Schwerhoff, Gerd. 1998. 'Zivilisationsprozeß und Geschichtswissenschaft. Norbert Elias' Forschungsparadigma in historischer Sicht'. *Historische Zeitschrift* 266: 561–605.

Senghaas, Dieter. 1995. 'Hexagon-Variationen. Zivilisierte Konfliktbearbeitung trotz Fundamentalpolitisierung'. In *Zivile Gesellschaft und zivilisatorischer Prozeß*, ed. Werner Goldschmidt and Thomas Mies: 113–28. Hamburg.

Small, Melvin and Singer, J. David. 1976. 'The War-Proneness of Democratic Regimes. *Jerusalem Journal of International Studies* 1, 4: 50–69.

Spehr, Michael. 2000. *Maschinensturm. Protest und Widerstand gegen Technische Neuerungen am Anfang der Industrialisierung*. Münster.

Stepan, Alfred. 1985. 'State Power and the Strength of Civil Society in the Southern Cone of Latin America'. In *Bringing the State Back In*, ed. P.B. Evans: 317–43. Cambridge.

Tenfelde, Klaus and Volkmann, Heinrich, eds. 1981. *Streik. Zur Geschichte des Arbeitskampfes in Deutschland während der Industrialisierung*. Munich.

Tester, Keith. 1992. *Civil Society*. London and New York.

Thomas, Hugh. 1997. *The Slave Trade. The History of the Atlantic Slave Trade, 1440–1870*. London.

Thoreau, Henry David. 1963 [1849]. *On the Duty of Civil Disobedience*. London.

Tilly, Charles, Tilly, Louise and Tilly, Richard. 1975. *The Rebellious Century 1830–1930*. Cambridge.

Tocqueville, Alexis de. 1994 [1835–40]. *Democracy in America* vol. 2. New York and Toronto.

Tolnay, Stewart E. and Beck, E.M. 1995. *A Festival of Violence. An Analysis of Southern Lynchings, 1882–1930.* Urbana.

Trentmann, Frank, ed. 2000. *Paradoxes of Civil Society. New Perspectives on Modern German and British History.* New York and Oxford.

'Über die Rationalität des Bösen'. Interview with Zygmunt Bauman. 1999. In *Auf den Trümmern der Geschichte*, ed. Harald Welzer: 91–125. Tübingen.

van Creveld, Martin. 1991. *The Transformation of War.* New York and Toronto.

van Krieken, Robert. 1989. 'Violence, Self-discipline and Modernity: beyond the "Civilizing Process"'. *Sociological Review* 37: 193–218.

Vogel, Jakob. 1997. *Nationen im Gleichschritt. Der 'Kult der Nation' in Waffen in Deutschland und Frankreich, 1871–1914.* Göttingen.

Volkmann, Heinrich and Bergmann, Jürgen, eds. 1984. *Sozialer Protest. Studien zu traditioneller Resistenz und kollektiver Gewalt in Deutschland vom Vormärz bis zur Reichsgründung.* Opladen.

Waldmann, Peter. 1998. *Terrorismus. Provokation der Macht.* Munich.

Waldmann, Peter, and Schmid, Carola, eds. 1996. *Der Rechtsstaat im Alltag. Die lateinamerikanische Polizei.* Ebenhausen.

Walzer, Michael. 1977. *Just and Unjust Wars. A Moral Argument with Historical Illustrations.* New York.

Weber, Max. 1978 [1925]. *Economy and Society. An Outline of Interpretive Sociology*, vol. 1, ed. Günther Roth and Claus Wittich, trans. Ephraim Fischoff. London.

———. 1988 [1921]. *Politik als Beruf.* In Max Weber, *Gesammelte politische Schriften*, 5th edn. Tübingen.

———. 1994 [1895]. *Political Writings*, ed. and trans. Peter Lassman and Ronald Speirs. Cambridge.

Weffort, Francisco. 1989. 'Why Democracy?'. In *Democratizing Brazil: Problems of Transition and Consolidation*, ed. Alfred Stepan: 327–50. New York and Oxford.

Wehler, Hans-Ulrich. 2001. 'Deutsches Bürgertum nach 1945: Exitus oder Phönix aus der Asche?' *Geschichte und Gesellschaft* 27: 617–34.

Weisbrod, Bernd. 1992. 'Gewalt in der Politik: Zur politischen Kultur in Deutschland zwischen den beiden Weltkriegen'. *Geschichte in Wissenschaft und Unterricht*, 43: 391–404.

———. 2000. 'Die Politik der Repräsentation. Das Erbe des Ersten Weltkrieges und der Formwandel der Politik in Europa'. In *Der Erste Weltkrieg und die europäische Nachkriegsordnung. Sozialer Wandel und Formveränderung der Politik*, ed. Hans Mommsen: 13–41. Cologne, Weimar and Vienna.

Windaus, Eberhard. 1986. 'Strafe und Zivilisationsprozeß'. *Jahrbuch der Kindheit* 3: 121–41.

Wirz, Albert. 1985. *Sklaverei und kapitalistisches Weltsystem.* Frankfurt.

7

IS THERE, OR CAN THERE BE, A 'EUROPEAN SOCIETY'?

Claus Offe

Curiously enough, it is not easy to find social scientists who seem to know – and are ready to explain – what a 'society' is. Yet it seems possible to put together a number of constituent notions that most authors, more or less implicitly, refer to when using the term. Among those notions, I submit, are the following.

(1) A society consists of individual actors, the number of which is relatively large (relative to members of families, business firms or localities), yet relatively small compared to the global human population, or 'mankind'.

(2) These actors are related to each other through a greater density of interaction, functional interdependence, and shared institutions than with outsiders or members of other societies.

(3) The internal density or cohesion of societies is generated by institutionalized rules. These impose constraints on the individually rational pursuit of gain (of power or wealth) or the avoidance of costs. Living in a society means sacrificing some kind of (short-term, individual) advantage for the sake of collective goods and the maintenance of social order.

(4) These constraining rules have the quality of trans-individual durability. They (are expected by members of a society to) last and stay valid for longer than the individual's lifetime and originate from a time that is prior to that lifetime. Some of these rules and

institutions are typically still around when, after about three generations, the entire 'personnel' of a society has been exchanged.

(5) Members of societies are reflexively aware of these rules as 'social facts', and they are also aware of their durability (or rootedness in some historical tradition and culture that is characteristic of their society); they are further aware of the contingency ('non-naturalness' and potential changeability) as well as distinctiveness (relative to other societies) of these rules.

(6) Given the inherent antagonism between these rules and individual self-interest and the temptations resulting from this antagonism, these rules (unlike pure coordination rules) are not self-executing through consensus, spontaneous sympathy or solidarity. On the contrary, relationships of trust, cooperation and the observance of traditional patterns depend upon the legal status and backing that the respective institutions enjoy. In modern, above all in 'postmodern' societies, society-wide rules are not self-supporting. Therefore, the making, enforcement and adjudication of these rules presuppose an apparatus of political rule and control. Beyond very low levels of either size (as in tribes) or cohesion (as in empires), societies depend upon states and their making, adjudication and enforcement of binding rules. Societies (as opposed to tribes) have always extended beyond the number of people with whom any of their members is likely ever to enter into direct interaction. Yet, in spite of the fact that most members of 'our' society are bound to remain strangers to each of us forever, we still find relationships of trust, common attachment, toleration, understanding and solidarity, as well as a sense of obligations to our 'strange' fellow citizens. All of this is due to the recognition that 'all of us' belong to some shared political community, the extent and content of which are defined by constituted state power. Even the ideally autonomous public sphere is a network of ideas and communications that is both guaranteed by and focused upon the constituted political authority of a state and its way of dealing with what we, due to this shared focus, think of as 'our' common problems.

(7) 'Princes' and other performers of these state functions have an intrinsic and private self-interest in providing and monopolizing the public good of rule.

(8) In order to be able to do so and to impose the rules (as well as to appropriate the benefits of rule to the rulers themselves), they have to make concessions to the ruled in order to secure their compliance/cooperation. This is what, from Hegel to Giddens, has been referred to as the 'dialectics of control'. If rulers want to impose duties upon society, they can do so only by granting rights to society, thereby binding/limiting themselves in the exercise of

rule. If ruling elites want to extract support, taxes and military resources, they must grant something in return, such as the effective protection of life, liberty and property, or the credible representation of the society's 'national' identity. The perfect equilibrium of rule from above and consent from below is reached when, as in all contractarian theories, the political regime can be thought of (or can present itself) as freely chosen by the enlightened will of the ruled. Military, legal and social security, as well as concessions in terms of representative and constitutional government, comprise the kinds of 'services' and concessions that states must deliver to society in order to 'earn' and preserve both the privileges of rule and their capacity to impose duties. These duties include, most importantly, the duty to pay taxes, to put one's life at the disposition of the military defence apparatus, and the duty to comply with the curricular regime of public education. Through the use of their military, fiscal and educational powers, states shape societies to the same extent that they must concede the right to being shaped by society in their practice of governance.

(9) Not only do societies depend upon states and their capacity for making and enforcing rules. In providing that service, states endow individuals and collective actors with rights and thereby engage in market making and other forms of 'society making'. Societies and states cohere in a relationship of circular mutual determination within the framework of a territorially bounded political community.

(10) There are three types of cases in which the precarious equilibrium of political regime and society can break down. For all of these cases, events in recent history can be invoked as illustrations. First, the regime fails to extract the societal resources of support and economic performance on which it depends for its survival; this is the case of post-communist and other post-authoritarian regime breakdown, where the balance between the regime's claims on society and the concessions it grants to society is fatally upset, the result being the disintegration of the regime and the constitution of a *new regime* in place of the old. Secondly, a political regime fails to maintain the unity and integrity of society because 'deep' (ethnic, religious, linguistic or historical) divisions lead to the separation of parts of its territory and constituent population through secession; this amounts to an *inward* revision of the regime's scope. Thirdly, the congruence of regime and society is upset by an *outward* revision of the regime's scope, or the fusion of two or more regimes into a new and unified one. The latter case has occurred historically through military conquest and the imposition of foreign rule through occupation. In the more recent past, it has occurred through the fusion of regimes and the creation of a multilayered

pattern of governance consisting of national and supranational regimes. The most interesting case in which such regime enlargement is currently taking place is (apart from German unification) the European Union (EU) and European integration. The question that I want to address is this: what are the causes, consequences and driving motives of the latter case of disarticulation between societies and political regimes?

The constitutional regimes of European nation states, of which the citizenry as a whole (the 'people') is thought of as the collective author, governs the scope and limits of the state's governance and at the same time creates and defines the society to which this governance applies. The problem of European political integration is that no such self-construction of the citizenry through an act of constitution-making exists. While the German Constitution (the *Grundgesetz*) ascribes, in its preamble, to the 'German people' the authorship of the document, nobody has ever claimed that the Treaties (of Rome, Maastricht and Amsterdam) that quasi-constitutionalize EU governance originate from some 'European people'. In these contracts, socie*ties*, not a society with its specific historical entity and distinctiveness, are subsumed under a supranational regime that applies to all of them with 'direct effects'. This regime is rightly seen to *dis*empower national political regimes and to render their autonomy increasingly nominal – often to the point, as is perceived within EU member states, of exercising a mild form of foreign rule. At the same time, 'Brussels' lacks the constitutional means and resources (as well as the mandate) to homogenize and 'Europeanize' the constituent societies of the EU in the same way as political elites were able to unify national societies in the process of nineteenth-century nation building. Short of a 'constitution-building coup', 'Brussels' lacks the capacities that have played a critical role in the formation of the societies of nation states: namely, the capacity to impose military conscription and action, to impose educational standards and curricular powers and to directly extract taxes from (what only then would be) a 'European people'.

While it is true that both economic transactions and the public sphere of communication are increasingly transnational ('globalized') in nature, each participant in these interactions is still enabled to participate in them by institutions and policies (ranging from corporate law to national educational systems) that are specific to and enforced by national state authorities. Even the most 'global' players pick their place of location or incorporation according to the most favourable conditions as provided by the respective host state and its (for example, tax) regime. This process has often and rightly been described as following a trajectory of 'negative' integration. This pattern of negative – or commercial, financial and monetary – integration of markets is designed to increase the options for economic 'exit' and to debase the governing capacity of national governments and their protectionist inclinations. But the process has not been complemented by some supranational 'positive' integration or the restoration of governing capacity at the European level. In fact, the residual elements of governing capacity that remain intact at the level of member states are used by them to obstruct – in the name of the 'national interest' and with the need to be (re-)elected by a national constituency in mind – the transfer of governance from the national to the European level. Thus negative integration both decimates national policymaking capacity *and* induces national governments to cling to whatever remains of it, rather than sacrificing it for the sake of 'positive' integration.

In fact, the prospects for uniting a 'European' society, i.e. the supranational equivalent and extension of national societies, are exceedingly discouraging. People belonging to a society will typically communicate in one (or a small number of) idiom(s), and they will presuppose their mutual familiarity with aesthetic and other forms of symbolic expression, ranging from styles and pieces of music to religious and national holidays. None of this is present – or could be created in any foreseeable future – at the European level. Within national societies, people will be shaped, both cognitively and motivationally, by a common cultural tradition that is reflexively known to them as being more or less different from the traditions of other societies and which is transmitted through schools, media, religious associations and cultural institutions (such as museums). The most extensive and wide-ranging form in which social integration and cohesion has been developed is the framework of the nation state, which, from the early nineteenth century on, has cultivated this distinctive type of societal integration and thus covered populations that before never belonged or thought of themselves as belonging to the same 'society'. Nation states 'make' societies and build a *demos* by imposing upon some pre-existing patchwork of heterogeneous regional cultures and political units (such as kingdoms and principalities) clearly defined borders, as well as, within those borders, a relatively homogeneous military, fiscal, educational, economic, religious, and judicial regime and institutional order.

This process of state-initiated nation building (or 'society building') does not have an equivalent at the European level. It has been studied in the case of France's nineteenth-century dynamic of transforming 'peasants into Frenchmen' (Eugen Weber). It has also been proclaimed as a (eventually successful) project that inspired the leaders of the Italian *risorgimento*: 'After we now have made Italy, let us proceed to make Italians', meaning people who feel and think of themselves as being tied to (and at the same time being the collective authors of) the encompassing political community of all other Italians, as defined by the scope of the Italian national state. Similarly, President Lincoln's Gettysburg address was part of an equally successful attempt to unite the population of a territorial state (that was torn by civil war) into a 'people', thereby creating the social and political unity and cohesion of a *demos* and its recognition of itself. These historical examples are instances of how representative political elites and their constitutive and unifying policies have actually helped to accomplish the project of *e pluribus unum*. But there are neither the incentives nor the resources available to accomplish a parallel process at the European level. (Note that virtually all types of collective and associative action, from the Red Cross to academic societies, from trade unions to business interest groups, are still based on an organizational domain that coincides with the territory of a state or its sub-territories. The principle that international communication is inter*national* also applies to organizations such as the United Nations, or, for that matter, the EU, the members of which are member *states*, the governments, corporate actors and citizens of which can then enter – by virtue of being constituted within the framework of a state – into transnational relations and activities, including the contractual formation of supranational institutions.)

The problem of creating both a European governing capacity that is capable of overruling nation states' regimes and of thus creating a European *demos* does not primarily reside with a prohibitive degree of diversity between the national components of such a *demos* nor with the aversion of national governments to cooperate. The core problem is, rather, the absence of a charismatic idea (*finalité*) that could drive attempts to overcome such obstacles to the building of a European *demos*. Here is one categorical 'dis-analogy' between the historical process of nation building and the hypothetical future process of building a European regime-*cum-demos*. Historically, nation states have come into being along two alternative trajectories: the fusion of small units into a bigger ones through national *unification*, or the splintering off of peripheries of empires (including colonial empires) in a process of national *liberation* and independence through separation. Unity and liberty have been the two driving forces and guiding values on the two alternative pathways to national statehood. Apart from cases of military conquest and occupation accomplished by outside forces,[1] all territorial reorganization (or redefinition of borders) that was initiated from within has been driven by the idea of 'liberation' – be it liberation from the rule of oppressive or exploitative foreign (e.g. colonial) powers or liberation from princely particularism, arbitrariness, unjust oppression, and belligerent passions. Thus the idea of 'unification' need not be conceived of as an alternative to liberation, but as a sub-case of it, notwithstanding the fact that the appeal to 'unity' can be used as a powerful device to constrain the liberty of individuals as well as of sub-collectivities. At the same time, 'unity' can be an instrumental value that serves the maintenance of liberty in defence against some perceived external threat or enemy.[2]

The core problem of European integration and political unity is not so much the extent of ethnic, historical, cultural, linguistic and economic diversities and cleavages, in spite of the vast discrepancies in the size of member states and their level of economic development, but the total absence of an appeal of *liberation* in the service of which unity might be pursued. 'Europe' does – perhaps – yield a surplus value in terms of prosperity, but no such surplus value in terms of liberty. European states and their societies, which have already adopted, recently or otherwise, a liberal democratic form of regime (and only such states are conceivable candidates for EU membership), are, as it were, 'saturated' concerning their quest for liberty; at the very least, 'Europe', whatever else its *finalité* may be deemed to consist of in terms of prosperity and power, does not stand for an ambition of further liberation. (This is true, at least, if we pass over the calculus of various regionalist movements that 'Europe' will weaken the nation state and hence assist them in the acquisition of *sub*-state 'autonomy'.) Europe does not hold the promise of liberation, certainly not the liberation from the fear of European international war (which has been made a practical impossibility by other, for example, 'Atlantic', means of supranational security policy) or from the fear of a loss of freedom (a motivation that informed much of the *West* European integration that occurred under Cold War conditions). To be sure, European integration along the lines envisaged by the Maastricht and Amsterdam treaties holds the great *instrumental* promise of reaping economies of scale, of global competitive advantage, of the pooling of civilian as well as of military resources, etc.; these benefits and economies of scale, however, can also be supplied within the framework of tight intergovernmental arrangements, beginning with common markets. But the promise of any kind of 'liberation' is not among the benefits a politically integrated Europe has to offer. Yet this promise is the *only* one which has historically driven (again, excepting international war, conquest, occupation, etc.) the territorial reorganization of states.

Classical political theorists (such as Machiavelli and Rousseau) believed that states, in order to engender a strong spirit of solidarity and patriotic commitment among their citizenry, should be *small*, modelled after the Renaissance city republics. Others have argued that, in order to accumulate the critical mass of economic and military resources needed to prevail over rival states and to allow for a favourable size of internal markets, states should, on the contrary, be *large* in terms of their population and territory, and hence their overall resources, in spite of the internal diversity of populations that this may entail. There is no compelling calculus by which a compromise of these conflicting logics of political cohesion vs. economic diversification and military strength could possibly be devised. But there is an almost universal rule of state building in the twentieth century. All large states, or the largest states of their region or continent – be they large in terms of territory or in terms of population – are *federal* states, combining, as it were, the two virtues of smallness and largeness in an ingenious synthesis. This rule applies to North America (USA, Canada), South America (Argentina, Brazil), Australia, Europe (Germany) and Asia (Russia, India). It does most conspicuously (and perhaps ominously) not apply to the People's Republic of China, the largest of all. Given the fact that political and economic/military reasoning about the optimal size of states points in opposite directions, any compromise between the two, including the adoption and design of a federal system, will be guided by considerations of unity and liberation.

What is Europe?

Europe is not a state and hence not a society. The building of European statehood and, by implication, the emergence of a 'European society' is not a goal that societies within Europe could credibly and plausibly pursue in the name of any notion of 'liberation' (as opposed to market liberalization – which, however, does not presuppose a common statehood.) But there is certainly a *type* of European society. These national societies share, to a lesser or greater extent, numerous affinities, similarities and common features. These common features are most clearly visible in regional clusters of national societies and their historical experience and cultural (including religious) profiles. Such partly overlapping clusters include the Scandinavian countries, the Baltic states, the central European countries, the Mediterranean countries, the German-speaking countries, the Orthodox countries, and so on. But there are a number of features that are virtually shared by all of them, such as their being liberal democratic by regime type, or their being both enabled and constrained by their (anticipated) membership in the supranational regime of the European Union. But it is exactly because European societies are so similar already that their fusion into a 'unitary' socio-political arrangement of a 'European' society is unlikely to occur: little is to be gained, and much is to be lost, from such a fusion. It is simply a *non sequitur* to deduce from the similarity of European societies the desirability and/or probability of their eventually becoming 'one' society. Let me briefly review seven (an incomplete list) of those similarities.

(1) The *circular* interaction of 'national' society shaping its state, with this state in turn shaping the institutional set-up of its society, is a peculiar European invention, which was, to be sure, transferred and

copied to other parts of the world (such as the USA) in characteristically modified versions. Societies, as I have argued, are arrangements of state-sponsored civility, with the state in turn being shaped and reshaped by representative collective actors. In contrast, state building in most of the former colonies was accomplished, as far as the territorial shape of the new states as well as their regime form are concerned, not by local populations, but either by (former) colonial powers or autocratic/military elites, if not warlords or big owners of land. But in Europe, too, the supranational institutions that exist are not made by, cannot be ascribed to and hence do not lead to the self-recognition of a 'European people', but are contracted by the governments of member states. As a consequence, the EU populations in total see themselves as affected by, but not the joint authors of, EU policies and programmes.

(2) Before the modern nation state, there emerged another peculiar form of territorial regime in Europe, the *city*. Cities often formed the nucleus of a future state, of which many of them became, or strove to become, capital cities (in political terms) or dominant centres of regions (in economic terms). The city (*Stadt*), with its spatial coexistence and condensation of production and commerce, residence and consumption, associative life and political self-government, and religious, aesthetic, educational and intellectual institutions is a uniquely European evolutionary accomplishment. Partly due to the dense population of Europe and the European history of outward (mostly transatlantic) rather than inward migration, these cities tend to be medium sized; only two of the world's twenty biggest cities are located in Europe (Istanbul and London). The city was similar to the state in that it was the result of the desires of city-dwellers for liberty (from princely rule) and unity (of its citizenry); it differed from states in its greater openness to inward migration, as well as in its institutionalized relations with other cities and the countryside. It was also similar to the state in that it provided the seedbed of diversity (of trades and commodities, of the ethnic and religious background of its citizens, of opportunities to enter into contractual relations). Only states and cities have 'citizens', whereas tribes have members and empires have subjects and estates, as well as centres and peripheries as constituent social entities.

(3) Throughout modern European history, *stateness was precarious and vulnerable*. This is so because states have been threatened by other states that were intent upon the project of empire building through the submission or occupation of other states. Such imperialist ambitions were executed, in a chronological sequence that is geographically clockwise, by the Ottoman empire, the Austro-

Hungarian empire, the French empire, the imperialist ambitions of Nazi Germany, and the Soviet empire. Partly in addition to this and partly as an alternative, the imperialist temptations of European states were directed at territories overseas, as in the cases of Denmark, Britain, the Netherlands, Belgium, France, Spain and (first of all) Portugal. The nature of European states is that they are unsettled, precarious, threatened or threatening in their relation with other states. This world of threatened and threatening states has come to an end, as far as Western Europe is concerned, with the end of the Second World War, the first steps towards international cooperation and the subsequently completed process of decolonization; as far as central and eastern Europe is concerned, with the end of the Cold War, the Iron Curtain, and the Soviet Union.

(4) Since that time, however, stateness is threatened in many places, as it were, from the opposite direction. The dangerous dynamic is no longer the expansion of states at the expense of other states, but the *implosion of states* challenged by internal ethno-territorial cleavages. The most horrifying example of the dynamic of such cleavages is the disintegration of Yugoslavia. More benign forms of analogous processes have occurred, or are presently under way, in France, Belgium, Spain, Great Britain, Denmark and, arguably, Italy. The state-seeking ethnic and sub-nationalist groups that are now emerging are not, as their predecessors were in the nineteenth century, splitting off from empires but from (multinational) states. Also, an increasingly prominent cleavage occurs between national populations, on the one hand, and non-territorial (migrant) minorities of *extracommunitari* within member states.

(5) European societies are specific in that they share a long history of international wars and attempts – frequently failed attempts – to neutralize the potential for international warfare. These wars, hot as well as 'cold', were, as far as the history of the twentieth century is concerned, driven by ideologies that we have come to speak of as 'totalitarian' belief systems and practices of domination. The crimes of these *totalitarian regimes* as well as their repressive, aggressive and genocidal conduct of rule, were rooted in ideas, it must be said, that were exclusively European in origin. But it can also be said that the standards by which they are to be judged and recognized *as* horrendous aberrations are also European by background. These standards derive from the intellectual legacies of Greek and Roman antiquity, Christianity, the Renaissance, the Reformation and the Enlightenment with its offshoots of both liberal and socialist ideas. The European history of ideas can be described as the coincidence in space of the worst crimes *and* the most elaborate and explicit standards of condemnation of those crimes. Throughout its history,

Europe has supplied itself with objects of its self-critical scrutiny. Due to this perplexing coincidence of opposites, the *self-critical appreciation* of the wrongs that have been committed by Europeans in their own history is something specifically European. This inclination to self-revision and self-doubt has no parallel, as far as I can see, in any of the non-European civilizations, e.g. those of the United States or Japan.

(6) The territorial and demographic situation of Europe did not, at the time of its breakthrough to economic and political modernization in the nineteenth century, allow for the benefit of nearby 'empty space' into which relative surplus populations could be 'exported'. To be sure, this was partly compensated for by populations threatened by immiseration transferring to the Americas. But the strategy of 'going West' to a 'new frontier' was not available within Europe itself. Hence in Europe, at an earlier point and to a larger extent than elsewhere, *institutional arrangements of social and political conflict resolution* came to be adopted. As explosive social conflict could not be dealt with through 'exit' or expulsion, provisions were invented (partly for the sake of preparing populations for international war, according to the 'welfare-warfare state' pattern) for the provision of 'voice', or the sharing of political power and, through it, economic resources. These arrangements of internal conflict resolution were premised upon the formation of strong intermediate and corporatist collective actors and forms of representation, the installation of which was in turn facilitated by the remnants of feudalism and a strong state apparatus (Crouch 1999). Reconciliation through compromise and the gradual inclusion of social categories was the prevailing European pattern, while elsewhere the maintenance of hierarchies of domination or unmediated class, ethnic and religious conflict and disparity remained in place, leading to the pattern of 'deeply divided societies'. European societies are privileged by the absence of two types of populations that make for deep divides in New World settler societies, namely, an indigenous population and the descendants of former slaves. But it remains to be seen how well Old World societies will be able to integrate two other types of populations, migrant labour and refugees (in addition to sub-national minorities). Note, however, that the European capacity for reconciliation and institutionalized conflict resolution is not just a matter of industrial relations, co-determination and social security policies. It is also evident in the abolition of capital punishment and the virtual absence of urban ghettoization, as well as in an effective enforcement of human and social citizenship rights.

(7) To conclude this list of admittedly rather daring generalizations about European societies, let us look at the distribution of states in

space. In between the two largest states, Russia and Germany, there is a strip of (mostly, with the exception of Poland) comparatively small countries, ranging from Finland to Cyprus, whose recent history is shaped by the threatening shadow or actual presence of imperial rule. These 'Central' European states are now in the process of 'returning' to Europe, whereas 'Eastern' Europe states (Russia, Ukraine, Belarus) are currently, and are likely to remain for the foreseeable future, outside the discourse of European identity and institutional belonging. With the exception of some still unsettled territorial issues of state building in former Yugoslavia (and arguably the Basque Country and Northern Ireland), *all states now have consolidated external borders*. None of them, except to an extent the regional cases just mentioned, can rightfully be described as a 'deeply divided society'. If new borders are drawn, these will be 'inward' redefinitions accomplished through peaceful means (granting autonomy rights, or 'velvet divorce', not civil war, as in the case of the Czech and Slovak Republics), not 'outward' redefinition through military aggression and imperial ambition. The possibility of both international war and intra-national civil war is effectively warded off by a set of effective supranational regimes, such as the Council of Europe, the Organization for Cooperation and Security in Europe (OSCE), the North Atlantic Treaty Organization (NATO) and the emerging framework of the EU's Common Foreign, Defence and Security Policy.

Diversities of States and Their Societies in Europe

Passports of EU countries identify their bearers first as EU citizens and second as citizens of a member country. Yet few (except for the residents of Luxembourg, 28 per cent of whom are non-nationals) would spontaneously respond to the question as to which political community they are citizens of in terms of 'European Union' citizenship. The predominant sense of belonging on the part of Europeans (except, perhaps, for members of the European elite who are asked this question in places like Hong Kong) is attached to countries (if not regions), not the EU (Kohli 2000). The awareness of both similarities and interdependencies within the framework of the EU's supranational institutions does not erode, but if anything strengthens, national frames of thought, action and the pursuit of interest and identity. This is entirely unsurprising. Why?

Suppose that what has been said above – about the enormous achievement of Europeans living today in countries between which war (and within which civil war) is a virtual impossibility – is not only true, but also *known* to be true by those to whom it applies: this still does not make them 'Europeans'. On the contrary – and as far as the former Comecon countries are concerned – the pride and pleasure people take in a national statehood that is, for the first time in at least two generations, not threatened by the imperial ambitions of great European powers to the West or to the East adds a special emphasis to their adherence to nation-state principles. The memories, fears and sense of distrust inherited from the past are much too strong and too widely shared – and very understandably so – for people to sacrifice part of or even to abandon these principles in favour of some European identity,. Also, people in EU countries (again with the exception of English-speaking elites) cannot communicate with most other Europeans. Patterns of religious affiliation and national cultures differ and are mutually *perceived* as constituting significant differences of collective identity, not as minor diversities within a cultural heritage that Europeans basically own in common. As there is no European idiom, there is no European public sphere that would have to be constituted by Europe-wide media and audiences, not just remote elite discourses and negotiations.

Furthermore, the national publics are strongly aware of political differences between their countries: different constitutions, parties, forms of government and welfare state regimes. They are further aware of the vast differences of size (the sizes of the biggest and the smallest, Germany and Luxembourg, are in a ratio of 204 : 1) and territorial location between countries (proximity vs. remoteness), as well as of the substantial differences in wealth and productivity, in spite of the fact that all member states are industrial societies with the institutions of liberal democracy in place. Most importantly, citizens of European countries form beliefs, accurate ones or otherwise, about how the interested behaviour of other European actors will affect 'our' or 'my' well-being and prospects. In this calculus, six concerns stand out. Taken together, they suggest the perception of the game of the European political economy as one of multidimensional rivalry clouded in deep uncertainties. Let us briefly remind ourselves of the nature of these concerns and fears.

(1) The concern with inward migration of labour, with all its ramifications in terms of loss of jobs, decline of wages in the rich countries, ethnic conflict and political backlash.
(2) The outward flow of investment to EU countries with lower costs of employment, and hence the loss of employment and prosperity on a national scale.
(3) The fiscal redistribution within the EU (and, in particular, a larger EU), consisting not only in a net transfer of funds from the rich to the less prosperous countries and regions, but also in the relative

deprivation that the previous net receivers (say, the Mediterranean countries) will suffer as a consequence of the accession of new and even poorer and therefore even more 'deserving' claimants amongst the new member countries in the east and south-east of Europe.

(4) The competition in markets for goods and services, which is likely (and, indeed, is intended) to drive productivity laggards in their respective industries out of business, thereby adding to the persistently high level of unemployment in most current member countries.

(5) The disadvantages imposed upon newly acceding countries by their being forced to adopt the entire *acquis communautaire* as a precondition of their accession; the disadvantages current member countries suffer in terms of the loss of protection as a consequence of European Court of Justice (ECJ) rulings; and the disadvantages that 'minorities' of one or more countries fear will result from majority decisions within the Council of Ministers that are contrary to their majoritarian national preferences – all of which give rise to the fear of 'Europe' becoming a new form of foreign rule.

(6) Finally, the fear that the intensification of cross-national interaction on all these levels will seriously curtail the remaining capacity for national policymaking, in particular in the policy area of social protection (which is nominally – in the name of a characteristically one-sided reading of the 'subsidiarity' principle – left to the national governments to design and adjust, but which may in fact be largely paralysed by the imperatives of competitiveness).

Taken together, these concerns have a corrosive impact precisely because it is so difficult to predict to what extent they will become reality and who is most likely to be negatively affected by them. These concerns are widely seen to have the potential to give rise to anti-European political forces, leading to an electoral backlash (particularly in countries providing for referenda in EU questions), thus blocking if not obstructing the further political integration of Europe. Pro-European enthusiasm is vanishing everywhere. Moreover, Eurobarometer findings on support for European integration provide a far too optimistic measure, as indicated by the actual voting behaviour of the very same constituencies: many still pay lip service to the standards of European political correctness in surveys, but behave differently in the voting booth (where concrete steps such as admitting new countries or adoption of the euro are at issue).

These six concerns apply to different current and prospective member countries to different extents. They are also controversial in terms of realism vs. paranoia, as well as of long-term versus short-term effects. Even if it were generally agreed (again, both by political elites *and* by national publics) that in the long run the game will turn out to be a strong positive-sum game, the usual 'valley of transition' scenario applies, with the two obvious questions: how wide will the valley turn out to be, and how deep?

The most interesting feature of these concerns is that they do not add up to a well-organized conflict that would divide current and prospective member countries along some clear-cut cleavage line. On the contrary, nobody is currently able to predict with any measure of certainty or authority who is going to win and lose, how much and for how long. It is *not* a game of small against large, rich against relatively backward, centre vs. periphery, old vs. new member countries. The conflict of interest is amorphous and poorly structured. Nor is it clear that the parties to the conflict are actually countries, as opposed to social classes, consumers versus producers, regions, sectors of industry, age groups or, in fact, time slices. Nor is the metric clear by which one would have to balance gains against losses. There are unanswerable questions, such as how much gain from international trade five years hence is worth how much increase in regional unemployment now or how much polarization in political conflict and the subsequent potential for government instability for the next two years. This lack of structure is exactly the problem, for well-structured conflicts can be embedded in an institutional bargaining framework in which demands, threats and promises can be exchanged and the losers can force the winners to compensate them by sharing part of their gains. This is how societies cohere, and this is why Europe is not a 'society': the authoritatively imposed institutional setting is lacking that would be able to transform the diffuse precariousness of a 'state of nature' into clear-cut social conflict and the rules for compromise.

The conflicts that we experience are not those among players in a game that can be adjudicated by neutral and recognized judges, assisted by the testimony of trustworthy experts. Instead, the scenery bears more resemblance to a minefield than a courtroom or, for that matter, a government. Yet there is the opposite risk as well – the largely economic risk of individual countries '*missing*' European integration or staying behind. The logic is simple and compelling: the more countries joining the Economic and Monetary Union (EMU), the less the remaining countries, for reasons of their economic prosperity, can afford *not* to join. A country must be uniquely rich in natural resources (such as Norway with its oil) to afford outsider status, but even then it will find it prudent to follow the regime of EU standards for long-term considerations (as Norway in fact does) in order not to foreclose the option of joining at a later point. At any rate, the definitive decision not to join is seen by all parties involved as a relative loss in prosperity for the country that decides to do so. This does not imply that there may not be non-economic reasons for a negative decision on joining. But these are largely, as the campaign preceding the Danish referendum of 2000 demonstrated, of a sinister and xenophobic nature and imply the deliberate forgoing of economic gain for the sake of asserting an exclusionary version of nationhood and the national interest. Confronted with the choice between two options, both of which involve substantial risks, European member state constituencies show declining enthusiasm (to put it mildly) and partly majoritarian opposition to their respective country's EU membership. To make things worse, countries that are in the process of becoming members and trying to negotiate a relatively safe and painless mode of accession are in a structurally weak bargaining position, since they cannot credibly threaten actually to stay out for good, as this would arguably hurt themselves more than others. For substantial parts of the populations of countries in Europe, and to an extent also for their political elites, Europe is a matter of deep uncertainty, fear and distrust.

Is the European Union, then, experiencing a relapse into a state of nature? It is most certainly not, as Europe's great asset after the end of the Cold War – as a result of the supranational security structures in place – is the *effective ban on inter-state violence* that Europeans enjoy at the turn of the millennium. (*military* violence, that is, and only if we optimistically disregard for the moment the still unfinished task of completing the civilization of the European system of states in the Balkans, which is not meant to belittle ongoing problems concerning the micro-violence of terrorism, on the one hand, and xenophobic aggressiveness on the other). But, arguably, Europe is in the somewhat oxymoronic situation of being in a 'peaceful state of nature'. If that is true, the task ahead is the building of a European regime that might eventually facilitate the rise of something that could seriously be called a 'European society'; the rationale of this society would be analogous to the logic according to which the uniquely European process of organizing civility through state building has taken place historically.

To be sure, and for the reasons mentioned above that condition a strong and legitimate attachment to nation states, this cannot possibly take place in the form of *one* European state emerging from the fusion of all existing European states. Part of the historical legacy of all European states is a strong sense of the precariousness and vulnerability of their statehood – something that was, by comparison, entirely absent when the component proto-states of what became the United States decided to merge. At the time of the federation, none of the states had ever waged war against any of the other states! European states are 'too old', burdened with too much history, and endowed with their own specific accomplishments achieved in the course of that history, to be plausible candidates for some outright fusion. (The only place where a fusion of states has taken place, namely the country I come from, has not experienced this merger as an unqualified success story, the celebratory pronouncements on the tenth anniversary of German unification in

October 2000 notwithstanding.) Nowhere would European societies be prepared to sacrifice their statehood as the institutional form by which they organize – and by which they have defended, if often unsuccessfully – their civility. (The only country whose political elites have occasionally gestured in this direction, namely Germany, has done so with the transparent aim of appeasing the concerns of its neighbours, which often enough has not actually put these concerns to rest, but exacerbated them by raising suspicions as to why a state should do such an 'unnatural' thing for reasons other than those of deceiving its neighbours.) Europeans have a lot in common, including a history that inspired them with a very rational reluctance to give up the stateness on which the coherence of their societies critically depends.

Nonetheless, the uncertain outcomes of the European integration of markets and countries do call for some kind of organizing capacity that is able to impose rules (voluntarily and rationally adopted rules, that is!) on the partial European state of nature. Such rules are the means for alleviating fear, generating certainties and engendering mutual trust. Again, the task of organizing civility is put on the agenda. This organizing capacity must be capable of not just making markets (through 'negative integration') but of beginning to build the rudimentary foundations of a European society (through 'positive integration'). This organizing capacity cannot be a state, as states are in place already and statehood is sacrosanct to the societies shaped by these states. National statehood is simply not seen by citizens as something they want to be 'liberated' from, but as something they depend upon for the sake of their protection and liberty. Hence this organizing capacity must respect and, indeed, strengthen national statehood. It must respect it by leaving substantial scope for national policymaking capacity in the hands of national (and even sub-national and regional) governments, which are and will remain accountable to and elected by national constituencies. It must strengthen and positively empower national governments so that these policymaking capacities are not rendered nominal, as in much of the field of social security, or through the facts of competition, interdependence and interpenetration.

What states have historically done to the citizens of their societies, namely civilize and regularize their common life so that they can live in a 'society', a constitutionalized European governing capacity must do to the multitude of member countries. The task is state building, but one level up and without the template of the nation state. We are now living through a fascinating and unprecedented period, in which Europe applies to itself the logic of the circular creation of state and society that shaped the modern history of European countries. To reiterate: the agency that will eventually accomplish a regime of 'organized civility' governing the entire European space will not itself be a state, but a 'union'. It will have to leave existing states in place. But it will also have to conform to two criteria that all European states have now come to accept as the standards of acceptable political rule: legitimacy and effectiveness.

By 'legitimacy' I mean a fair and impartial way in which societies create their political authority (which, as legitimate, enjoys the compliance and support of members), and by 'effectiveness' I mean the capacity of political authorities actually to achieve their goals and impose their rules. There is little disagreement today that the EU in its current institutional state lacks both. This is the rational core of the sceptical attitudes displayed by citizens, media, and voters. It can be summarized in the question: 'As Europe (Brussels) evidently does not owe much of value to us, what do we owe to Europe?'

The holders of union powers must be *legitimate*. This is a simple thing that is hard to accomplish. Through the European institutions of governance, Europeans must be seen, and must be able to see themselves, as *governing themselves*. That is, no group of 'advanced' European countries (presumably consisting of countries that pride themselves on being more advanced and Europe-minded than others) should be seen as governing other European countries by devising a system of governance that is good for all. There is a disparity between 'founding members' and 'latecomers' anyway, and this should not be exacerbated by some core countries assuming pioneering roles and setting rules for the rest. Nor is some 'neutral' committee of benevolent experts, judges or commissioners good enough to decree the rules and institutions of European governance. In either of these two cases, the resulting regime would be insufficiently good due to the paternalist mode by which it had been brought into being, simply because opposition to such paternalism provides ample reason to defect or to disobey what actually would have to function as a European constitution. Only if the regime can be robustly presented as a self-governing and 'self-binding' (rather than 'other-binding') regime does it have a chance of winning the loyalty of all of its citizens.

Furthermore, the regime would have to be compatible with the major ideas and principles that are enshrined in existing constitutions of European states (Abromeit 1998), most notably the democratic principle that whoever wields governmental powers must be accountable to those over whom they are wielded. There is currently no convergent view, to the best of my knowledge, as to how this task of European constitution-making could be accomplished. The tendency in this situation would be to use gag rules, i.e. to start with the little that is relatively uncontroversial and leave the rest to later debates, foreclosing its discussion for the moment.

However, this 'wait-and-see' approach collides with the somewhat urgent requirement of *effectiveness*. In order to overcome the market-driven European state of nature and create Europe-wide institutions of bargaining and conflict resolution, the European governing capacity that is to be created on top of nation states must be highly potent. It must basically be able to accomplish two things. First, it must have at its disposal credible devices to reduce both the depth and width of the valley of transition. Only if European citizens have strong reason to believe the pains that the common market inflicts upon them – hopefully for a limited period of time – will be equitably compensated for and distributed fairly, will they become prepared to surrender some of their (increasingly nominal) reserved domains of national policymaking. That is, Europe must be more than a framework for the military security of states; it must become the source and active promoter of the social and economic security of its citizens. And such security must come as a right attached to European citizenship, not as a set of discretionary programmes tabled (or withdrawn) by the Commission, as is the case with structural funds programmes.

Secondly, and as an obvious consequence of the above, the holders of European governing capacity need, if they are to honour European citizenship rights, the authority to tax and to extract the resources that are needed to finance programmes of meaningful burden-sharing and compensation. To be sure, it is the undebatable virtue of markets to pose challenges for adjustment, learning and innovation. But it is equally beyond debate that some challenges are too demanding to be met without substantial assistance, by those (individuals, countries, sectors, regions, occupations, generations) who are affected by them. Other challenges resulting from the Commission and ECJ's quest for negative integration (e.g. concerning the way in which countries run their pension system, electronic media or alcohol regime) can be rejected as inappropriate and illegitimate. The question is obvious: which challenges belong to which of these three categories? Which pains can we be expected to live with, which call for pain relief to be administered, and which are simply unacceptable in the first place? We can begin to speak of the reality of a European society only after European authorities set up bargaining tables that allow these and related questions to be answered.

Notes

1. Such conquest was the rationale of Nazi Germany's notion of a 'new European order' that was to be established under German hegemony by military means (see Kletzin 2000).
2. Swedberg (1994) and Münkler (1995) have demonstrated that European 'unity' has always been invoked in situations when collective liberty was deemed to be in need of defence against internal or, more often, external threats and enemies.

References

Abromeit, Heidrun. 1998. *Democracy in Europe: Legitimising Politics in a Non-State Polity*. New York.

Crouch, Colin. 1999. *Social Change in Western Europe*. Oxford.

Immerfall, Stefan. 1995. *Einführung in den europäischen Gesellschaftsvergleich. Ansätze – Problemstellungen – Befunde*, 2nd edn. Passau.

Kaelble, Hartmut. 1987. *Auf dem Wege zu einer europäischen Gesellschaft* Munich.

———. 1997. 'Europäische Vielfalt und der Weg zu einer europäischen Gesellschaft'. In *Die westeuropäischen Gesellschaften im Vergleich*, ed. Stefan Hradil and Stefan Immerfall: 27–68. Opladen.

Kletzin, Birgit. 2000. *Europa aus Rasse und Raum. Die nationalsozialistische Idee der Neuen Ordnung*. Münster.

Kohli, Martin. 2000. 'The Battlegrounds of European Identity'. *European Societies* 2, 2: 113–37.

Morin, Edgar. 1991. *Europa denken*. Frankfurt.

Münkler, Herfried. 1995. 'Die politische Idee Europa'. In *Herausforderung Europa. Wege zu einer politischen Identität* , ed. Mariano Delgado and Matthias Lutz-Bachmann: 9–27. Munich.

Swedberg, Richard. 1994. 'The Idea of "Europe" and the Origin of the European Union'. *Zeitschrift für Soziologie* 23, 5: 378–87.

Weber, Eugen. 1976. *Peasants into Frenchman: The Modernization of Rural France, 1870–1914*. Stanford.

8

SOCIAL MOVEMENTS CHALLENGING NEOLIBERAL GLOBALIZATION

Dieter Rucht

'Look at it this way. We have the numbers
on our side, because there are far more
losers than winners in the neo-liberal game.'
Susan George (1997: 7)

Introduction

According to the American sociologist Douglas Kellner, globalization is *'the* buzzword of our times' (Kellner 1998: 23). The British sociologist Anthony Giddens echoes this statement: 'Every business guru talks about [globalization]. No political speech is complete without reference to it. Yet as little as 10 years ago the term was hardly used, either in the academic literature or in everyday language. It has come from nowhere to be almost everywhere' (Giddens 1999).

The term 'globalization' has indeed spread at a breathtaking pace since the late 1980s (Gerhards and Rössel 1999).[1] In the beginning, it had largely positive associations. More recently, however, globalization, both as a term and as an empirical process, has become a highly contentious matter. In the last few years, Seattle, Prague, Genoa, Florence and many other places have become signifiers for large-scale protest mobilizations directed, in most media portrayals, 'against globalization'. My aim here is not to provide a detailed account of these protests. Instead, adopting a more general approach, I shall try to put them in context. This may help me answer two questions: What are the background and the common denominator of these protests? To what extent are these mobilizations new?

First, I shall sketch the major ideological positions *via-à-vis* globalization and draw some parallels with a similar, earlier debate centred on modernization. Secondly, the link between globalization or, more precisely, neoliberalism[2] and civil society will be discussed, with special emphasis on aspects of democracy. Thirdly, some characteristics of the campaigns and movements against neoliberal globalization will be highlighted. Finally, I shall speculate about the prospects of these protests.

Debates about Modernization and Globalization

The debate surrounding globalization both benefits and suffers from the inclusiveness and vagueness of its key term.[3] The debate benefits in so far as the term provides a convenient denominator for a broad range of phenomena that are considered by many to be extremely important for the present and future of humankind. Phenomena previously seen as more or less isolated from each other are now perceived as facets of one trend, globalization – a trend already described in the Communist Manifesto in 1848.[4] In its most abstract, formal versions, globalization can be described as 'the shrinking of distance on a world scale through the emergence and thickening of networks of connections' (Keohane 2002: 325) or as 'the widening, intensifying, speeding up and growing impact of worldwide interconnectedness' (Held 2002: 306). Many people feel that these processes affect, or may soon affect, their lives, and that they can therefore relate to the debate on globalization. In addition, the theme of globalization has attracted wide attention because it has become so controversial, both with regard to political activities and as a matter of debate in the media and science.[5] On the other hand, the theme of globalization suffers from the fuzziness of its key term inasmuch as the parties in conflict with each other often conduct their struggle on muddy terrain and in foggy air – a struggle characterized by mutual misrepresentations and misunderstandings, threatening gestures, 'sieges enforced in the wrong location', and the like.

When one considers the most extreme poles in this debate, it appears as if they are referring to two totally different worlds. One side greets globalization enthusiastically. Globalization is not only inevitable, but desirable. It creates – in many ways – progress for humankind. It strengthens economies in both the Western/Northern and the Southern hemispheres; it sets free forces of creativity and entrepreneurship that have been confined within political and cultural boundaries; it implies the free flow not only of capital, goods, services and labour forces but also of ideas such as democracy and human rights; it brings countries and cultures closer together and, as a result, fosters a sense of interdependence, mutual support, understanding, and tolerance. This positive perspective is expressed in the official statement issued at the end of the G8 summit in Cologne in June 1999:

> Globalization ... has cast us together as never before. Greater openness and dynamism have contributed to the widespread improvement of living standards and a significant reduction in poverty. Integration has helped to create jobs by stimulating efficiency, opportunity and growth. The information revolution and greater exposure to others' cultures and values have strengthened the democratic impulse and the fight for human rights and fundamental freedoms while spurring creativity and innovation.[6]

At the other end of the spectrum, people remain not just sceptical but hostile towards globalization. They use two main arguments. First, globalization, intentionally or not, widens the gap between the rich and the poor, destroys indigenous cultures and increases the exploitation of human and natural resources. Secondly, globalization is not under the control of (national) political institutions and thus incapacitates the people as the democratic sovereign. According to McChesney (1999: 11), globalization or, more precisely, neo-liberalism 'is the immediate and foremost enemy of genuine participatory democracy, not just in the United States but across the planet, and will be for the foreseeable future'.

Whereas in the early phase of the debate the promoters of globalization were the dominant voice, it seems that we have now entered a stage in which the critics are gaining ground. Regardless of which side is on the defensive or the offensive, it is likely, for various reasons, that this struggle will last for quite a while. First, as mentioned above, the struggle suffers from a lack of clarity about both the meaning of globalization and the phenomena to which this generic label refers; this is likely to prolong, not shorten, the debate. Secondly, even when the subject is clearly defined, there is usually no solid, empirical information that would allow certain phenomena, such as economic prosperity or disaster, to be causally attributed to globalization or to any of its more specific dimensions. We still do not know how precise empirical investigation will answer a number of crucial questions about the consequences of globalization. Thirdly, and probably most importantly, the struggle is not just about arguments and frames; it is also a clash of values and interests. Such a clash cannot easily be moderated, let alone transformed into compromise. We shall probably learn more about the structure and implications of this struggle if we compare it with the earlier debate about modernization.

As a scholarly concept, *modernization* took shape in the 1960s, in an era marked by impressive economic growth rates in Western countries, the Cold War and decolonization in many Third World countries. In its truly naïve versions, modernization theory regarded the most advanced states, in particular the US, as *the* model that the rest of the world, including the so-called underdeveloped countries, would sooner or later adopt.[7] It was assumed that, at the end of this process, the whole world, still conceived as a plethora of nation states, would be 'modern', that is economically developed, politically stable and democratic and culturally secular and liberal. In this perspective, those who remained essentially sceptical or even hostile towards modernization were characterized as irrational (Berger et al.: 1973, chap. 8).

Some critics pointed to the arrogance, ethnocentrism and underlying neocolonialist assumptions of this view; they rejected the concept of modernization altogether (Frank 1967; Wallerstein 1976). Others, Jürgen Habermas (1987) and Zygmunt Bauman (1989), for example, have pointed to some negative consequences of Western modernization, with its emphasis on instrumentality, commodification, standardization and shallowness. Partly drawing on classical sociologists, such as Marx, Weber and Simmel, these critics of modernization have pointed to its inherent ambivalence: with regard to both individuals and societies, it offers choices *and* pressures and generates winners *and* losers. Even in the long run, modernization is not necessarily a positive-sum game in which virtually everyone profits. Moreover, other cultures, for example, the Muslim world, were, and still are, highly suspicious of modernization as they associate it with secularization, shallowness and the pursuit of Western hegemony.

In retrospect, it is obvious that modernization has not happened as its proponents had predicted. The economic gap between the 'developed' and the 'underdeveloped' world has remained and, on aggregate, become even wider.[8] Fundamentalism of any kind is far from disappearing in both the non-Western and Western worlds. Even in the West, not all countries are taking the same path to further modernization. In short, modernization has lost much of its appeal, particularly since well-respected intellectuals, who hardly fit the image of romantic backwoodsmen, have characterized modernization as implying both liberalization and estrangement, if not colonization.

Today, it appears that the concept of *globalization* has in many ways replaced that of modernization. Again, since we are still in a relatively early period of the debate about globalization, we can find, as mentioned before, its enthusiastic proponents; and, just as arguments were levelled against modernization, critics, who stress the negative aspects of globalization, have begun to raise their voices. The spectrum of critics is wide even in Western countries: it ranges from those who argue against globalization from a chauvinist and nationalist position (the extreme right), to those who essentially accept globalization but seek to control some of is negative side effects (social democrats and New Labour), to those who decisively reject globalization in so far as it consists of a neoliberal strategy on the part of Western elites to pursue their economic goals based on the exploitation of the weak (the extreme left). In addition, we also find critical groups that cannot be located easily on a left–right scale. Thus, there are religious and humanitarian groups in the West that, adopting an advocate's role, promote the rights of the victims of (economic) globalization. There are also people in the Muslim world and, more generally, in the Southern hemisphere – for instance, peasants and small shopkeepers – who are desperately trying to defend their own, vital, economic survival and cultural integrity in an era in which capital and other resources enjoy unprecedented mobility.

Like modernization, globalization is widely perceived as something that simply 'happens'. In this view, similar to how Alexis de Tocqueville perceived democratization,[9] globalization can probably be accelerated or delayed to some degree. but it cannot be halted or reversed. Globalization appears to follow an inherent evolutionary logic that leads to ever more interconnectedness and conformity. Even among those who reject the idea of globalization as being a process from which everybody will, at least in long run, derive advantage, probably the vast majority perceive it as a quasi-natural process. Just as rain falls, globalization occurs. Those who happen to be outdoors get wet; others indoors are protected. And, like rain, which is greeted by farmers on dry land but cursed by tourists on the beach, globalization can be perceived from quite different angles – privileging some, depriving others. Globalization, however, cannot be politicized as long as the perception of globalization as a quasi-natural process prevails. At best, people, by appealing to the mercy of the welfare state or of private charity, may seek some protection from the downside of globalization.

Yet there is also a minority that does not share this view of globalization as 'natural' or 'inevitable'. Like earlier critics of modernization processes, these new critics characterize globalization as a deliberate political, economic and ideological project promoted by those who will profit most from it: that is, in Leslie Sklair's (1997) words, the 'transnational capitalist class'. These critics argue that globalization does not occur as a uniform process but is shaped, mediated and filtered by specific structural and cultural contexts. These cannot be characterized – simplistically – as playgrounds; they are, rather, arenas in which power struggles take place. Globalization, if unravelled, is perceived as a hegemonic project that serves the needs of those groups and states that are already in an advantageous position. Seen in this perspective, globalization is essentially an extension of the earlier project of modernization. However, while modernization was perceived as a process that would stretch over a long period, with every state more or less advanced on a developmental scale, globalization is a kind of modernization in one stroke.

Again, we find a similar pattern on the side of globalization's proponents as they try to discredit its critics by describing them as romantic, idealistic and uninformed, if not simply ill-intentioned. A German journalist, for example, claimed that the fierce protests against the G8 summit in Genoa in July 2001, with their 'moral ardour', resembled a 'children's crusade'.[10]

A closer look, however, reveals that the protesters in Seattle or Genoa could be adequately characterized neither as a bunch of noisy children nor as mere 'anti-globalists'. This becomes apparent when evaluating their concerns, which, as stated above, are not only driven by a call for global solidarity and global justice, but are also related to the question of democracy in a globalizing world. This aspect will be discussed in the following section.

Globalization, Civil Society and Democracy

Civil society, as a concept, has fundamentally changed its meaning during its long history. Initially, it included political and legal institutions and referred to the 'whole realm of the political' (*societas civilis; état civile; bürgerliche Gesellschaft*) (Kumar 1996: 89). From about the middle of the eighteenth century the concept was gradually 'modernized' in response to the actual differentiation between society and the state (Keane 1988). In early liberal thought, as represented, for example, in the writings of John Locke, the state and civil society were not clearly juxtaposed as two entities based on different principles. Adam Smith heralded a change with his notion of the 'political society', referring to what was later called the 'state'. More explicitly, writers such as Adam Ferguson and Thomas Paine emphasized the existence of a society distinct from, and in tension with, the state. Since then, the modern nation state, with its monopoly of formal power and its tendency to assume more responsibilities, has been widely perceived as a potential threat to civil society. Strengthening civil society has become synonymous with reducing the role of the state.

Today, in the era of globalization, or 'de-nationalization' as Michael Zürn (1998) puts it, states are seen as losing power and competencies, particularly in economic matters, while businesses, especially multinational corporations, are gaining greater influence. In a strictly formal sense, this process may be interpreted as empowering civil society relative to the state. In this view, the shrinking role of states not only is advantageous to the economy as a whole – as many neoliberals argue – but may also be interpreted as strengthening democracy. This line of reasoning, however, has a number of deficiencies. First, it is based on a simplistic assumption about the distribution of virtues (associated with civil society) and evils (associated with the state). This belief, held not only by neoliberals but also by radical libertarians in the tradition of David Thoreau, grossly idealizes civil society. The latter is understood as a pluralistic entity with little concentration of power. Moreover, this view portrays civil society as promoting basic common goods and having a very high capacity for self-regulation; but it neglects the dark and 'uncivil' side of societies, even their liberal variants.[11] In addition, this picture ignores the fact that the state is not simply a mechanism of dominance, intrusion and control. At least as far as democratic welfare states are concerned, the state, rather than being a tool in the hands of repressive elites, is a means for securing internal peace, elementary human and civil rights and material security for those who are economically weak or deprived. Historically speaking, monopolizing power was instrumental in (1) eliminating or reducing civil war; (2) establishing the rule of law and democratic rights, thereby self-limiting state power; and (3) redistributing societal wealth in order to reduce, at least to some extent, the gap between the rich and the poor and to guarantee minimal standards of social security.

The second flaw of the neoliberal perspective is that it conceives the relationship between state and society in a mechanical fashion – as if it were a simple zero-sum game. The assumption is that weakening the state necessarily strengthens civil society. In many respects, however, this does not hold true. A lack of state control, for example, can also undermine the functioning of a proper civil society in so far as some groups, usually those who are already more powerful or wealthier than others, can impose their will on the rest of society. The state may also be instrumental in empowering deprived social groups to organize themselves and raise their voices in order to improve their situation.

Thirdly, it is also important to unravel the notion of civil society and, accordingly, to investigate the understanding and interests of its respective advocates. Some of those proponents of civil society who want to reduce the role of the state allegedly for the sake of civil society do so in fact primarily to satisfy their own particularistic interests. As in the slogan 'What is good for General Motors is also good for America', they suggest, at least implicitly, that an identity exists between civil society and private interests and, in particular, business interests. This, of course, is more easily proclaimed as long as civil society remains a vague generic label.

However, business should not be equated with civil society. Many authors, therefore, promote a more restrictive concept of civil society.[12] They perceive non-state groups who care about public goods – for example, certain kinds of voluntary associations and social movements, often called public interest groups – as the centrepiece of civil society. These groups do not act 'for the sake of any particular formation ... but for the sake of sociability itself' (Walzer 1991: 298). Civil society, in this view, is not the ensemble of all non-state actors but a 'public ethical-political community' based on a common ethos (Cohen and Arato 1992: 84). In a normative perspective, profit-oriented business is marginal to the idea of civil society, if not outside it. This idea implies other standards than those of the business community. In Bauman's words: 'The human quality of a society ought to be measured by the quality of life of its weakest members' (Bauman 2000: 9).

In sum, if certain normative connotations of the idea of civil society promoted by philosophical 'pragmatists' (John Dewey, for instance), 'communitarians' (Amitai Etzioni) or radical republicans (Benjamin Barber) are evoked, the global reach of neoliberalism appears highly problematic; it represents a potential evil, not an asset. If neoliberalism implies ruthless economic competition, the dismantling of the welfare state and the survival of the fittest, it threatens to jeopardize the 'civility' of society in the sense of mutual respect, bonds of solidarity and society's moral obligation to protect those who are marginalized and deprived. Neoliberalism, understood in this manner, results in the hegemony of some parts of civil society over others, both within and across nations (Chomsky 1999). Globalization is then only a euphemism for 'turbo-capitalism' (Luttwak 1999): the pursuit, both domestically and transnationally, of profit maximization and market shares.

The welfare state, 'one of the greatest gains of humanity and the foremost achievement of civilised society' (Bauman 2000: 11), was created to overcome or prevent Manchester capitalism. Yet today, in the name of economic progress and global competition, the wheel of history seems to be rolling back towards an unleashed market liberalism with its call for a minimal state. Ironically, many states tend to support neoliberalism, since they perceive each other – either as individual entities or as parts of a larger bloc of countries such as the European Union (EU) – as competitors whose political strength is heavily dependent on a flourishing economy. Such an economy, neoliberals argue, is only feasible to the extent that it is 'liberated' from high taxes, from restrictions on imports and exports, the flow of capital and of the labour force, and from rules concerning minimum wages, as well as from limits on working hours and layoffs.[13]

Critics of globalizing neoliberalism not only point to its negative aspects, such as growing inequality and the erosion of social security standards; they also, in several ways, worry about the state of democracy. First, to the extent that states and, more specifically, national governments are losing control over, or are deliberately withdrawing from, major economic decisions – these are being left to 'the market' as an abstract system (see Self 1993) or to major private players, in particular big multinational corporations.[14] However, critics argue, neither the market nor major economic actors can claim to represent the people; they do not operate on the basis of democratic principles. As a consequence, those who are negatively affected by economic developments no longer have an addressee for their demands; someone who can be called to account (Mander and Goldsmith 1997).

Secondly, even when national and international governments are included in economic decision-making processes, an extreme asymmetry exists between the respective weight and influence of individual states and institutions. The US has become – more than ever before – a dominant player in world politics. Formally or informally, the US is the key actor in institutions such as the North Atlantic Treaty Organization, the United Nations (and its sub-organizations), the World Bank, the International Monetary Fund (IMF), the G7 and G8 summits, the World Trade Organization (WTO), the Organization for Economic Cooperation and Development and the North American Free Trade Organization (NAFTA). The role of the US in these institutions reflects its military and economic power, but it certainly does not correspond to its population size – which, from a democratic viewpoint (according to the principle of 'one person, one vote'), would be a more adequate measure for granting influence.

Thirdly, there is a more general problem in international politics as a result of the dominance of executive power over legislative bodies. While in domestic politics the parliament usually controls and limits the government, there is really no functional equivalent of parliaments at the international level,[15] let alone directly elected decision makers in international bodies. In addition, the spatial and functional distance between ordinary citizens and those who make decisions about international policies – the two are barely informed about each other – is mediated less than on the national level by parties, interest groups and social movements.

Scholars have begun to promote various solutions to the problem of the obvious democratic deficit at the international level. McGrew (1997: 241–54), for instance, identifies three 'models of global democracy'; he labels these 'liberal-internationalist', 'cosmopolitan' and 'radical communitarian'. In addition to academic discussions of this matter, transnational non-governmental organizations (NGOs) and social movements are exerting pressure for greater democracy by challenging not only established methods of international policymaking but, in a more general sense, the existing global power structure. If it is true that social movements have often been 'the central bearers of democratizing pressures within Western societies' (Foley and Edwards 1996: 47), one could also expect them to play a role when it comes to democratizing international policymaking.

Campaigns and Movements
against Neoliberal Globalization

Most ordinary people do not link their fate to globalization, or they simply consider this fate to be a quasi-natural process. A minority, however, assumes a different stance. In part, this minority actively intervenes in matters of globalization, as demonstrated by the protests against the policies of the WTO in Seattle in December 1999.[16] Many observers perceive the 'Battle of Seattle' to have been the start of a new protest movement – as indicated, for example, by questions such as : 'Why are the protests expressed only now, after many years of trade liberalization?' and 'What will the stance of the EU on the "post-Seattle" world be?'[17] A closer look, though, reveals that these assumptions are highly debatable. Seattle is not the beginning of a wave of protest, nor is the label 'post-Seattle world' justified. Nevertheless, Seattle is of importance, as will be argued below.

Activism before Seattle

The protest in Seattle was, in at least two senses, not a sudden eruption in a hitherto quiet terrain. First, as with many other large protests, it was the result of an orchestrated campaign. 'The demonstrators of Seattle were far from being a disorganized rabble. For months, a dozen or more groups ... had been planning the protests, working under the umbrella of the Direct Action Network, united by a commitment that the demonstrations remain non-violent' (Brown 2000: 32f.; see also Lori's War 2000: 47–50). Secondly, and more important, Seattle was not the first campaign against neoliberalism in general and institutions such as the WTO, the IMF, the World Bank, the G7 summits, NAFTA and the EU Council in particular (O'Brien et al.: 2000). It may have taken many journalists by surprise, but not close observers of similar activities in the past and present. Let us consider some examples.

On the occasion of the G7 summit in Bonn in May 1985, about 30,000 demonstrators gathered in the West German capital and in Cologne to demand more justice and equality at the global level. An even more powerful mobilization occurred when the representatives of the IMF and World Bank held their meetings in Berlin in 1988. After nearly two years of planning and dozens of preparatory meetings, teach-ins and so on, the mobilization against these institutions culminated during the official conference in many protest activities, including a rally of 40,000 to 80,000 people. Although the protesters were mainly – though not exclusively – from West Germany, the range of groups was similar to that in Seattle: it included trade unions, leftist parties, feminists, ecologists, civil rights groups, and Third World groups (Gerhards and Rucht 1992; Gerhards 1993). In the following years, most IMF and World Bank meetings continued to attract protest, though on a much smaller scale than in Berlin.

Similarly, international gatherings of the World Economic Forum (WEF) and other institutions have become the foci of protest mobilizations directed, in part, against neoliberal free trade policies. For example, sizeable protests accompanied the WTO Ministerial Conference in Geneva in 1998, the Birmingham G7 summit in the same year [18] and the EU summit as well as the G7/8 summit in Cologne in June 1999. Among those protesting in Cologne were the participants of the *Intercontinental Caravan 99*, some 370 activists from Mexico, Brazil, Bangladesh, India and Nepal, who toured Europe and North America. Their aim was to inform the public about the problems of farmers and fishermen in their countries who were threatened by, among other things, the liberalization of the economy and by the aggressive marketing of genetically modified seeds and pesticides. These activists overlap with the network *Peoples' Global Action*, which was founded in February 1998 in Geneva to bring together such diverse groupings as the movement *Sem Terra*, an organization of landless peasants from Brazil; the *Frente Zapatista* from Mexico; and Ogoni people from Nigeria: all these groups are fighting the free trade policies promoted by WTO and similar institutions.[19] Other groups that participated in the June 1999 Cologne protest were part of *Jubilee 2000*, a loose alliance of groups and networks from more than fifty states that demanded a considerable debt reduction for poor countries in the Southern hemisphere. All these groups and their claims were represented in the Seattle protests.

Likewise, various North American organizations and networks mobilized against neoliberal policies in the years before the 'Battle of Seattle'. Some of them, for example the US *Network for Global Economic Justice*, specifically targeted the IMF and the World Bank.[20] Others, amongst them many trade unions in North America, opposed NAFTA (Shoch 2000). Even if one focuses exclusively on the US north-west, a chain of labour protests can be identified in which the 1999 Seattle actions were just the most recent link (Levi and Olson 2000). In addition to US workers, there were also many young people in Seattle who, in part, had been trained in tactics of direct action and civil disobedience by semi-professional groups such as the *Ruckus Society*.[21] In other words, the call for action in Seattle fell on fertile ground.

Seattle and Beyond

In the light of all these activities preceding the Seattle events of 1999, we can hardly define the latter as a watershed separating an era of calmness from an era of significant and unruly mobilization against the globalization of the economy and free trade policies. Most of the groups performing on stage in Seattle had already been active in prior struggles. None of the arguments raised and most probably none of the strategies applied in Seattle were new. Also, the alliance between official delegations from a number of Southern countries and many Northern NGOs outside the conference venue were also forged at several earlier international conferences. Nevertheless, Seattle was special in so far as (1) the WTO was confronted with more internal and external opposition than ever before; (2) the link between labour unions and other groups, including those from Third World countries, was particularly strong; (3) the conference was considerably disrupted by massive protests; and (4), at least partly because of the close interaction between some NGOs and some official delegates, particularly those from the Alliance of Small Island States, no agreement in the official conference could be reached.[22] Given these factors, together with the tremendous media coverage of the Seattle event and some signs of sympathy for the ideals and aims of the protesters by political leaders such as Bill Clinton, it is not surprising that Seattle became an important reference point for subsequent debates and mobilizations.

The following years have been filled with transnational protests, mainly at official meetings, such as, in 2000, the IMF and World Bank conference in Washington, DC., in April, the IMF and World Bank meeting in Prague in September, the G20 meeting in Montreal in October and the EU summit in Nice in December; in 2001, the Quebec meeting in April on the creation of the Free Trade Area of the Americas (FTAA), the EU summit in Götenborg in June, and the G8 summit in Genoa in July; and, in March 2002, the EU summit in Barcelona (Pianta 2001; Rucht 2002). In most of these cases, the protesters referred positively to Seattle as a kind of model – see, for example, the slogan 'Turn Prague into Seattle'. Their activities were flanked by other groups and networks that so far are hardly known within the wider public, but which are gradually gaining strength. The German branch of *Jubilee 2000*, for example, comprised about 1,500 organizations and groups. One of them, WEED (*World Economy, Ecology and Development*), has, since its creation in 1990, become very active in matters of free trade and debt relief. Another example is *Eurodad* (*European Network on Debt and Development*), a network with similar aims that is represented in 16 European countries. More recently, ATTAC (*Association for the Taxation of Financial Transactions for the Aid of Citizens*[23]) has emerged as a significant player. Established in France in 1998, by autumn 2004 ATTAC had branches in fifty countries, from Argentina to Switzerland to Tunisia, and claimed to have 90,000 members. In addition, there is a plethora of smaller groups that are all critical of neoliberal policies: the French groups *Agir-ICI* and *Raison d'Agir*, for example; the British network *Critical*

Mass, which links aspects of globalization and ecology; and the *Halifax Initiative*, created on the eve of the G7 summit in Halifax in 1995.[24]

Though such groups have flourished and are networking actively, for various reasons the relative success of the Seattle protests could not be repeated. One general reason is that in some subsequent events both police and conference organizers were better prepared to deal with the protesters. In Genoa, where, with some 200,000 protesters, the biggest transnational mobilization to date took place,[25] the protesters were physically kept out of the 'red zone' reserved for the official conference. Another reason, which applies to the May Day protests in London and Berlin, is the absence of a specific institution representing a clearly identifiable target. Moreover, there was no coalition between labour unions and other groups in the May Day campaigns, and only small and fragile links could be detected in the Götenborg and Genoa protests. As a rule, as long as protesters mounted attacks on official summits, they received considerable attention but little sympathy in the media, as the London event in 2000, above all, shows (Rucht, forthcoming, 2005). Thus, from the viewpoint of most organizers and activists, the post-Seattle protests were not overly successful and encouraging, with Genoa being more difficult to evaluate.[26]

Perhaps because of the limited effects achieved by targeting official summits, the global justice movement – as it is increasingly called – has begun to organize its own, independent meetings: the Social Forums (Anand et al. 2004). In sheer quantitative terms, these meetings have been a roaring success. While the first Global Forum in Porto Alegre in January 2001 attracted some 15,000 participants, the third, in January 2003, was attended by 100,000 people. Similarly, the first European Social Forum in Florence in November 2002 attracted some 50,000 people and culminated in a mass demonstration of half a million of people: the largest event in the history of such groupings. On the other hand, there are voices criticizing these meetings for having no strategic ambition, for being a kind of political tourism, a marketplace for self-expression and fuzzy slogans ('Another world is possible!').

Conclusions and Perspectives

In the 1990s, protests against 'globalization' broadened and intensified. 'Anti-globalization' is, as an official report states, 'a spreading phenomenon' (Canadian Security Intelligence Service 2000). However, labels such as 'anti-globalization movement' are misleading.[27] Those associated with such labels promote globalization in certain ways: for example, solidarity, justice and democracy at the global level (Smith 2000b). Not accidentally, these groups call themselves Peoples' Global Action, Global Action Project,

Earthwatch, EarthAction and the like. Furthermore, they profit from global communication structures to coordinate their activities. Yet they also challenge globalization in other respects. It appears that at the heart of their struggle is an attack on neoliberalism or, to use another loaded term, the 'Washington consensus' (Stiglitz 2002: 16). The ideological spectrum of the protesters is broad, ranging from Christian groups to social democrats to anarchists. Among these groups, the critique of capitalism, or even outspoken anti-capitalism, is gaining ground. This critique differs from its earlier forms to some extent: (1) 'real socialism', as practised in the Soviet bloc and a number of other countries, is no longer a relevant reference point; (2) hopes for revolutionary change are mainly absent and an overwhelming number of protesters reject the use of violence; (3) the key concerns of the protesters are the peoples in the Southern hemisphere and, more generally, global social, political and ecological problems, rather than the fate of workers in the industrialized world; (4) the main targets are multinational corporations and international governmental bodies; and (5) more than ever oppositional movements are truly transnational – and they increasingly incorporate groups from the Southern hemisphere. Some even claim that a 'movement of movements' is emerging. Because globalization is geographically unlimited and has so many thematic implications and repercussions, it can become the focus of a great variety of groups; these groups can sometimes form broad coalitions that link specific issues and territories. In other words, the critique of globalization is becoming increasingly global; this is best exemplified by the World Social Forums.

The Seattle protests of December 1999 were not the starting point of such a wave of protest, nor were they fundamentally new in character. There were, from the mid-1980s, many earlier, similar protests; these usually focused on G7 and EU summits, UN world conferences, IMF and World Bank meetings, and conferences of the WTO and its forerunner GATT (General Agreement on Tariffs and Trade). However, Seattle played a great symbolic role in so far as it revealed the broad range of protest groups that can come together in a single, orchestrated campaign. Seattle also exhibited the disruptive potential of these groups and the extensive media coverage they are able to elicit. At least for the moment, Seattle has weakened the self-confidence of some politicians who want to promote a truly global free trade economy.

Whether or not the protests against neoliberal globalization mark the emergence of a new type of social movement is not clear (Tarrow and della Porta 2004). Obviously, the answer depends much on the criteria applied. As with many so-called new social movements in the past, lines of continuity exist that tend initially to be neglected but come to the fore, above all, when historians dig into the past. I would argue that the campaigns we have witnessed in the last few years are not new in terms of their ideological basis, the social background of participants, the means of mobilization and tactics. However, in all these respects there are some elements that were at first marginal or just hardly noticed, but which have become more distinct. For example: neoliberalism has become a focal point; labour unions and non-labour groups have moved closer together; the transnational component has become stronger, with groups from the Southern hemisphere no longer just spectators; and the idea of non-violence and of using the tactics of civil disobedience is gaining ground.

What are the consequences of these numerous efforts to change the world? Seattle has inspired subsequent campaigns by critics of neoliberalism, although none of these campaigns has had the same immediate impact on the official event or such relatively positive media coverage. For example, it was not possible to 'Turn Prague into Seattle'. In summary, the various campaigns before and after Seattle have resulted mainly in symbolic rather than substantial gains (Roth 2000).[28] In relative terms, some of the UN institutions have probably become more supportive of the demands of protest movements and NGOs (see Otto 1996; Weiss and Gordenker 1996; Willets 1996; Oliver 1999). In contrast, those international institutions seeking to steer the global economy have done little more than pay lip service to their challengers. In the last few years, the World Bank and the IMF have been reassessing their strategies; they have indicated they will pay more attention to social issues, including poverty in Third World countries (Fox and Brown 2000; Udall 2000). This is reflected by their emphasis on concepts such as ownership and participation in the framework of a new set of initiatives such as the *Comprehensive Development Framework* (CDF), the *Poverty Reduction Strategy Paper* (PRSP) and the *Poverty Reduction and Growth Facility* (PRGF). Whether this is more than rhetoric remains to be seen (Goldberg 2000). As far as the opposition to the WTO is concerned, Scholte (2000: 116) draws a sobering conclusion:

> These long efforts have booked only modest gains to date. Thanks in good part to pressure from certain civic groups, the WTO has since 1996 added competition issues, development concerns, environmental problems, and labour standards to its agenda. However, little has happened on these matters beyond occasional meetings of committees and working groups. The core mission of the WTO has remained that of the widest and fastest possible liberalisation of cross-border flows of goods and services.

Similar assessments can be found regarding the World Bank (Nelson 1995) and other international governmental bodies. Although it is unlikely that the campaigns against neo-liberalism will have an immediate and profound impact in the near future, I doubt that the protests will soon fade away. Rather, given the scope of the problems they address – the dissatisfaction of many young activists with the 'new world order', the democratic deficit of international policymaking and the increased ease of coordinating movements across issues and space – I would, rather, expect the protests to intensify and broaden (Keck and Sikkink 1998; della Porta et al. 1999; Rucht 1999; Cohen and Rai 2000; Florini 2000). But we can also assume that the targeted institutions will react to this challenge, for instance by applying a stick-and-carrot strategy. The stick would be not only tear gas, batons, bullets, arrests (including the abuse of arrested protesters of the kind perpetrated, above all, in Genoa) and criminal proceedings, but also the refusal to offer debt relief, aid and/or credits. The carrot could entail both a symbolic embrace of the needs of civil society in order to co-opt those critics who appear to be 'reasonable', and, at best, the granting of limited concessions – though these, I would guess, would not pacify most challengers.

Calls for more solidarity and democracy have characterized many movements in the past active within national boundaries. Now, in an era of globalization, these calls refer to a 'cosmopolitical democracy' (Archibugi and Held 1995). This idea may be a dream, but so was 'national democracy' in most countries in the eighteenth century.

Notes

This is a revised and slightly expanded version of a published article with the same title (Rucht 2003). It is based on two earlier papers, the first presented at a conference in Santiago de Compostela in March 2000 ('The Construction of Europe, Democracy and Globalization'), the second at a workshop of the European Commission in Brussels in December 2000 ('Global Trade and Globalising Society: Challenges to Governance and Sustainability. The Role of the EU'). I am grateful to Jesus Casquete, John Keane and Jackie Smith for their comments, and to Janice Cornwall and Amanda Dalessi for their editorial assistance. Author's address: Rucht@wz-berlin.de

1. My own investigations support the findings of Gerhards and Rössel. According to a key-word search in the German left-alternative newspaper *die tageszeitung*, which is available on CD-ROM, the term 'globalization' did not appear before 1988 (with two hits in that year). It was still relatively rare until 1994 (twenty two hits) but then became quite common with about 350 to 400 hits in the late 1990s and close to 1,000 hits in both 2001 and 2002. Whether or not the actual process of globalization is occurring as rapidly as most observers assume is less clear. Even in the realm of economics, where such a process seems evident, some scholars argue that, in historical perspective, globalization started earlier and is advancing less quickly than we tend to assume (Hirst and Thompson 1999).

2. Broadly speaking, neoliberalism is a new wave of a predominantly economically driven liberalism. It promotes free trade, a supply-side economy, deregulation, low taxes, privatization and self-reliance and self-responsibility on the part of the citizenry (See Barry et al. 1993; Cloclough and Manor 1994; for critical assessments, see George 1999; MacEwan 1999).

3. Whichever positions are taken in this debate, it is clear that globalization is a multidimensional process: it has economic, technological, ecological, political, social and cultural features, and occurs at different levels (Held and McGrew 1993; Chase-

Dunn 1999; Keohane and Nye 2000). Taking this into account, it usually makes little sense to label either camp simply as pro- or anti-global. Even most of those who generally favour globalization would concede that it has some negative side effects for some people in some places. Even its harshest opponents would admit that globalization might have some advantages, for instance the facilitation of communication which allows the creation of a *global* 'anti-globalization' movement.

4. The need of a constantly expanding market for its products chases the bourgeoisie over the entire surface of the globe. It must nestle everywhere, settle everywhere, establish connections everywhere. The bourgeoisie has, through its exploitation of the world market, given a cosmopolitan character to production and consumption in every country. To the great chagrin of reactionaries, it has drawn from under the feet of industry the national ground on which it stood. All old-established national industries have been destroyed or are daily being destroyed. They are dislodged by new industries, whose introduction becomes a life and death question for all civilized nations, by industries that no longer work up indigenous raw material, but raw material drawn from the remotest zones; industries whose products are consumed, not only at home, but in every quarter of the globe. In place of the old wants, satisfied by the production of the country, we find new wants, requiring for their satisfaction the products of distant lands and climes. In place of the old local and national seclusion and self-sufficiency, we have intercourse in every direction, universal inter-dependence of nations. (Marx and Engels 1888/1848; see http://csf.Colorado.EDU/psn/marx/Archive/1848–CM/)

5. Like the political world, the allegedly more neutral scientific world is also deeply divided over the effects of globalization. While one side praises it as beneficial also for the 'developing' countries (e.g. Sachs and Warner 1995; Gwartney and Lawson 2000), the other side sees these countries as the main victims of globalization (e.g. Chomsky 1999; Gray 1999; Mander and Goldsmith 2001). Both sides try to substantiate their positions with statistics and empirical examples, sometimes even referring to the same country to make their point. Stiglitz (2002) is somewhere between these positions. He is optimistic about the potential benefits of globalization but critical of the prevailing strategies used to steer these processes.

6. G8 communiqué of the Cologne G8 Summit, 18–20 June, 1999. Cited after May (1997: 4). On the other hand, the communiqué also mentions that 'globalization has been accompanied by a greater risk of dislocation and financial uncertainty for some workers, families and communities across the world'.

7. Lerner (1968: 386) defines modernization as 'the process of social change whereby less developed societies acquire characteristics common to more developed societies'.

8. According to a report of the United Nations Development Programme, the GINI coefficient, which measures differences in income of the poorest and wealthiest fifths of the population, was – at the global level – 1 to 30 in 1960, 1 to 60 in 1990 and 1 to 74 in 1997 (UNDP 1999: 3). Three hundred and fifty eight billionaires earned the same amount of money as the poorest 45 per cent of the world population, that is, nearly 3 billion people (UNDP 1996: 2).

9. In the introduction to *Democracy in America* Tocqueville states, with respect to the movement towards democracy and social equality: 'it cannot be stopped, but it is not yet as rapid that it cannot be guided' (1994: 7).

10. Thomas E. Schmidt, in *Die Zeit*, August 2, 2001, p. 4.

11. For a more realistic view on civil society, see, for example, Carothers (1999/2000). On the dark side of democracy, see Mann (1999).

12. Yet there are also authors, John Keane for instance, who perceive the economy, or markets, as a constitutive part of civil society: 'Where there are no markets, civil societies find it impossible to survive. But the converse rule also applies: where there is no civil society, there can be no markets' (Keane 1998: 19).

13. As Chomsky (1999) and many others have shown, the major proponents of free trade policies have not applied the latter necessarily to themselves. Great Britain and the US have tended to protect and subsidize their own industries as long as they face powerful foreign competitors. In contrast, free trade policy is promoted when the aim is to conquer new markets abroad. Also, the neoliberal call to reduce the state has not always been implemented. For example, contrary to what most people would assume, in Britain under Margaret Thatcher the share of the gross national product taken by state expenses did not decrease; and, in the US during Roland Reagan's administration, the state hardly shrank.

14. For early critical discussions of the role of multinational companies, see Tugendhat (1972) and Vernon (1977).

15. This holds true even when taking into account the existence of the UN General Assembly and European Parliament. The first is a body of representatives of national governments and, compared to the Security Council, relatively weak; the second, though having directly elected members, still lacks many of the competencies that characterize most national parliaments.

16. For a critical assessment of WTO policies, see Wallach and Sforza (1999) and Smith and Moran (2000). On the Seattle events, see Bayne (2000), Cockburn and St Clair (2000); Epstein (2000), Gill (2000), Scholte (2000), Smith (2000a); Thomas (2000).

17. From the announcement to the Brussels conference referred to at the beginning of these notes.

18. For an analysis of the protest against this summit, see Pettifor (1998). According to Pettifor, more than 70,000 people participated in this protest.

19. In its Geneva manifesto, *Peoples' Global Action* presents itself as 'a worldwide coordination of resistance against the global market, a new alliance of struggle and mutual support' with the following hallmarks:

    '1. A very clear rejection of the WTO and other trade liberalisation agreements (like APEC, the EU, NAFTA, etc.) as active promoters of a socially and environmentally destructive globalization, 2. A confrontational attitude, since we do not think that lobbying can have a major impact in such biased and undemocratic organisations, in which transnational capital is the only real policy-maker, 3. A call to non-violent civil disobedience and the construction of local alternatives by local people, as answers to the action of governments and corporations, 4. An organisational philosophy based on decentralisation and autonomy.' (http://www.tao.ca/fire/gather/0049.html)

20. This network was partly inspired by Danaker's study (1994) of the World Bank and the IMF.

21. See the detailed report of the *Ruckus* training camp in Florida (Brown 2000). See also www.ruckus.org

22. According to many close observers, the tactics of the US delegation were another major reason why an agreement could not be reached: the delegation locked out from informal negotiations during the conference many delegations that they perceived as potential troublemakers. This fact leaked to the 'outsiders', who, for this reason amongst others, were no longer inclined to compromise.

23. Among other things, ATTAC promotes the taxation of transactions on the stock markets (the Tobin tax). See http://www.attac.org/indexen.htm.

24. It mainly comprises Canadian groups 'currently focused on the issues of multilateral debt relief, World Bank energy policy and practice and international currency speculation'. See http://www.web.net/~halifax/index.htm

25. How many people participate in mass protests is usually a matter of debate. Initially, lower numbers were given for Genoa. In later reports, however, both journalists and representatives of the Italian administration referred to 200,000 participants.

26. The sheer number and broad spectrum of protesters could be seen as an asset. However, the violent clashes, of which the police, in some instances and places, were the initiators, can be seen as a burden in so far as the *form of action* overshadowed the *reasons for the protest*. Many commentators, and probably more so large parts of the populace, tended to regard the protesters as mindless vandals.

27. Susan George, the vice president of ATTAC France, states: 'Actually, I refuse the term "anti-globalization" that the media have lumbered us with. This combat is really between those who want inclusive globalization based on cooperation and solidarity and those who want the market to make all decisions' (George 2001: 1). As for the latter attempts, George uses labels such as 'market-driven' or 'corporate-led' globalization.

28. However, there are a few exceptions to this rule. For example, the Multilateral Agreement on Investment (MAI) failed due to the combined critique of grass-roots movements and some governments, most notably the French government (Goodman and Ranald 1999). Another example of a movement's success is the campaign for a ban of landmines (Rutherford 2000).

References

Anand, Anita, Escobar, Arturo, Sen, Jai and Waterman, Peter, eds. 2004. *Eine andere Welt. Das Weltsozialforum*. Berlin.

Archibugi, Daniele and Held, David. 1995. *Cosmopolitan Democracy: An Agenda for a New World Order*. London.

Barry, Andrew, Osborne, Thomas and Rose, Nicholas. 1993. 'Liberalisms, Neoliberalism and Governmentality: Introduction' *Economy & Society* 22, 3: 265–66.

Bauman, Zygmunt. 1989. *Modernity and the Holocaust*. Ithaca.

———. 2000. 'Am I My Brother's Keeper?' *European Journal of Social Work* 3, 1: 5–11.

Bayne, Nicholas, 2000. 'Why did Seattle Fail? Globalization and the Politics of Trade'. *Government and Opposition* 35, 2: 131–51.

Berger, Peter L., Berger, Brigitte and Kellner, Hansfried, 1973. *The Homeless Mind*. New York.

Brown, Nick, 2000. 'Having a Nice Riot'. *Telegraph Magazine* (London), 15, April: 29–37.

Canadian Security Intelligence Service. 2000. *Anti-Globalization – A Spreading Phenomenon. Report # 2000/08*. http://www.csis-scrs.gc.ca/eng/miscdocs/200008e.html

Carothers, Thomas. 1999/2000. 'Civil Society'. *Foreign Policy* 117, Winter: 18–29.

Chase-Dunn, Christopher. 1999. 'Globalization: A World-systems Perspective'. *Journal of World-Systems Research* 2, 2: 165–85.

Chomsky, Noam. 1999. *Profit Over People: Neoliberalism and Global Order*. New York.

Cloclough, Christopher and Manor, James, eds. 1994. *States or Markets? Neo-Liberalism and the Development Policy Debate*. Oxford.

Cockburn, Alexander and St Clair, Jeffrey. 2000. *5 Days that Shook the World: Seattle and Beyond*. London and New York.

Cohen, Jean and Arato, Andrew, 1992. *Civil Society and Political Theory*. Cambridge, Mass.

Cohen, Robin and Rai, Shirin M., eds. 2000. *Global Social Movements*. London and New Brunswick, NJ.

Danaker, Kevin, 1994. *50 Years is Enough: The Case against the World Bank and the International Monetary Fund*. Boston.

della Porta, Donatella, Kriesi, Hanspeter and Rucht, Dieter, eds. 1999. *Social Movements in a Globalizing World*. London.

Epstein, Barbara. 2000. 'Not Your Parents' Protest'. *Dissent* Spring : 8–11.

Florini, Ann M., ed. 2000. *The Third Force: The Rise of Transnational Civil Society. Tokyo: Japan Center for International Exchange*. Washington, DC.

Foley, Michael W. and Edwards, Bob. 1996. 'The Paradox of Civil Society'. *Journal of Democracy* 7, 3: 38–52.

Fox, Jonathan A. and Brown, David. 2000. 'Assessing the Impact of NGO Advocacy Campaigns on World Bank Projects and Policies'. In *The Struggle for Accountability: The World Bank, NGOs, and Grassroots Movements*, ed. Jonathan A. Fox and David Brown: 485–551. Cambridge, Mass. and London.

Frank, André Gunder. 1967. *Capitalism and Underdevelopment in Latin America*. New York.

George, Susan. 1999. 'A Short History of Neo-liberalism'. Paper presented at the Conference on Economic Sovereignty in a Globalising World, Bangkok, 24–26 March. www.zmag.org/CrisesCruEvts/Globalism.htm

———. 2001. 'Another World Is Possible.' *Dissent* Winter. http://www.dissentmagazine.org/archive/wi01/george.shtml

Gerhards, Jürgen. 1993. *Neue Konfliktlinien in der Mobilisierung öffentlicher Meinung. Eine Fallanalyse*. Opladen.

Gerhards, Jürgen and Rössel, Jörg. 1999. 'Zur Transnationalisierung der Gesellschaft der Bundesrepublik. Entwicklungen, Ursachen und mögliche Folgen für die europäische Integration'. *Zeitschrift für Soziologie* 28, 5: 325–44.

Gerhards, Jürgen and Rucht, Dieter. 1992. 'Mesomobilization: Organizing and Framing in Two Protest Campaigns in West Germany'. *American Journal of Sociology* 98, 3: 555–95.

Giddens, Anthony. 1999. *Globalization*. BBC Reith Lectures. http://news.bbc.co.uk/hi/english/static/events/reith_99/week1/week1.htm

Gill, Stephen. 2000. 'Toward a Postmodern Prince? The Battle of Seattle as a Moment in the New Politics of Globalization'. *Millenium* 29, 1: 131–40.

Goldberg, Jörg. 2000. 'Front gegen die Armut? Neue Strategien der Bretton-Woods-Institutionen'. *Blätter für deutsche und internationale Politik* 45, 4: 456–64.

Goodman, James and Ranald, Patricia, eds. 1999. *Stopping the Juggernaut: Public Interest vs. the Multilateral Agreement On Investment*. Annandale, NSW.

Gray, John. 1999. *False Dawn: The Delusions of Global Capitalism*. London.

Gwartney, James and Lawson, Robert. 2000. *Economic Freedom of the World. Annual Report*. Vancouver, BC.

Habermas, Jürgen. 1987. *The Theory of Communicative Action*, 2 vols. Boston.

Held, David, 2002. 'Cosmopolitanism: Ideas, Realities, Deficits'. In *Governing Globalization: Power, Authority and Global Governance*, ed. David Held and Anthony McGrew: 305–24. Cambridge.

Held, David and McGrew, Andrew. 1993. 'Globalization and the Liberal Democratic State'. *Government and Opposition* 28, 2: 261–88.

Hirst, Paul and Thompson, Grahame. 1999. *Globalization in Question* 2nd (revised and updated) edn (1ˢᵗ edition: 1996). Cambridge.

Keane, John. 1988. 'Despotism and Democracy: The Origins and Development of the Distinction Between Civil Society and the State, 1750–1850'. In *Civil Society and the State: New European Perspectives*, ed. John Keane: 35–71. London and New York.

———. 1998. *Civil Society: Old Images, New Visions*. Stanford, Calif.

Keck, Margaret E. and Sikkink, Kathryn. 1998. *Activists beyond Borders: Advocacy Networks in International Politics*. Ithaca and London.

Kellner, Douglas, 1998. 'Globalization and the Postmodern Turn'. In *Globalization and Europe*, ed. Roland Axtmann: 23–42. London and Washington.

Keohane, Robert O., 2002. 'Governance in a Partially Globalized World'. In *Governing Globalization: Power, Authority and Global Governance*, ed. David Held and Anthony McGrew: 325–47. Cambridge.

Keohane, Robert O. and Nye, Joseph S. 2000. 'What's New? What's Not? (And So What?)'. *Foreign Policy* 118, Spring: 104–19.

Kumar, Krishan. 1996. 'Civil Society'. In *The Social Science Encyclopedia*, 2ⁿᵈ edn, Adam Kuper and Jessica Kuper: 88–90. London and New York.

Lerner, Daniel, 1968. 'Modernization. Social Aspects' In *International Encyclopedia of the Social Sciences*, vol. 10: 386–95. New York.

Levi, Margret and Olson, David. 2000. 'The Battles in Seattle'. *Politics and Society* 28, 3: 309–29.

Lori's War. 2000. 'The FP Interview: Lori's War'. *Foreign Policy* Spring: 29–55.

Luttwak, Edward N. 1999. *Turbo-Capitalism: Winners and Losers in the Global Economy*. New York.

MacEwan, Arthur. 1999. *Neo-Liberalism or Democracy? Economic Strategy, Markets, and Alternatives for the 21st Century*. London.

McChesney, Robert W. 1999. 'Introduction'. In *Profit Over People: Neoliberalism and Global Order*. ed. Noam Chomsky: 7–16. New York.

McGrew, Anthony. 1997. *The Transformation of Democracy: Globalization and Territorial Democracy*. Cambridge.

Mander, Jerry and Goldsmith, Edward, eds. 1997. *The Case against the Global Economy*. San Francisco.

Mann, Michael, 1999. 'The Dark Side of Democracy. The Modern Tradition of Ethnic and Political Cleansing'. *New Left Review* 235: 18–45.

Marx, Karl and Engels, Frederick. 1888. *Manifesto of the Communist Party*, trans. Frederick Engels (orig. 1848). http://csf.Colorado.EDU/psn/marx/Archive/1848–CM/

May, Bernhard. 1997. 'Globalisierung – Gewinner und Verlierer auf globaler Ebene.' http://www.politik-im-netz-com/po...z_3.lasso&Ident_such=A-20&-search

Nelson, Paul J. 1995. *The World Bank and Non-Governmental Organisations: The Limits of Apolitical Development*. New York.

O'Brien, Robert et al. 2000. *Contesting Global Governance. Multilateral Economic Institutions and Global Social Movements*. Cambridge, Mass. and New York.

Oliver, Michael, 1999. 'Learning New Steps: UN Agencies and Programmes and Civil Society'. In *Whose World is it Anyway? Civil Society, the United Nations and the Multilateral Future*, ed. John W. Foster (with Anita Anand): 313–35. Ottawa.

Otto, Diane. 1996. 'Nongovernmental Organisations in the United Nations System: The Emerging Role of International Civil Society'. *Human Rights Quarterly* 18: 107–41.

Pettifor, Ann. 1998. 'The Economic Bondage of Debt – and the Birth of a New Movement'. *New Left Review* 230: 115–22.

Pianta, Mario. 2001. 'Parallel Summits of Global Civil Society'. In *Global Civil Society 2001*, ed. Helmut Anheier, Marlies Glasius and Mary Kaldor: 169–94. Oxford.

Roth, Roland. 2000. 'NGOs and International Politics'. Contribution to the UNESCO Programme 'EUROPA-MUNDI', October. Unpublished paper.

Rucht, Dieter. 1999. 'The Transnationalisation of Social Movements: Trends, Causes, Problems'. In *Social Movements in a Globalizing World*, ed. Donatella Porta, Hanspeter Kriesi and Dieter Rucht: 206–22. London.

———. 2002. 'Rückblicke und Ausblicke auf die globalisierungskritischen Bewegungen'. In *Globaler Widerstand. Internationale Netzwerke auf der Suche nach Alternativen im globalen Kapitalismus*, ed. Heike Walk and Nele Boehme: 57–82. Münster.

———. 2003. 'Social Movements Challenging Neo-liberal Globalization'. In *Social Movements and Democracy*, ed. Pedro Ibarra: 211–28. New York.

———. Forthcoming (2005). 'Attention but No Support: Press Resonance to Mayday Protests in London and Berlin'. *Mobilization*.

Rutherford, Kenneth R. 2000. 'The Evolving Arms Control Agenda. Implications of the Role of NGOs in Banning Antipersonnel Landmines'. *World Politics* 53, 1: 74–114.

Sachs, Jeffrey and Warner, Andrew. 1995. *Brookings Papers on Economic Activities. Economic Reform and the Process of Global Integration*. Washington, DC.

Scholte, Jan Aart. 2000. 'Cautionary Reflections on Seattle'. *Millennium. Journal of International Studies* 29: 115–21.

Self, Peter. 1993. *Government by the Market? The Politics of Public Choice*. Boulder, Colo.

Shoch, James. 2000. 'Contesting Globalization: Organized Labor, NAFTA, and the 1997 and 1998 Fast-track Fights'. *Politics and Society* 28, 1: 119–50.

Sklair, Leslie. 1997. 'Social Movements for Global Capitalism: the Transnational Capitalist Class'. *Review of International Political Economy* 4, 3: 514–38.

Smith, Jackie. 2000a. 'Globalizing Resistance: The Battle of Seattle and the Future of Social Movements'. *Mobilization* 6, 1: 1–19.

———. 2000b. 'Made in (Corporate) America: Looking Behind the Anti-Globalization Label'. Unpublished manuscript.

Smith, Jackie and Moran, Timothy Patrick. 2000. 'WTO 101: Myths about the World Trade Organisation'. *Dissent* 2: 66–71.

Stiglitz, Joseph E. 2002. *Globalization and Its Discontents*. New York and London.

Tarrow, Sidney and della Porta, Donatella. 2004. 'Conclusion: "Globalization", Complex Internationalism, and Transnational Contention'. In *Transnational Protest and Global Activism*, ed. Donatella della Porta and Sidney Tarrow: 227–46. Lanham.

Thomas, Janet. 2000. *The Battle in Seattle: The Story Behind and Beyond the WTO Demonstrations*. Golden, Colo.

Tocqueville, Alexis de. 1994 [1835, 1840]. *Democracy in America*. New York.

Tugendhat, Christopher. 1972. *The Multinationals*. New York.

Udall, Lori. 2000. 'The World Bank and Public Accountability: Has Anything Changed?' In *The Struggle for Accountability: The World Bank, NGOs, and Grassroots Movements*, ed. Jonathan A. Fox and David Brown: 391–436. Cambridge, Mass. and London.

UNDP. 1996. *Human Development Report 1996*. Oxford.

———. 1999. *Human Development Report 1999*. New York.

Vernon, Raymond. 1977. *Storm over the Multinationals: The Real Issues*. Cambridge, Mass.

Wallach, Lori and Sforza, Michelle. 1999. *Whose Trade Organisation? Corporate Globalization and the Erosion of Democracy*. Washington, DC.

Wallerstein, Immanuel. 1976. 'Modernization: Requiescat in Pace'. In *The Uses of Controversy in Sociology*, ed. Lewis A. Coser and Otto N. Larsen: 131–35. New York.

Walzer, Michael. 1991. 'The Idea of Civil Society'. *Dissent* Spring: 293–304.

Weiss, Thomas G. and Gordenker, Leon, eds. 1996. *NGOs, the UN, and Global Governance*. Boulder, Colo.

Willetts, Peter, ed. 1996. *'The Conscience of the World': The Influence of Non-Governmental Organisations in the UN System*. Washington, DC.

Zürn, Michael. 1998. *Regieren jenseits des Nationalstaats*. Frankfurt am Main.

9

ENTANGLED HISTORIES: CIVIL SOCIETY, CASTE SOLIDARITIES AND LEGAL PLURALISM IN POST-COLONIAL INDIA

Shalini Randeria

Cartographies of social ties seem to have changed so rapidly that it is difficult today to read the old and new maps of social connectedness together. In the heyday of modernization theory just thirty years ago, solidarities of caste, community and religion were considered to be undesirable relics of the passing of 'traditional' societies destined for the dustbin of history. There were no communitarians then who would have shared the prevailing Indian 'backward' belief that individual identities were shaped by communities whose ways of life must be preserved and protected. Theorists of social capital had yet to discover that dense social networks of any variety were good for civil society and democracy. Those were the days before bowling together, or rather playing cricket, had been found to further civic ties or democratic values. Religious communities were viewed with deep suspicion in India; they were believed to be an obstacle to the realization of a secularist ideal that societies in the West were assumed to have achieved long ago. We were brought up to believe that the ills of traditional societies like ours, and these societies' inability to modernize rapidly, were due to the existence of too dense a network of social ties, or at least of social ties of the wrong kind. Affiliations of caste, solidarities of religion, parochial loyalties of language, ethnicity or region were seen as signs of backwardness. It was considered imperative in the interest of national progress and prosperity that Brahmins, Bengalis or Muslims be turned into Indians. Ties of citizenship and nationhood were viewed as modern, and desirable, forms of social connectedness. The Marxists, who were equally nationalistic, preferred class solidarity as the quintessential form of modern social ties – but that is another story.

Prior to the celebration of multiculturalism in the West, an urgent task of the post-colonial state was seen to be the overcoming of diversity rather than the recognition of difference. Constitutional safeguards for religious and cultural minorities in the Indian constitution of 1950, including the right to be governed by religiously defined family laws of one's own community, was a legal novelty without Western precedent. The provisions in the Indian constitution of quotas in education and public employment for underprivileged and disadvantaged groups were bold innovations (with roots, however, in colonial legacies of the institutionalization of difference). Such collective compensatory measures to redress centuries of discrimination were equally unknown then in Western democracies. Both the numerical quotas and the right to one's own religiously defined family laws were regarded as temporary measures necessary to facilitate the transition to a mature modernity characterized by legal homogeneity and individual rights of citizenship. By accepting several group-specific rights and devising a set of policies for the recognition of cultural differences in the public domain, which granted minorities autonomy and equal treatment while seeking to redress inequalities between groups, the Indian constitutional experiment departed from the then current models of Western liberalism (Mahajan 1995). It chose instead what Thomas Pantham has termed a 'communitarian-liberal democracy' (1995: 171), a post-colonial precedent still unrecognized in contemporary Western debates on minority rights and multiculturalism.

Ironically, while Western societies, faced with a crisis of national political culture (as the chickens of the Empire come home to roost), discover multiculturalism and group rights, in India minority rights come under serious attack in the name of cultural homogeneity and national integration. The militant Hindu nationalist attack against minority rights in India today is animated by the desire for a homogeneous political community based on a unitary and uniform culture and on the religion of the Hindu majority as the foundation of a strong nation state modelled on the Western image. Central to the rhetoric of political Hinduism is its insistence on righting the wrongs of history, that is, the loss and humiliation suffered by the Hindu majority at the hands of the Muslim minority. Couched in the vocabulary of religion, this is – as Khilnani (1997) has pointed out – a highly modern statist project that aims to eradicate any legal and political recognition of cultural and religious differences. It thus includes plans for the reform of the Indian constitution in order to introduce a uniform legal code, which would replace the plurality of civil codes of law for different religious communities. In such a conception, the possibility of a plurality of cultures in the public sphere is precluded, as is the desirability of a dialogue among communities with very different visions of the good life out of which a shared national culture, which embodies more than only procedural commitments, could evolve. If it is assumed that the national culture should be the culture of the dominant group, usually the majority (Offe 1998) (an issue which exercised the political imagination in the recent German debate on *Leitkultur*), then the question of whom the nation belongs to culturally does not arise. However, if a shared and inclusive national culture appears just and desirable, such a composite culture must be the product of a dialogue between different groups irrespective of size and degrees of similarity.

There remains an uneasy fit between the legal recognition of the collective rights of communities to their culture and the fact that such adherence may end up cementing those very social ties which the political process of nation building seeks to dissolve. In the process, particularistic ties may well change their form but not necessarily in the direction of universalistic ties of individual citizenship. Nation building is seen to entail the fashioning of individual citizens, governed by a uniform common civil code, out of members of castes and religious communities owing primary allegiance to these 'primordial' sub-state entities and governed in personal matters by their own 'traditional' collective norms. A society with a plurality of religions, linguistic communities, ethnic groups, castes and indigenous peoples strove for decades, therefore, to find 'unity in diversity', to use the official vocabulary, even as it sought to wear the garb of modernity differently, as Prime Minister Nehru put it. That this garb was fashioned out of a traditional social fabric very different from that of the West, and one that had been cut according to colonial design, was a much later realization that post-colonial theory was to use in the 1990s to formulate the idea of multiple or alternative modernities.

Recent attempts to pluralize modernity have been concerned with two sets of issues: (1) differences in the trajectories of modernity in different parts of the world; and (2) differences in the outcomes of these processes in different societies. Conceptualizations of plural modernities, such as those of Eisenstadt (2000) or Therborn (1995), raise several questions concerning the relationship of European to non-European modernities under highly asymmetrical conditions of domination and exploitation. What status would be accorded to the paradigm of 'Western' modernity (which must be pluralized as well) in a conceptualization that recognizes historical and contemporary entanglements between Western and non-Western societies? Can multiple modernities be conceived of in terms of different elements of modernity variously combined at different points of time in different societies?

Anthropologists working with the idea of a pluralization of modernities, or of a vernacularization of modernity, have usually emphasized the creative and selective appropriations of various aspects of Western modernities in different colonial and post-colonial contexts to produce a variety of hybrid outcomes. Once modernity is pluralized, it becomes possible to conceptualize trajectories and outcomes that diverge from the ideal-typical historical experience of Western societies. But, even more importantly, it is possible to analyse the unevenness of processes of modernization in different spheres *within* a society. Consequently, the idea of a homogeneous Western modernity travelling, more or less imperfectly, to the rest of the world must be replaced by a more messy and complex picture of what I have termed disparate and divergent but uneven and entangled modernities (Randeria 1999a, b). Rather than reconceptualizing multiple or alternative modernities at the level of the nation state (Indian or Japanese modernity) or in terms of 'cultures' or religions (African modernity, Islamic or Confucian modernity), it would be more fruitful to explore uneven modernities within a society. For modernity as social experience varies in the understandings and practices of different groups of people. Modernity has always been in tension with its others (the non-modern or anti-modern) but it has now also become a contested concept with a multiplicity of meanings which vary with actors and contexts. Its status has, therefore, altered significantly from that of a teleological and a historical-philosophical category, as part of the Enlightenment project, to that of a dimension of social experience and a part of the social imaginary that is acted and reflected upon.

In the universal language of modern social theory, the history of the West is always written as world history. Of course, by globalizing the categories of Western modernity, capitalism and imperialism have lent some truth to this claim (Conrad and Randeria 2002). But discourses of multiple or alternative modernities may, paradoxically, cement rather than destabilize the categories of Western modernity as a universal narrative against which local difference in the experience of non-Western societies is measured. I would suggest replacing a 'history of absences' (Mamdani 1996), as in discourses of modernization theory, or a history by analogy, as in discourses of alternative modernities, by a relational perspective that foregrounds processes of interaction and intermixture in the entangled histories of uneven modernities (Randeria 1999a, b). Such a perspective would not privilege Western historical experience or trajectories and would be sensitive to the particularities of the non-Western society under study.

This chapter seeks to connect the sequestered histories of civil society and legal pluralism in the West and outside it, and to locate them within the framework of (post-)colonial governance. The first section delineates the entangled histories of civil society as the *locus classicus* of social ties independent of state and market (I have discussed this elsewhere in detail: Randeria 2001b). Indian debates on civil society, which I discuss in the second section, interact with different Western imaginings of civil society and help one understand how local and trans-local ideas, institutions and workings of civil society are inextricably intertwined. Civic activism against the state, and political as well as scholarly debates about it, in many parts of the 'Third World' pre-date the rediscovery of this activism in the 'Second World'. A Eurocentric perspective on civil society often overlooks the fact that many of these debates in Latin America, Africa (Bayart 1996, Mamdani 1996) and India (Sheth 1984; Kothari 1988, Gupta 1999) are independent of the resurgence of interest in the idea of civil society in the West in the light of the East European experience. A more cosmopolitan understanding of civil society would, therefore, include those debates along with analyses of the workings of civil society outside Europe.

The third section is concerned with what Dirks (1992) sees as the Indian variant of civil society instituted by colonial rule – the ties of caste. Using Sudipto Kaviraj's distinction between traditional 'fuzzy' identities and modern enumerated ones, I critically examine the refashioning of multiple, fluid, contextually shifting personal identities and collective ties in pre-colonial India into monolithic, stable and homogeneous identifications and belongings, based on common interest rather than social interaction. This process of transformation is illustrated with reference to the so-called 'untouchable' castes, or Dalits as they prefer to call themselves collectively today. The status of these castes at the bottom of the social hierarchy is also examined with reference to the vexed issue of their inclusion in a pan-Indian 'Hindu' community, the boundaries of which were defined and shaped by the discourses and practices of the colonial state.

The final section of the chapter engages with the controversial issue of legal pluralism in the sphere of family law in India; this legal pluralism has been framed by its advocates and opponents in terms of the choice between community identity/autonomy, on the one hand, and national integration/social cohesion, on the other. In my view both protagonists and detractors of legal pluralism have a narrow understanding of the issue: they restrict the legal sphere to that of state law, thus according it a primacy it does not enjoy in social life. I look at the question instead from the vantage point of autonomous informal institutions of justice, outside the reach of the state or in limited interaction with state courts, which set and adjudicate their own norms for the majority of lower castes among Hindus and Muslims in western India.

My argument is that caste or *jamat* assemblies, as the sphere of the self-regulation of communities through an autonomous production and adjudication of family law, form an important domain of civil society in (post-)colonial India. The workings of a civil society containing such collectivities challenges the liberal Western conceptualization of civil society as the sphere connecting autonomous individuals to the state. If civil society is, rather, understood as being concerned with establishing and maintaining bonds of social solidarity and as a sphere of relatively autonomous self-regulation, then castes and caste councils offer interesting material for thinking about civil society as being governed and organized in a very different way from a liberal understanding of it. A liberal conception of civil society would include only formal associations based on voluntary membership – and on that criterion exclude from the ambit of civil society castes based on ascription. Caste councils do not merely reflect the 'tyranny of cousins' as against the freedom to choose one's identity – which Gellner (1995) sees as characteristic of modern civil society. In my view, the modernist bias inherent in such a narrow and Eurocentric conception leads one to overlook rich forms of associational life in non-Western societies, just as it leads one to overemphasize the contrast between choice and ascription and to represent tradition and modernity as binary opposites.

Contemporary caste-based associations are as much traditional ascriptive bodies as they are modern organizations of colonial origin (Randeria 1992a). The form of these associations does not adequately reflect their purposes. Some of them own considerable property, have elected office bearers, have their accounts audited, are registered with the Commissioner of Charities and publish regular newsletters. Many caste councils, which set norms and adjudicate family and marital disputes, are also associations that perform a variety of services for their members: they run secondary schools, colleges and hostels for students in urban areas; provide scholarships for education; run *dharamshalas* (dormitories) at large temple complexes and places of pilgrimage; provide medical aid; form networks for political mobilization; and organize meetings in large towns – announced in daily newspapers – at which marriages between younger caste members can be arranged by their families. A view of civil society in India that disregards these often lower-caste organizations that straddle the traditional-modern divide underestimates the often chaotic and messy pluralism of associational life in modern Western societies. The modernist and individualist bias of such a liberal position, based on the trajectory of civil society in a few Western societies, precludes it – when, for example, judging which associations to include in civil society – from considering why the criteria of voluntary membership should take precedence over the criteria of autonomy from the state and internal self-regulation.

If, as my empirical material suggests, normative conflict *within* the local community of caste members is pivotal to its constitution, then multiculturalism and value pluralism cannot be understood in terms of the opposition between state and communities. In arguing that processes of internal disputation and of contestation of norms within each group (rather than the difference between 'traditional' or customary law and state law) are central to the collective identity of a caste, I interrogate the communitarian representation of communities as internally culturally homogeneous entities. If the state is a contested terrain, communities are equally so. If one does not romanticize communities – as communitarian discourse often does – or read legal pluralism as a sign of a deficient modernity – as jurists often do – it is possible to map the changing contours and the intertwining of state and society, the shifting boundaries between the public and the private spheres in the domain of family law. An analysis of the hybrid institutions in this domain reminds us of the unevenness of modernity in India, where social ties of caste have neither dissolved nor been entirely transformed by state processes of codification and enumeration. If there is a convergence of Western and non-Western modernities, it is Western discourses of communitarianism and practices of multiculturalism that have come to resemble the uneven modernities of post-colonial societies.

Entangled Histories of Civil Society

Adam Seligman (2002) suggests that the idea of civil society in late seventeenth- and eighteenth-century Europe developed in response to a crisis of social order not unlike the one that has led to its recent renaissance: the growth of market economies, the commercialization of land and labour and the need to reconcile individual interests with the public good. It represented then, as today, an attempt to conceive of a new ethical model of the workings of society in the face of a crisis of social order. In eighteenth-century Europe, civil society came to be conceived of as the new moral source of social order in the wake of the questioning of God and King as transcendental and external foundations of order (Seligman 2002). The preoccupation with the idea at the end of the twentieth century is clearly due to the dismantling of socialist states, the disappointment with the overreach of capitalist welfare states and the disillusionment with the unfulfilled promises of modernizing post-colonial states. Debates about civil society are also debates about modernity, pluralism, social cohesion and value consensus, individualism and communitarianism; they are about the shifting boundaries between the public and the private spheres.

Most recently – on the neoliberal agenda of restructuring the state – civil society, whittled down to a depoliticized sphere of non-governmental organizations (NGOs), is seen as a cheaper and more efficient alternative to the state. Represented as a domain of civic virtue and voluntary associations, communitarian solidarity and self-help, this redefined domain of civil society excludes political struggles and challenges to state power. Instead, it is seen as a sphere of market-friendly institutions and service delivery agents outside and independent of the state. Such a vision overlooks the fact that civil society can hardly substitute for state functions since it depends in part on state regulation for its functioning. A strong state is a necessary concomitant to a strong civil society, as Jürgen Kocka (2000) has pointed out. Similarly, Neera Chandhoke (1995) has argued forcefully that state and civil society constitute, support and may even impede one another. Delinking the two to conceptualize them as separate and distinct spheres impoverishes our understanding of both.

Civil society is a relational term. It can only be understood in the matrix of a set of interdependent ideas and institutions – nation state, market, public sphere, citizenship, rights-bearing individuals. As John and Jean Comaroff (1999) remind us, these terms have had a highly chequered history in former colonies still struggling to free themselves of the intellectual and institutional legacies of European imperialism. Concomitant with the setting up of the colonial state, the idea of civil society travelled to the colonies in the nineteenth century. It designated a sphere outside the colonial state, either because the rulers sought to demarcate a sphere in which the state would not interfere, or because colonial subjects – using this newly available political vocabulary – sought to delimit the influence of colonial rule with respect to certain areas of their lives (Kaviraj and Khilnani 2001). If civil society in nineteenth-century Europe came to be defined within and in relation to the nation state, its emergence in the age of discoveries was related in part to the interest in very different modes and models of organizing social life in the non-European world (Seligman 2002: 14–15). Civil society in the colonies was a product of imperial rule, with, from its inception, transnational referents.

John and Jean Comaroff have suggested that the broad contemporary transnational appeal of the idea of civil society as a 'trope for these uncertain times' (1999: viii) is predicated upon the fact that it is not a concrete entity waiting to be explicitly defined and analytically demarcated once and for all. Rather than viewing civil society, with Gellner (1994) or Hall (1995), as a unique Western achievement and its specific contours in non-Western societies as a sign of difference or deficiency, it may be important to see that the substance of the idea of civil society is inherently elusive, both in and outside the West. This is in part due to the complex intellectual history and uneven political realization of this ideal over several centuries in the West, as well as to the chequered history of its translation and conflictual domestication within the framework of colonial rule in most of the non-Western world. A preoccupation with the European roots of the idea often obscures an understanding of the routes through which various, often divergent and incompatible, ideas of civil society and the institutions it encompasses have travelled to, and been received in, other regions.

I think it is important to emphasize that there is no single coherent idea of civil society that has travelled from the West and has been, or could be, replicated elsewhere. Its contours within and outside Europe have been redrawn in various social and political theories of which it has been an element, and in political visions that it has been mobilized to support. Various ideas of civil society were produced in Europe in the context of political practice answering specific historical needs, as Kaviraj and Khilnani have shown (2001). Their appropriation and cultural translation outside the West relate in creative ways to a diversity of Western traditions, and were shaped by the political context in which they were forged – usually in opposition to colonial rule. The strategies of defiance crafted by Gandhi in the Indian national movement against British domination, for instance, owed as much to a recontextualization of Indian religious traditions of non-violence and everyday strategies of domestic resistance as to Ruskin's writings on civil disobedience. But they were also a deeply deliberated civil response to the incivility of colonial rule. Asked once by a young British journalist, 'Mr Gandhi, what do you think of Western civilization?', Gandhi's famous reply was 'I think it would be a good idea.'

Anthropologists have often cast doubt on the value of using an ethnocentric term like civil society for comparative purposes (Goody 2001). They have made their own contribution to particularizing the term by exploring its very different referents in different societies, including various European societies (Hann and Dunn 1996). The usual mode of engaging in a comparative exercise idealizes and abstracts from Western experience in order to then compare (more often than not negatively) non-Western trajectories, transformations and institutions of civil society as deficient or different. These narratives, whether Marxist or liberal, view social reality through the lens of binary oppositions (West/non-West, modern/traditional, societies with history/societies without history, secular/religious). Non-Western societies, as the term signifies, are defined by negation. As André Béteille (1991) has argued, the dominant traditions of comparative research in the social sciences assign a priority to contrast over comparison, to difference over similarity and to discontinuity over continuity; all non-Western societies are compared in terms of their contrast to the West. The historical and contemporary experience of non-Western societies is understood in such a framework not in terms of what it is but in terms of what it is not. But, as Mamdani (1996) has suggested, an ahistorical essentialization takes place on the Western side of the binary opposition as well. An idealised image of civil society in the West is created against which, for example, a 'marginal' African civil society (Mamdani 1996) or an 'embryonic' Indian one (Heins 2001) is measured and found wanting. Such an exercise partakes in a grand narrative of world history cast in terms of binary contrasts, in which European historical experience is seen as both unique and universal.

One consequence of such a narrative, as Mamdani (1996) has argued, is that it accords the European experience both an analytical value and a universal status, while regarding the non-European experience as residual. But, if such a perspective caricatures the experience summed up as residual, it also homogenizes and mythologizes the experience postulated as normal. It ascribes a 'suprahistorical trajectory' (Mamdani 1996) of development to Western societies; it posits a necessary rather than a contingent path unaffected by the struggles that produced it. It renders the experience of both European and non-European societies ahistorical by robbing them of their historical specificity. An exploration of these historical specificities would situate different meanings and trajectories of civil society in a framework sensitive to 'multiple modernities' (Eisenstadt 2000); this approach would map the very different paths and patterns of civil society both *within* and outside Europe. Moreover, it would enable a delineation of the entanglements, of varying degrees and kinds, of different European societies with their imperial and colonial projects overseas at different points in time (Cooper and Stoler 1997). Viewing metropolitan self-understanding through the prism of the (post-)colonial would enable a discussion of the complex play of inclusion/exclusion, disenfranchisement, recognition and exploitation of subjects and citizens, the incivility of civil society not merely 'at home' but when intertwined with racism and violence abroad (Said 1993; Gilroy 2000). Such a perspective of what I have termed 'entangled histories' of modernities within and outside the West overcomes both the methodological nationalism and Eurocentrism of the social sciences by seeing colonialism as constitutive of, not external to, European modernity. By drawing attention, for example, to the fervent missionary activities of modern Europeans in the colonies, such a perspective would unsettle the modernist narrative of a progressive secularization of Europe, a narrative that makes it possible to overlook, or at least underplay, the role of the churches, missionary societies and religious associations in modern Western civil societies and to regard these as characteristic of backward or imperfect non-European ones.

A perspective of entangled histories would argue not only against seeing a single coherent idea of civil society as emerging fully formed in Europe; it would also show how various European ideas of civil society were creatively used and developed further outside the confines of Europe, and how these in turn affected metropolitan discourses and practices. After all, there is little in common between Tocqueville's idea of civil society as a realm of secondary associations; Hegel's use of it as an analytical category to designate a sphere of ethics differentiated from the family and the state where societal ethics and individual morality can be reconciled; Gramsci's view of it as the sphere where the capitalist state establishes hegemony over society; and a Foucauldian perspective that interrogates the neat demarcation between state and civil society through a conception of the state as a disciplinary formation whose capillary power flows into all social institutions and into the very constitution of its subjects. Therefore, instead of tracing the diffusion of the ideas and institutions of civil society as a near universal with purely Western roots, it may be more fruitful to analyse the contestation and deployment of various conceptions of civil society in the service of diverse theoretical positions and political agendas in both Western and non-Western societies today. These dialogues with Western modernity expand or modify some of its ideas, but remain in part uncomfortable with it, as the Indian debates on civil society I review briefly in the next section illustrate.

Traditional Solidarities vs. Modern Institutions: Civil Society as Contested Terrain

The current controversies about questions of civil society in India are fuelled by concerns about the nature of democratic politics and citizenship rights on the subcontinent; by the widespread disillusionment with the failures of the post-colonial state to deliver the goods; by fears that undue state interference undermines the functioning of intermediate institutions; and by an interest in the revival or strengthening of indigenous traditions of civility. Activists and scholars alike have adopted the language of civil society to frame the legitimate rights of people in a democracy to make demands on the state, to render it accountable, to redress its malfunctioning and to curb its authoritarian policies.

Rajni Kothari, the leading theorist of civil society in India, premises his call for a 'humane governance' (1988b) – rooted in the subcontinent's own civilizational values and pre-colonial moral ordering of social relations – on a diagnosis of the ills of the modern state. He views violence as inherent in the modern state, not merely as endemic only to its post-colonial formations. For him the creation of civil society must draw

> upon available and still surviving traditions of togetherness, mutuality and resolution of differences and conflict – in short, traditions of a democratic collective that are our own and which we need to build in a changed historical context. This is the basic political task facing Indians – the creation of a civil society that is rooted in diversity yet cohering and holding together. (Kothari 1991: 29)

Critics of such a culturalist–communitarian perspective point out that its nostalgic and selective rendering of tradition overlooks the inequalities, hierarchies and denials of individual freedom – continuing into the present – in these pre-modern traditions (Gupta 1999). Such a sweeping critique, however, obscures the fact that these neo-traditionalist critiques of modernity do not advocate an unqualified romantic return to tradition. Rather, they emphasize the need for cultural moorings if alien institutions are to be successfully domesticated, a process which, in their view, requires a sensitivity to traditions in order to recover their best characteristics. Ironically, the communitarian concept of civil society implies a return to a traditional moral ordering of community: the very hierarchical and pre-modern past from which Locke, Rousseau and Hegel sought to break away with the concept of civil society in order to move towards a shared public sphere of civic ties and trust among citizens/strangers.

Indian scholars of civil society (Nandy 1984, 1989; Sheth 1984; Kothari 1988b, 1991; Chatterjee 1997, 2001) are not alone in privileging community ties over modern institutional arrangements. This seems also to be a relatively dominant trend in current renditions of civil society in Western scholarship. It is against a background of disappointment with state performance, or the perceived 'overreach' of the state, that a tendency to romanticize 'society' can be seen, especially those aspects of society least coloured by the (post-)colonial or the welfare state – and, therefore, more 'civil' or authentic. Protagonists of this view of civil society tend to define the current malady in India as the result of the colonial rupture with tradition and the neglect of the subcontinent's distinct cultural roots when building modern institutions. Civil society, as Gupta (1999) has pointed out, is thus understood as a realm before and/or outside modernity and the modern state. It is represented as a sphere sensitive to cultural plurality and social heterogeneity, a diversity that the state has sought to homogenize into a national monoculture.

An interesting contrast to this perspective is the view of the Indian sociologist André Béteille (1994), for whom the social value of an idea or an institution exists irrespective of, and can never be reduced to, the idea's or institution's geographical origins. His is a powerful critique of the search for more authentic ideas and institutions in tune with the cultural logic of Indian civilization. His argument for strengthening constitutional democracy in India (Béteille 1991) emphasizes – following Tocqueville – the role of modern intermediate and voluntary associations. He sees the well-being of modern institutions in India guaranteed only if civil societies are understood as comprising truly autonomous bodies – even if these bodies are of modern colonial origin (Béteille 1996). For him, citizenship and constitutional democracy cannot be built out of primordial ties of caste, kinship and religion, as these have formed the basis of a hierarchical social integration in the past. These traditional solidarities and exclusionary loyalties, therefore, are as responsible as is intervention by the state for the fragility and malfunctioning of modern institutions. A plurality of inclusive, secular, mediating institutions, relatively autonomous from the state and insulated from particularistic ties, is indispensable for the development and functioning of democracy in India. The success of the modern project of nation building is predicated on the expansion of this realm of civil society (Béteille 1998).

Placing himself squarely in the Hegelian tradition, Dipankar Gupta (1999), too, argues that a modern state – rather than traditional ties of caste and religious community, collective norms and customary law – is indispensable for the functioning of civil society. The primary task of civil society is, therefore, to constitute a community of citizens bound by the ethics of freedom, not by the particularities of tradition or the calculus of market interests. At the centre of his discussion of civil society is the issue of individual freedom and citizenship, in contradistinction to the neo-traditionalist and communitarian views, which centre on the collective rights and autonomy of communities. From the neo-traditionalist or culturalist-communitarian viewpoint a civil society based on the civilizational values of the subcontinent is the way to contain the violence of the modern post-colonial state. For modernists, liberals and Marxists alike, it is important, instead, to strengthen – and expand the ambit of – intermediate, rational-legal institutions; the well-being of these institutions also needs to be protected, both from the state and from the particularistic ties that can corrupt them.

For Gupta, civil society would include only those rational bureaucratic institutions compatible with individual freedom, equality, citizenship, deliberative procedures of decisionmaking, autonomy and the freedom of entry and exit. Partha Chatterjee (2001) concurs with this conceptualization of civil society, but argues that the history of modernity in non-Western settings is replete with the emergence of 'civil-social institutions' that do not conform to these principles and remain restricted to a small section of well-off citizens. The incomplete modernization of Indian state and society, which modernists like Gupta and Béteille would like to see completed along a Western trajectory, is, for Chatterjee, a distinctive feature of non-Western modernity, a marker of its colonial origins and its cultural difference.

Colonial Transformations of Caste Solidarities

The following two sections attempt to historicize and contextualize the ideas and institutions of civil society in India. By examining the workings of actually existing civil society – that is, the social practices of its inhabitants in a (post-)colonial context – these sections explore some of the ambiguities and tensions inherent in the idea of civil society. Apart from contributing to a less Eurocentric and a more cosmopolitan understanding of the uneven texture and changing contours of this domain of social ties as coloured by the policies of the state, the analysis also challenges a Western definitional monopoly on ideas and institutions that have travelled worldwide. Moreover, it counters the easy essentializations and binary contrasts that characterize the current debates on the Western origins of civil society and its less than perfect realization in non-Western societies.

The institutionalization of group rights and legal pluralism in India is part of the entangled histories of liberalism in Western and non-Western societies. Western liberalism attempted to create homogeneous universal citizenship in the metropolis while simultaneously instituting and cementing difference in the colonies. Unlike European polities conceived within a liberal democratic framework, colonies were never imagined as homogeneous. As Dirks (1992) has argued, despite its rhetoric of universalizing modernity, colonial governance was concerned with the management and often even the production of difference. Castes and religious communities as we know them today are very much a product of enumeration, classification and categorization by the colonial state in the nineteenth and twentieth centuries (Cohn 1984; Kaviraj 1992; Appadurai 1993). Thus the groups that bear collective rights in contemporary India, and the kinds of rights they claim, are shaped by processes of collective identity formation and community representation in colonial India. Whereas the ideology of colonialism pointed towards secular modern rights-bearing free citizenship and eventually nationhood, its reality dealt not only with the essentialization of racial inequality but also with the institutionalization of an elaborate grammar of cultural diversity through bureaucratic and administrative practice.

There are two variants to the thesis that communalism in contemporary India is of colonial origin. The provision of separate electorates for religious minorities and the reservation of caste-based quotas in the administrative services have been regarded as powerful historical factors in the formation of caste and religious identities. Bipan Chandra (1981) has argued that these measures were an important instrument of the divide-and-rule strategy of the British, whereas Sarkar (1983) is of the view that the element of calculated incitement of communal hatred through these policies has been exaggerated. More recently, the emphasis in historical scholarship has shifted from colonial policy to colonial discourse. Exploring the knowledge/power nexus, this scholarship has argued that colonial historiography, ethnography, cartography and census operations shaped and strengthened the collective identities of castes (Cohn 1968, 1984), religious communities (Pandey 1990), and 'tribes' or indigenous peoples (Devalle 1992).

The multiple identities based on cultural differences in pre-colonial India were fluid and flexible, not exclusive and exhaustive, partitions of the world. The prevalence of overlapping and cross-cutting idioms of difference meant that personal and collective identities were situational and segmented. For example, the community of Mole-Salam Garasia Rajputs in Gujarat had until recently a Hindu and a Muslim name for each of its members. There was no monolithic overarching ethnic identity cutting across caste, region, village of origin, religious denomination or sect. Moreover, the sense of distinctiveness on which each of these identities was predicated was not based on the reification or essentialization of 'cultural' features that characterizes modern ethnicity. Kaviraj (1992) has argued that these *Gemeinschaften*, in Toennies's sense, were based on a sense of belonging and solidarity that had little to do with a convergence of economic or political interests. In such a conception, pre-colonial communities are seen as based on organic bonds of kinship: pre-political primordial groups bound by tradition rather than constituted through voluntary ties of association of a contractual legal nature (Shodhan 2001). As I argue in the final section, such a contrast misrepresents the nature of communities in that it overlooks the fact that castes were, and most lower castes continue to be, largely self-governing local collectivities, which have authority and jurisdiction over their members. Although ascriptive in nature and bound by multiplex ties of social, marital and gift exchange, they were nonetheless political and jural entities, and have remained so.

Kaviraj (1992: 20–26) has tried to capture the difference between pre-modern, genuinely communitarian ways of conceiving a community and modern conceptions of it, in the contrast between 'fuzzy' and 'enumerated' communities. 'Fuzzy' communities belonged to a world that was unmapped and unenumerated. These communities had fuzzy boundaries because some collective identities, such as caste or religion, were not based on territory. Their members were not concerned to draw exact geographical boundaries of their communities, nor were they interested in unambiguously defining and counting all other members of the same region, caste, linguistic group or denomination. Numbers were not the basis of political legitimacy in pre-colonial India. It was only in the colonial and post-colonial states that they came to be used to bargain for economic resources and political privileges. Just how new the idea of exclusivist religious identities is can be seen from the fact that, in the 1911 census, 200,000 Indians declared themselves to be 'Mohammedan Hindus' (Lokhandwala 1985).

Kaviraj suggests that the difference between fuzzy and enumerated communities has important consequences for the action orientation of their members. Fuzzy traditional communities 'did not see historical processes as things which could be bent to their collective will if people acted concertedly on a large-enough scale' (Kaviraj 1992: 26). The enumeration of communities, introduced as part of colonial governmentality, brought about a radical change in this regard. Not only was enumeration a source of psychological strength regarding the size of the 'we' group; numerical majority became the basis of political legitimacy in the emerging nation state – it thus became imperative to define and draw precisely the boundaries of nations and regions and of communities within them. In the following section, I show that an evolutionary view of the transformation of traditional multiple belongings and diffuse identities into modern monolithic interest-based ones obscures an important fact: even in a world of enumerated collectivities, many castes continue to function as local, territorially demarcated groups, kin and affines with their own norms, procedures and practices of self-government (which they jealously guard from state intervention). However, the fact that castes enjoy relative autonomy, as ascriptive groups, in the domain of family law does not prevent them from engaging in collective interest-based mobilization at elections in terms of the arithmetic of vote banks. Different kinds of ties based on different logics of connectedness are deployed by caste members in different contexts.

To return to the colonial context of the objectification of ties with the help of the technologies of counting and codification: in order to enumerate the entities that were to form the basis of colonial policies, unambiguous definitional criteria were necessary. That these were messy categories was often clear to those that administered them. Nevertheless, the colonial state adopted caste and religion for the purpose of census enumeration, for the allocation of seats in representative bodies and for job appointments in the administration. For example, with regard to the term Hindu, the Madras Census Report stated, as early as 1881: 'Regarded as a definition of religion, or even of race, it is more liberal than accurate' (quoted in Lütt 1993: 1). But, perhaps even more importantly, the decennial census operations, and the policies based on them, led to these categories becoming intensely contested. Being perceived as a member of a community was no longer a matter of changing interactional contexts, but, rather, of being subject to definitive bureaucratic classification. This not only touched on questions of self-identity but involved high political and economic stakes for the elites of the different castes and communities. By the early years of the twentieth century, communal parties and caste organizations mobilized their respective all-India constituencies, created in the process of enumeration, in defence of their interests and for a greater share of political and economic power.

The logic and dynamic of the transformation of fuzzy local communities into enumerated regional or national entities can be illustrated with reference to the so-called 'untouchable castes' at the very bottom of the caste hierarchy. It is important to remember – as I have pointed out above – that this did not lead to the erosion of other modes of belonging but added another dimension to them, which could be deployed according to context. There are three reasons why I have chosen communities at the very bottom of the caste system – their existence interrogates the construction of a homogeneous Hindu majority – to illustrate the new forms of social connectedness. First, these are the castes whose practices of self-regulation are the focus of the next section on legal pluralism and the autonomy of caste councils.

Secondly, it will be argued that, by separating out these communities and constituting them as an all-India category, colonial discourse and policy set in motion a process that acquired a dynamic of its own; this, in turn, had several unintended consequences. It had important consequences for the subsequent self-identity of these collectivities at the all-India level, and for the formulation and implementation of state policies in relation to them even today. The reflexive process of social ties being moulded by the way they are conceptualized by the state is reflected in the hundred-year-old career of the term 'untouchable castes', which spans local, regional, national and global levels (Randeria 1992a). Varying practices of discrimination against several communities at the margins of local caste hierarchies were first reified at a regional level in colonial ethnographies; they were then elevated in the census to form an all-India category that embodied the essence of this discrimination in terms of 'untouchability'. The colonial policy of caste-based quotas, which continues in contemporary India, is a bone of contention for liberal secular intellectuals and the propounders of a Hindu nationalism alike. For the former, state policies based on particularistic identities contravene the principles of modern nation building based on the equality of all citizens; while, for the latter, a monolithic majoritarian Hinduism is difficult to maintain in the face of the politicization of caste identities and growing caste conflicts (Randeria 1996).

Finally – on the implicit assumption that majorities and dominant groups have few problems in this regard – problems of collective identity and boundary maintenance have usually been studied with reference to minorities and disadvantaged groups. But the massive public controversy in the 1920s on the question of whether untouchables were Hindus – a question that would have been meaningless only a century earlier – shows that the construction of a Hindu identity encompassing these groups was a highly contested process in colonial India. Moreover, their inclusion was perceived to be so vital for a Hindu majority in the political numbers game that, in the early decades of this century, the need for a reform of Hinduism was advocated to avert the danger of a dwindling of the Hindu population through conversions. The concerted efforts of Hindu nationalists to 'reconvert' to Hinduism those untouchables who have become Muslims or Christians and to prevent such conversions, if possible, show that the identity and integration of these communities remain a problem for political Hinduism in the present (Randeria 1996).

The arrangement of castes in an orderly hierarchy was chosen by the British administrators as the most important categorization with which to map and control Indian society. Although administrative necessity was said to be the official rationale for recording information on castes, nationalist Indians felt that it was part of the design 'to keep alive, if not exacerbate, the numerous divisions already present in Indian society' (Srinivas 1966: 100). In order to collect 'objective' information, the fluid contours of a caste unit, as well as situational and segmented identities and belongings, had to be resolved in favour of unambiguous categories. A standardization of caste names and definitional criteria became necessary in order to ensure all-India comparability.

The groups separated out at the bottom of the local caste hierarchies as the repository of 'untouchability' came thus to constitute a distinct all-India category embodying this essence. The group of castes so demarcated became not only the object of missionary activity and conversions, of philanthropic practice and Hindu reformist zeal, but also of administrative interest and political concessions. In order to ascertain their numerical strength, a few defining features – out of the diversity of local cultural practices – were used to construct an all-India community.

The estimate of the 'depressed classes' population, as the 'untouchables' were then called, varied widely depending on the specific criteria of ritual and social exclusion that were used, for example, non-access to temples, wells, association with an impure occupation or, more broadly, low status in the caste hierarchy. Around 1917, pollution by touch for the upper castes (that is, 'untouchability') came to be the chief criterion for inclusion in the category. I am not arguing that, if castes had not existed, the British would have invented them. What the British did, however, was to use 'untouchability', an attribute of *all* inter-caste relations, to characterize and set apart as beneficiaries of political concessions and welfare measures a particular group of castes in every region. But, once these categories were used by missionaries, administrators and Orientalists, they functioned in a recursive manner and – as ethnic labels – were appropriated by the people so designated for the conceptual reification of groups.

The boundaries of an all-India category of 'untouchable castes' were drawn once and for all in terms of a checklist of 'civic disabilities' (put together by the Census Commissioner in 1931) from which they suffered. These included access to services of Brahmans, to 'public utilities' like wells and schools, to temples, and so on. To conceive of these exclusions in terms of 'civic disabilities' is to impose a modernist category. This category presupposes the existence of a civil society, not a world of caste divisions and interactions governed in different situations by different idioms of ritual ranking, in which exclusion is a matter of degrees and contexts. Galanter (1984: 122–31) has pointed out that it was also unclear what would count as evidence with regard to a local practice, since services of Brahmans, access to wells and temples, and so on, were all matters of claims and counterclaims. Particular local practices did not reflect the *rights* of groups (which is what the state wanted to ascertain with regard to public utilities) but, rather, continual contestation about ranking.

How far colonial rule and modern competitive politics were responsible for the reshaping of collective identities and the role of indigenous agency in the process remain matters of deep division among historians of modern India. But here it is enough to have shown the historically changing character of ties of communities of caste and religion in interaction with the state. Recognizing the historical processes of community formation does not, however, render contemporary identifications, belongings and claims based on these processes illegitimate. But it does point to a central dilemma inherited by the post-colonial Indian state – how to institutionalize the recognition of difference in a way that does not essentialize and cement difference. Can bureaucratic and legal mechanisms for coping with cultural heterogeneity be made compatible with the constructivist insights that cultures are not immutably bounded wholes and that identities are flexible, plural and contextually shifting? One of the challenges for future social and political theory will be simultaneously to address the claims of both equality and identity, the unresolved tension that continues to trouble the Indian model of communitarian liberal democracy. The Indian experience in this regard has much to contribute to Western debates – carried out in ignorance of non-Western experiences of diversity and pluralism – on differentiated citizenship, cultural rights of communities and affirmative action.

Legal Pluralism and Autonomous Caste Councils

These theoretical debates among historians, political scientists and sociologists/social anthropologists in India serve to frame my discussion of local castes, and especially caste councils: these are a relatively autonomous arena for the setting, implementing and interpreting of norms with regard to engagement, marital conflicts and affinal gifts, inheritance, divorce, remarriage and the custody of children. If civil society is the space of social self-organization between, family, state and market (Kocka 2000: 4), it must – in the Indian context – include not only caste councils and associations but a variety of other non-state legal institutions of self-government and regulation of social life that are relatively autonomous from the state. Given the pre-colonial and colonial history of relative legal autonomy and pluralism in India, the state has never had a monopoly over the production, administration or interpretation of personal law. In post-colonial India, non-state legal institutions span a wide variety of institutions, from 'traditional' caste councils that exclude women from participation to 'modern' hybrid women's bodies. The latter include newly established women's courts (*nari adalat*) under an Indian-government directed and Dutch-government financed project of women's empowerment (*Mahila Samakhya*); and experiments in gender justice by NGOs in Rajasthan that support the inclusion of women in traditional caste councils and the setting up of parallel women's caste councils.

Women's organizations like Jyoti Sangh in Ahmedabad (Gujarat, Western India) also belong in this category. Jyoti Sangh has a long history, dating back to pre-independence India, of settling marital disputes of women from all castes and classes and a formidable reputation for following up and enforcing the terms of reconciliation it has worked out with the couple (after extensive consultations with the extended family). The category of autonomous hybrid institutions in the field of dispute resolution (which straddle the traditional and modern divide) would also include Gandhian organizations or Jesuit missionaries in south Gujarat who mediate in family and property disputes among the indigenous communities (*adivasi*) (for whom they also provide various other educational and medical services). With the exception of the women's courts (*nari adalat*), none of these organizations is recognized by the state as a legal forum. However, the organizations' decisions, based on norms woven together from a variety of sources, are accepted, and sometimes even sought, by lower state courts. Compared with rulings by state courts, these usually elicit much greater compliance from the disputants, and for two reasons: not only do disputants recognize these decisions as morally binding and closer to their own quotidian values and practices, but the parties to the conflict have also participated, along with the entire community, in arriving at these compromises.

Six distinct sets of phenomena must be distinguished analytically within the contemporary plurality of legal regimes and civil society institutions in the domain of family law in Gujarat:

(1) the prevalence of separate religiously based family laws for members of different religious communities throughout the country (Hindu, Muslim, Christian, Parsee). Codified by the British colonial state and reformed by the post-colonial state in the case of the Hindu Personal Law, these are administered by state courts.

(2) The de facto toleration by the state of a multiplicity of 'traditional' legal authorities and institutions, along with a multiplicity of

'customary' and scriptural sources of norms as administered by caste, 'tribal' or *jamat* councils (*panchayats*), which both adjudicate and reform these laws for the members of their own local communities.

(3) The explicit constitutional provision for communities of indigenous peoples (so-called 'Scheduled Tribes') to be governed by their own set of customary family laws in state courts as well as their own autonomous forums.

(4) The toleration by the state of the role of several voluntary organizations including women's organizations, Gandhian institutions and church-based NGOs, which seek to resolve family conflicts in accordance with a diverse set of legal norms, using mediation.

(5) The setting up by the state of 'people's courts' as a speedy, cheap and accessible alternative to state courts as a way of lessening the pressure on the state system.

(6) The introduction of 'women's courts' (*nari adalat*) by the '*Mahila Samakhya*' programmes (which were set up under a state-initiated programme for women's empowerment and gender justice funded by Dutch development aid).

All these institutions operate parallel to and in varying degrees of interaction with state law and state courts. An analysis of their complex articulation with state-centred legal regimes would help to transcend the dichotomies in terms of which discussions of legal pluralism are often framed: tradition/modernity, state/community, state/civil society and secular/religious. These relatively autonomous 'traditional' institutions, such as caste councils, fit neither the liberal model of civil society based on individual rights of citizenship nor the liberal assumption of the monopoly of the state over law. Nor do they fit Partha Chatterjee's idea of 'political society' discussed above, as they are not arenas of collective bargaining and negotiation with the state but, rather, arenas in which communities govern their own internal affairs. My argument is that caste- and community-based institutions should be seen as part of the specificity of the workings of civil society and of the uneven texture of post-colonial modernity in India; they should not be defined out of the public sphere of civil society as representing 'primordial' ties as opposed to 'civic ties' or be seen – as modernists like Dipankar Gupta are wont to – as administering 'customary law'.

An examination of the concepts and conduct of 'informal justice' in post-colonial India poses a challenge to liberal social and political theory derived from Western historical trajectories of individual rights of citizenship and the monopoly of the state over law. This examination also reveals a fracturing of sovereignty in the nation state that contemporary academic and political debates about a uniform civil code in India obscure. By reducing law to state law, these accord it a primacy and a privileged status it does not have in practice. Academic and public debates in India have been largely concerned only with religiously based personal law of colonial provenance, administered in upper-level state courts; this leads to a rather narrow understanding of legal pluralism. The exclusive focus on state law has eclipsed the role of civil society institutions like NGOs, women's organizations and Jesuit and Gandhian institutions, as well as the workings of caste councils and popular justice in the field of family law. Keeping the wide variety and hybrid institutions of informal justice and legal plurality in mind would enable a mapping of the changing contours of state and civil society relations and of shifts in the boundary between the public and the private spheres.

Nivedita Menon (1996) has argued that, from the point of view of gender justice, feminists should reject the homogenizing thrust of a uniform family law that seeks to subordinate women's interests in the name of national integration. She cautions against the tendency to naturalize communities in order to claim rights in the name of primordial ties represented as prior to other identifications and belongings. As argued in the previous section, contemporary communities are far from immutable entities with unalterable contours and customs; they have been formed, rather, in the process of historical interaction with both one another and the practices of the colonial state. Any attempt to subordinate the interests of women to the interests of communities defined as internally homogeneous and conceived of as the collective bearers of rights is equally problematic. The rights of autonomy and difference that communities claim *vis-à-vis* the state must also be extended to women as members of communities. In this context the right to exit from or to choose whether or not to belong to a community – rather than simply ascriptive membership of it by virtue of birth – has come to define the community's civility for many feminists.

Another, perhaps unusual, argument for the civility of castes could be made in this context: this argument contrasts with the stress, in the literature on modern civil society, on castes' unfree character and the coercive nature of this realm of the 'tyranny of cousins' (Gellner 1995). The caste assembly, or *panchayat*, composed of adult male members of a territorial unit of a caste, functions as the primary local unit of identification and belonging. Collective identity, patterns of solidarity, ties of kinship and affinity but also community power structures and the authority of caste elders, are all constituted with reference to the *panchayat*. Following Moore (1994), a *panchayat* can be understood more as a process with changing participants than as an institution or an event. It is an important forum in which local community norms are subject to continual deliberation and periodic revision. Processes of internal disputation and contestation of norms within each caste (rather than the difference between community and state law) are central to the collective identity of a local sub-caste (Randeria 1992a). My ethnographic material – generated during fieldwork among the Dalits, or 'untouchable' castes, in north Gujarat (in western India) – reminds us of the workings of local subdivisions of castes as communities of discourse. Caste assemblies, comprising adult men, set the rules and procedures by which they are collectively governed, commit them to writing and interpret and change these norms in long-winded processes of public negotiation. Legal and rhetorical skills are well distributed in the community, and the informal and non-professional nature of the proceedings ensures greater accessibility and participation.

Each Dalit caste in the area is subdivided into several, named, local units constituted by a set of villages spread over a particular area. These local units, or *paraganu*, often do not encompass contiguous villages. Following Max Weber, Klass (1980) treats each subdivision of a caste as an autocephalous *Verband*, a corporate group with its own leadership and internal control mechanisms, which admits no other level of authority. Rather than emphasizing their corporate character, I have chosen to follow my Dalit interlocutors in conceiving of them as territorially defined autonomous politico-jural units; these may function as units of endogamy, but their main function is the administration of all local caste matters, including the rules of connubium and commensality, which bind members together. Interestingly, the Gujarati word for caste is either *nat* (derived from the Sanskrit *gynati*, meaning species), or *samaj* (society); these are used synonymously. The latter usage is a pointer to the fact that the social world of a caste is not conceptualized by its members as the arena of private particularistic interests – as opposed to a larger public sphere defined in relation to the state or seen as encompassing the entire nation. Caste members see the ties of solidarity marked by reciprocal food exchange and the exchange of women and gifts (exchanges that characterize castes as local communities), as belonging to the public sphere of sociality *par excellence*; and they contrast this sphere with the private sphere of narrow individual self-interest (Randeria 1992b, 1999d).

Each local caste unit, or *paraganu*, has its own written and printed 'caste constitution' (*bandharan*), which contains all the rules of gift exchange with kin, affines and service castes to be followed at life-cycle rituals; in addition, the *bandharan* contains the procedures and punishments for breaking an engagement, for divorce, for the remarriage of widows and divorcees, and for the custody of children. Caste assemblies legislate, administer and adjudicate the internal affairs of the *paraganu*, enforce and interpret the norms, punish transgressions and collect fines, or even excommunicate the offending families from membership of the local caste. Written caste constitutions all over Gujarat seem to have been a response to the process of collection and codification of caste norms under colonial rule. In 1827, the British Collector of Ahmedabad, Borrodaille, launched a large-scale administrative inquiry to collate – through interviews with selected male caste leaders – the 'customs' of all castes; his aim was provide the colonial judiciary with information on which to base its decisions. This seems to have given a fillip to caste assemblies to commit to writing and to publish their hitherto flexible, oral and highly contextual local norms. The form of present-day caste constitutions corresponds closely to the structure of the colonial questionnaires administered almost two centuries ago (Randeria 1992a).

The process of codification, however, has not completely frozen the highly flexible norms in question. In the long, acrimonious public contestation of the rules and their interpretation at caste assemblies, the written document remains only one source of norms; others include precedent and the practices of neighbouring subdivisions of the same caste. Caste councils handle disputes very differently from the way courts do.[1] As Hayden (1981, 1983) has shown, conflicts between individuals are transformed in the assembly into a dispute between each party and the caste as a whole. Rather than treating the offending persons, or rather families, as parties to a conflict, the offending family or, rather, all families of the caste resident in a particular village are considered to have committed an offence against the caste. In speeches by caste leaders before the assembly, disputes are attributed to narrow self-interest and are represented as polluting the purity of the collective body of the caste, whose sacredness is compared to the River Ganges or to God. Dispute resolution on these occasions does not follow a set trajectory that begins with the statement of a complaint and ends with a final resolution, culminating in the crafting of a compromise capable of generating consensus.

In these attempts at mediation, which last as long as it takes to reach a consensus, each side loses some and gains some. The family held guilty is made to a pay a price for transgression of norms, but an attempt is made to avoid a rupture in social relationships. Discussions proceed in a meandering manner, in which mobilization of kin and affinal networks, past alliances, behind-the-scene bribes and relationships of power determine the course of the proceedings (which may stretch over months of negotiations at various caste assembly meetings). These factors, along with the rhetorical skills of the disputing parties and their allies, influence which issues are brought up, how they are framed, which issues are kept out, how long the deliberations take, whether consensus can be reached, which set of norms is applied, which precedents are considered relevant, how heavy a fine is levied and whether the offenders are excommunicated from membership of the caste.

If normative conflict *within* a spatially defined caste unit (*paraganu*) is pivotal to its constitution as a community, then community justice is as contested a terrain as state law. Villagers told me in interviews that they often used both these forums in parallel for different purposes. State courts are used to delay the resolution of a dispute interminably, demonstrate one's networks of influence outside the caste and harass an opponent and ruin him economically by pushing up the costs of a prolonged conflict. Justice is then sought in the caste assembly using familiar local idioms, supported by one's network of kin and affinal ties and according to the norms of one's community. There is a great deal of continuity between everyday social interaction and dispute settlement in caste assemblies. Even women, who may not speak for themselves in these forums but have to be represented by their fathers and uncles, usually prefer the familiar arena of caste assemblies – embedded within their social world – to the unfamiliar and distant world of state courts. Usually only young upwardly-mobile men, resident in urban areas and with good salaries of their own, prefer – in a bid to cut the ties of caste and to escape from family pressure – to use state courts for divorces. It is not that villagers often prefer caste *panchayats* to courts as speedier or cheaper options: bribes have to be paid in both cases. But the money spent in caste assemblies builds on and strengthens multiple social ties and contributes to social capital – which can be used for other, future, purposes. Money paid to lawyers, judges, police and witnesses is seen, on the contrary, as a waste. It nurtures no social relationships, builds no new bonds of trust and cannot be put to any other use in future.

Unpacking categories like civil society or community enables one to delineate some of the richness, the complexity, but also the ambiguities and paradoxes of contemporary processes of legal pluralism. Perhaps the uneven modernities of the semi-periphery make available political spaces for non-state actors – especially in the sphere of legal production – eclipsed in the advanced capitalist countries by a statist imaginary. Rather than merely seeing these political spaces as a sign of the weakness or failure of the state in post-colonial societies, one could also see it as a chance for justice to be realized by a diversity of actors with varying capabilities. Many women's NGOs in rural areas have, therefore, preferred to struggle for the inclusion of women in traditional caste councils or have set up alternative women's councils, rather than relying on state law and courts for gender-just family laws and their implementation.

Veena Das (1995) has argued that an authentic 'traditional' *telos* is as unavailable in contemporary Indian society as in any modern institution that has not been coloured by its location. All major institutions in India are reconstituted through their double articulation in tradition and modernity. It is this texture of Indian modernity, with its failure to escape from the bonds of caste, class and gender, that a conceptualization in terms of unevenness is meant to capture. As my account of caste solidarities and non-state legal regimes in India reminds us, 'traditional' ideas, values and institutions are not residual traces of a vanishing past in colonial and post-colonial settings; they are constitutive features of modern life. My material on the plurality of sources of norms and of arenas of conflict resolution in the area of family life shows how uneasily the 'traditional'-'modern' dichotomy fits into the easy quotidian intermingling of discourses and practices (which theories of modernization posit as contradictory, binary opposites).

The scholarly debates and everyday practices I have outlined here allow an analysis of the actual workings of civil society and the dilemmas of its actors *vis-à-vis* the state. State intervention in the lives of poor and marginalized communities in India is highly selective. Indifferent to the governance of domestic discord among the poor, to their caste conflicts and marital strife, the state is ever vigilant, and even coercive, in its control over the fertility of the poor and the sizes of their families – as the history of dirigist population policy in India amply illustrates (Randeria 1995, 1999c). Unconcerned about the lives and livelihoods of these citizens, the state is highly interventionist in its control over the natural resources held in common by these communities (Randeria 2002, 2003b). It recognizes the cultural rights of communities but not their collective rights over natural resources (land, water, forests). Thus the multiple or fractured sovereignties characteristic of the domain of family law cannot be extended to cover the commons. The cunning state, as I have argued elsewhere (Randeria 2001a; 2002, 2003b), chooses to exercise selective and partial sovereignty over its territory and its citizens. However, what would appear in liberal theory, and from a statist perspective, as the failure of the state, or its weakness, can also be seen as an opportunity. The absence of state hegemony in some areas of social life, along with the state's inability, or unwillingness, to colonize completely the everyday life-worlds of its citizens, also provides a space for dissenting imaginaries. Rather than seeking statist solutions based on Western models, the challenge is to be able to develop alternatives, and experiment with them, as tools of a new moral and social imagination sensitive to the textures and rhythms of uneven modernities in India.

Notes

This chapter has had a long history and has been presented to several audiences in its various reincarnations. Originally written to address issues of multiculturalism, group rights and practices of citizenship in India for a conference of the 'Theory, Cultural and Society' group in London in 1999, it benefited greatly from the comments of Stuart Hall, Mike Featherstone and Scott Lash. Its focus shifted to include a consideration of legal pluralism and community justice, thanks to intensive dialogues with Boaventura de Sousa Santos during my participation in the project of his Centre for Social Studies, Coimbra, and the MacArthur Foundation on 'Reinventing Social Emancipation'. A first draft of the present version was presented at the conference on 'Bindung' (Ties) as part of the Wissenschaftskolleg, Berlin AGORA 2000 project, of which I was a member. Comments by Richard Schweder and Sally Humphreys helped me to clarify several issues in the last two sections. An earlier version of the paper was published in the conference volume edited by Yehuda Elkana et al., *Unraveling Ties: From Social Cohesion to New Practices of Connectedness* (Berlin, 2002). I am grateful to John Keane for several discussions that helped give final shape to the section on civil society. In its present form the paper was presented at the conference organized by the Civil Society Network at the Wissenschaftszentrum für Sozialforschung Berlin (WZB) in November 2002 and incorporates some of the invaluable suggestions made by Shmuel Eisenstadt.

1. However, the differences between the two are often exaggerated by seeing upper-level courts as the prototype of state law. Lower courts, though of course not embedded in the social life of the community, often exhibit greater similarity to community justice: for example, in their use of mediation, or in their application of the community's own norms instead of state law.

References

Appadurai, Arjun. 1993. 'Number in the Colonial Imagination'. In *Orientalism and the Postcolonial Predicament:Perspectives on South Asia*, ed. Carol Breckenridge and Peter van der Veer. Philadelphia.

Bayart, Jean-Francois. 1996. *The State in Africa. The Politics of the Belly.* London.

Béteille, André. 1991. *Society and Politics in India.* London.

———. 1994. 'Secularism and the Intellectuals'. *Economic and Political Weekly* 29.

———. 1996. *Civil Society and its Institutions.* First Fulbright Memorial Lecture. Calcutta.

———. 1998. 'The Conflict of Norms and Values in Contemporary Indian Society'. In *The Limits of Social Cohesion: Conflict and Mediation in Plural Societies*, ed. Peter Berger: 265–92. Colorado.

Chandhoke, Neera. 1995. *State and Civil Society: Explorations in Political Theory.* Delhi.

Chandra, Bipan. 1981. *Nationalism and Communalism in Modern India.* New Delhi.

Chatterjee, Partha. 1993. *The Nation and its Fragments. Colonial and Postcolonial Histories.* Princeton.

———. 1997. 'Beyond the Nation? Or Within'. *Economic and Political Weekly* 32: 30–34.

———. 2001. 'On Civil and Political Society in Post-colonial Democracies'. In *Civil Society. History and Possibilities*, ed. Sudipta Kaviraj and Sunil Khilnani: 165–78. Cambridge.

Cohn, Bernard. 1968. 'Notes on the Study of Indian Society and Culture'. In *Structure and Change in Indian Society*, ed. Milton Singer and Bernard S. Cohn: 3–28. Chicago.

————. 1984. 'The Census, Social Structure and Objectification in South Asia'. *Folk* 26: 25–49.

Comaroff, John L. and Comaroff, Jean, eds. 1999. *Civil Society and the Political Imagination in Africa*. Chicago.

Conrad, Sebastian and Randeria, Shalini. 2002. *Jenseits des Eurozentrismus: Postkoloniale Perspektiven in den Geschichts- und Kulturwissenschaften*. Frankfurt am Main.

Cooper, Frederic and Stoler, Ann, eds. 1997. *Tensions of Empire. Colonial Cultures in a Bourgeois World*. Berkeley.

Das, Veena. 1995. *Critical Events: An Anthropological Perspective on Contemporary India*. Delhi.

Devalle, Susana. 1992. *Discourses of Ethnicity: Culture and Pin Jharkhand*. New Delhi.

Dirks, Nicholas. 1992. *Colonialism and Culture*. Ann Arbor.

Eisenstadt, Samuel N. 2000. 'Multiple Modernities'. *Daedalus* 129, 1: 1–29.

Galanter, Marc. 1984. *Competing Equalities: Law and the Backward Classes in India*. New Delhi.

Gellner, Ernest. 1995. 'The Importance of Being Modular'. In *Civil Society: Theory, History, Comparison*, ed. John Hall. Cambridge.

Gilroy, Paul. 2000. *Against Race: Imagining Political Culture beyond the Color Line*. Cambridge, Mass.

Goody, Jack. 2001. 'Civil Society in an Extra-European Perspective'. In *Civil Society. History and Possibilities*, ed. Sudipta Kaviraj and Sunil Khilnani: 149–64. Cambridge.

Gupta, Dipankar. 1999. 'Civil Society or the State: What Happened to Citizenship?' In *Institutions and Inequalities. Essays in Honour of André Béteille*, ed. Ramachandra Guha and Jonathan P. Parry: 234–58. Delhi.

Hall, J.A. ed. 1995. *Civil Society: Theory, History and Comparison*. Cambridge.

Hann, Chris and Dunn, Elizabeth, eds. 1996. *Civil Society: Challenging Western Models*. London.

Hayden, Robert. 1981. 'No One is Stronger than Caste: Arguing Dispute Cases in an Indian Caste Panchayat'. Unpublished dissertation. University of New York at Buffalo.

————. 1983. 'Excommunication as Everyday Event and Ultimate Sanction: the Nature of Suspension from an Indian Caste'. *Journal of Asian Studies* XLII, 2: 291–307.

Heins, Volker. 2001. *Der Neue Transnationalismus. Nichtregierungsorganizationen und Firmen im Konflikt um die Rohstoffe der Biotechnologie*. Frankfurt and New York.

Kaviraj, Sudipta and Khilnani, Sunil. 2001. 'Introduction: Ideas of Civil Society. In *Civil Society. History and Possibilities*, ed. Sudipta Kaviraj and Sunil Khilnani: 1–8. Cambridge.

Kaviraj, Sudipta. 1992. 'The Imaginary Institution of India'. In *Subaltern Studies VII*, ed. P. Chatterjee and Gyanendra Pandey: 1–40. New Delhi.

Khilnani, Sunil. 1997. *The Idea of India*. Delhi.

Klass, Morton. 1980. *Caste: the Emergence of the South Asian Social System*. Philadelphia.

Kocka, Jürgen. 2000. 'Zivilgesellschaft als historisches Problem und Versprechen'. In *Europäische Zivilgesellschaft in Ost und West. Begriff, Geschichte, Chancen,* ed. Manfred Hildermeier et al.: 13–39. Frankfurt am Main.

Kothari, Rajni. 1988a. 'Integration and Exclusion in Indian Politics'. *Economic and Political Weekly* 23: 2223–27.

———. 1988b. *State against Democracy: In Search of Humane Governance.* Delhi.

———. 1991. 'Human Rights: A Movement in Search of a Theory'. In *Human Rights: Challenges for Theory and Action,* ed. Smitu Kothari and Harsh Sethi. New York.

Lokhandwala, S.T. 1985. 'Indian Islam: Composite Culture and Integration'. *New Quest* 50: 87–101.

Lütt, Jürgen. 1993. '"Hindus – a Dying Race". Census and Identity in India before the First World War'. Paper for the Conference *Identität im Wandel,* Berlin 21–22 October.

Mahajan, Gurpreet. 1995. *Identities and Rights: Aspects of Liberal Democracy in India.* Delhi.

Mamdani, Mahmood. 1996. *Citizen and Subject: Contemporary Africa and the Legacy of Late Colonialism.* Princeton.

Menon, Nivedita. 1996. 'Uniform Civil Code: Debates in Feminism Today'. In *Sites Of Change: The Structural Context for Empowering Women in India,* ed. Nitya Rao et al.: 445–59. Delhi.

Moore, Erin. 1994. 'Law's Patriarchy in India'. In *Contested States: Law, Hegemony and Resistance,* ed. Mindie Lazarus Black and Susan Hirsch: 89–117. New York.

Nandy, Ashis. 1984. 'Culture, State and Rediscovery of Indian Politics'. *Economic and Political Weekly* 19: 2078–83.

———. (1989). 'The Political Culture of the Indian State'. *Daedalus* 118, 1–26.

Offe, Claus. 1998. '"Homogeneity" and Constitutional Democracy: Group Rights as an Answer to Identity Conflicts'. In *Rules, Laws and Constitutions,* ed. Satish Sabarwal and Heiko Sievers: 188–208. New Delhi.

Pandey, Gyanendra. 1990. *The Construction of Communalism in Colonial North India.* New Delhi.

Pantham, Thomas. 1995. *Political Theories and Social Reconstruction.* New Delhi.

Randeria, Shalini 1992a. *The Politics of Representation and Exchange Among Untouchable Castes in Western India (Gujarat).* Dissertation, Free University Berlin.

———. 1992b. 'Kings, Brahmans, "Untouchables": Caste-Hierarchy and Gift-Exchange Western India'. In *Wissenschaftskolleg Jahrbuch 1990–1991,* ed. W. Lepenies: 294–312. Berlin.

———. 1995. 'Die sozio-ökonomische Einbettung reproduktiver Rechte: Frauen und Bevölkerungspolitik in Indien'. *Feministische Studien* 1: 119–32.

———. 1996. '"Hindu-Fundamentalismus": Zum Verhältnis von Religion, Politik und Geschichte im modernen Indien'. In *Kulturen und Innovationen: Festschrift für Wolfgang Rudolph,* ed. G. Elwert et al.: 333–61. Berlin.

————. 1999a: 'Geteilte Geschichte und verwobene Moderne'. In *Zukunftsentwürfe. Ideen für eine Kultur der Veränderung*, ed. Jörn Rüsen et al.: 87–96. Frankfurt.

————. 1999b. 'Jenseits von Soziologie und soziokultureller Anthropology: Zur Ortsbestimmung der nichtwestlichen Welt in einer zukünftigen Sozialtheorie'. *Soziale Welt* 50, 4: 373–82.

————. 1999c. 'Through the Prism of Population: State, Modernity and Body Politics in India'. Paper presented for the Agora-2000 Project.

————. 1999d. 'Mourning and Mortuary Exchange: the Construction of Local Communities among the Dalits of Gujarat'. In *Ways of Dying Death and its Meanings in South Asia*, ed. E. Schombucher and Claus Peter Zoller: 88–111. Delhi.

————. 2001a. *Local Refractions of Global Governance: Legal Plurality, International Institutions, the Postcolonial State and NGOs in India*. Habilitation. Faculty Politik- und Sozialwissenschaften, Free University Berlin.

————. 2001b. 'Zivilgesellschaft in postkolonialer Perspektive'. In *Neues über Zivilgesellschaft aus historisch-sozialwissenschaftlichem Blickwinkel*, ed. Jürgen Kocka et al. WZB Arbeitspapier. Berlin.

————. 2002. 'Globalising Gujarat: Environmental Action in the Legal Arena-World Bank, NGOs and the State'. In *Development and Deprivation in Gujarat – Festschrift for Jan Breman*, ed. M. Rütten and G. Shah. Delhi.

————. 2003a. 'Neo-liberal Discipline and Negotiations over Law: Nation-States, International Organizations and NGOs'. In *Shared Histories and Negotiated Universals*, ed. W. Lepenies. Frankfurt am Main.

————. 2003b. 'Which State is Globalization in? International Institutions, Social Movements and the Cunning State in India'. In *Another Knowledge is Possible*, ed. Boaventura de Sousa Santos. London.

Said, Edward. 1993. *Culture and Imperialism*. New York.

Sarkar, Sumit. 1983. *Modern India 1885–1947*. New Delhi.

Seligman, Adam. 2002. 'Civil Society as Idea and Ideal'. In *Alternative Conceptions of Civil Society*, ed. Simone Chambers and Will Kymlicka: 13–33. Princeton.

Sheth, D.L. 1984. 'Grass Roots Initiatives in India'. *Economic and Political Weekly* 19: 259–62.

Shodhan, Amrita. 2001. *A Question of Community: Religious Groups and Colonial Law*. Calcutta.

Sollors, Werner. 1989. *The Invention of Ethnicity*. New York and London.

Srinivas, M.N. 1966. *Social Change in Modern India*. Berkeley.

Therborn, Göran. 1995. 'Routes to/through Modernity'. In *Global Modernities*, ed. Mike Featherstone, Scott Lash and Ronald Robertson: 124–39. London.

10

THE TEMPTATIONS OF UNFREEDOM:
ERASMUS INTELLECTUALS IN THE AGE OF
TOTALITARIANISM

Ralf Dahrendorf

For a long while now, I have been concerned with the question why so many intellectuals in the two decades following the First World War succumbed to the great temptations of communism or fascism. This is, in the first place, a historical question but one that has lost none of its relevance, even if it is not quite clear in what form the new temptations of the twenty-first century will beguile intellectuals.

That communism was a temptation has long been clear. For good reason the thoughtful British intellectual and Labour MP Richard Crossmann gave his 1949 collection of the memoirs of prominent ex-communists like Arthur Koestler and Ignazio Silone the title *The God That Failed*.

To many young intellectuals, particularly those who had lost the God of their Jewish or Christian parents, the hope of a socialist paradise seemed to be more than a substitute, especially because it was a paradise on earth. Manès Sperber, the great novelist of the period, author and psychologist, once wrote of the 'suprapersonal relationship compulsion' under which he and his communist friends suffered.

The nature of communism as a temptation is probably most apparent in the pain of abandoning the true faith, that is, the discovery that the god is not a god. The events that brought such insight, if not *en masse* at least for many, are all milestones in the history of the twentieth century: the first show trials of Stalinism, the Ukrainian Harvest of Sorrow (to use

Robert Conquest's words) that was collectivization, the Spanish Civil War, the Hitler-Stalin Pact; then, after the war, Khrushchev's revelation speech and the brutal suppression of the Hungarian Revolution, both in 1956, Solzhenitsyn and the Gulag, the bloody end to the Prague Spring in 1968. Was there a single intellectual communist left? Yes, there was one, the great historian Eric Hobsbawm, who has never quite explained why he was so keen to be the last to put out the scarcely flickering light of the (British) Communist Party.

That National Socialism, too, was a temptation is not quite so evident. Like Italian Fascism before it, it had not so much vision as power, so that it was not quite clear whether its supporters were acting from conviction, opportunism or purely as fellow travellers. However, in a particularly fine essay entitled 'National Socialism as a Temptation', Fritz Stern showed that a 'religious-mystic element' was not lacking. Hitler was the 'saviour', who brought 'national rebirth'. He willingly evoked 'Providence'. Above all, however, fascism, especially in its National Socialist variant, promised something for which the people of the period thirsted, namely commitment: commitment to the abstract community, the nation, to the concrete order, the rallies and Speer's mass stagings, commitment to the community, including the often evoked *Volksgemeinschaft* or 'national community'.

Few resisted the allure of such temptations. The summer of 1933 offers a particularly ominous and disquieting spectacle. Thomas Mann, already in exile, found that there were good sides to the Nazi regime. Karl Mannheim, dismissed from his professorial chair and forced to emigrate, nevertheless believed Hitler had his uses for Germany. In prison, Julius Leber, the great Social Democrat, wrote that there had been really no future left for Weimar. Even Martin Heidegger fitted into this picture with his self-assertion speech; and Hannah Arendt, who, in spite of everything, did not deny Heidegger her personal sympathy.

How was this possible? The question has often been put. A generation, now two generations, of German historians have contributed to answering it with an unusual corpus of material and studies. The Wissenschaftszentrum Berlin is in the fortunate position of being headed, in the person of Jürgen Kocka, by an outstanding representative of these new historians. His authority forbids me to venture too far into his territory. I take a different point of departure, anyway. I wish to reverse the question of why so many major intellectuals succumbed to the temptations of communism and fascism to ask: who among the important figures of intellectual life did not succumb? Who was immune to the temptations of totalitarianism? And what in the intellectual habitus of these untemptables gave them the strength to resist?

In answering this question, I devote special attention to those who were in their prime at the zenith of temptation, that is to say, in the early

1930s. They are all people born in the first decade of the twentieth century. Some have already been mentioned in passing: Manès Sperber, for instance (1905), who had, however, to fight for his immunity; and Hannah Arendt (1906), who had very personal problems with it. My most important heroes are three men whom I had the pleasure of knowing rather well: Karl Popper (1902), Raymond Aron (1905) and Isaiah Berlin (1909). All three were Jews and hence, so to speak, constitutionally exempt from temptation by fascism. My most important witness in this regard is Norberto Bobbio (1909), although there is no lack of others.

When I come to write something about the subject, the biographies of these and others will play a role. For my present purpose, however, I must concentrate on the general question of what these immune people had in common, what gave them the strength to resist the temptations of the period? My answer is that they shared certain fundamental attitudes, perhaps also certain intellectual characteristics. By no means were these traits only appealing, but they were decisive for holding out in times of trial. So far I have been struck by four such characteristics, four virtues, as I choose to call them.

The first of these virtues can be described as the *courage to stand up for the cause of freedom in solitude*. This could perhaps be better formulated, but the concepts courage, solitude and freedom should not be omitted. At least in later life, Isaiah Berlin was often disturbed by his lack of courage. 'I'm a coward,' he said over and over again, and meant that he had not dared to join any of the movements of his time. He did not share the prevailing passions, even though they deserved Max Weber's label of 'sterile excitement'. Berlin's biographer, Michael Ignatieff, has graphically described the dilemma, coming to the wise conclusion that 'romantic standards of heroism are a form of moral tyranny': 'People should not be judged by whether they are prepared to risk their lives but by whether they keep their heads, morally and politically, when others are losing theirs.' Joachim Fest describes Hannah Arendt in very similar terms, coming to the succinct but profound conclusion: 'she willingly accepted the isolation in which she soon found herself as the price of freedom'. This is the virtue I mean, and it requires courage in a world in which the strength of battalions counts more than that of arguments. It means rejecting the battalions ('Where there is talk of intellectual camps', writes Hannah Arendt, '*Ungeist* usually holds sway') and being able to stand up for freedom quite alone if need be.

The second virtue of those who remain immune in the face of all illiberal temptations is the *ability to live with contradictions*. Possibly the greatest weakness of those who succumb to the temptations of totalitarianism is that they cannot resist seeking a god, or at least a providence, in whom all the perturbing contradictions of reality are cancelled out. The Hegelian core of the Marxian philosophy of history, the overcoming of struggles in the finite synthesis of communist society, played a fateful role. This is no less true, indeed, it is much more primitively so, of the yearning for community and the Führer cult in National Socialist fascism. Isaiah Berlin can supply a counter-image: for him, pluralism was not mere arbitrary diversity but the co-existence of the incompatible. This position is brought still more strongly to bear in Karl Popper, who elevated the imperfections of the world almost to a principle of his open society. Paradise is lost. 'There is no way back to a harmonious state of nature.' 'If we wish to remain human beings ... , we must advance into the unknown, uncertain, and unsecured.' Self-determinacy, enlightenment in the Kantian sense, requires the acceptance of antinomies, not the search for their dissolution or cancellation, be it in the sense of Rousseau or of Hegel.

The third necessary virtue for immunizing intellectuals in times of trial is that of the *engaged observer*. This is a peculiar figure that the French philosopher and sociologist Raymond Aron invented for himself. In the course of a long discussion with two students, he was asked: 'Didn't you pave the way by stating your opinion on events and analysing them at the same time?' Aron answered: 'Yes. I believe I have already pointed out that I decided my intellectual line of conduct when I was an assistant at the University of Cologne [in 1933, which gives the statement particular weight]. I decided then to be an "engaged observer".' What he meant was to observe the unfolding of history as objectively as possible without remaining completely distant. Whether this is possible in theory is questionable. It is as if one wished forcibly to amalgamate 'science as a vocation' and 'politics as a vocation', each of which demands such a fundamentally different attitude. In practice, however, a few have indeed managed to achieve this. Noone will want to accuse Aron of remaining neutral towards the various forms of 'opium of the intellectuals', but he was never seduced by the ever-new enthusiasms of his *petit camarade* Jean-Paul Sartre (who, incidentally, was in Germany at the same time and succeeded Aron in his Berlin position at the Institut Français). Perhaps the most important characteristic of the engaged observer is that he cannot be silenced; he describes and analyses and judges and writes and writes and writes, but he does not act.

He is thus entirely dependent on the fourth virtue that gives one immunity to illiberal temptations, *the passion of reason*. The two concepts seem not to belong together. As a rule, reason is considered to be cool and passion the lure of unreason. But the intellectuals I am examining are all passionately rational. Perhaps we should speak of a quiet passion: it does not go onto the streets to chant 'Rea-Son'; the Goddess of Revolution figures in another chapter. But the intellectuals concerned do not allow themselves to be diverted from their insistence on discourse, argumentation, the rational examination of all allegations.

Courage for freedom in isolation, living with contradictions, engaged observation, the passion of reason – is there a single concept that can subsume all these in a convenient description of the position? The concept is a person. He was an intellectual and, like all those we have been talking about, a public intellectual. He lived at a time of upheaval in which it was almost impossible not to take sides. Nevertheless, he said: 'I love freedom and I will not and cannot serve any party.' His contemporaries had little understanding for this stance. One of the most prominent among them wrote to him: 'If you so wish, remain what you have always claimed you wanted to be: a mere spectator of our tragedy.' This was a little unjust, for the spectator was always engaged in some way or other; indeed, he was considered by some to be the ideal source of reform. But he did not become dogmatic. One of his biographers said of him that he loved 'the world precisely because of its diversity, and its differences do not daunt him. Nothing is farther from his thoughts than wanting to abolish these differences in the manner of the fanatic and systematician.' Another biographer sums it up better than I could: 'As an intellectual type he belongs to the rather rare group of those who are unconditional idealists as well as being thoroughly moderate.' The quiet passion of reason.

The title of my remarks will have already betrayed who the mystery man is: Erasmus of Rotterdam. (It was Martin Luther who scolded him for being a 'mere spectator of our tragedy'.) The disputes of Erasmus's time, 500 years ago, were quite different from those of the twentieth century. Although they invited fanaticism on both sides, among the contested Roman Church and the Protestants, and were the cause and medium of one-and-a-half centuries of armed conflicts, they can be described as temptations of unfreedom only in unnecessarily audacious analogy. Nevertheless, Erasmus in his tempestuous times represented an intellectual habitus very much like that with which I am concerned, that is to say, a habitus which, I suspect, contains the answer to the question of what makes people immune against the temptations of totalitarianism. I therefore speak of Erasmus intellectuals, or more simply of Erasmians.

Like Erasmus himself, Erasmians are not necessarily agreeable; they are certainly not all agreeable. Luther was not the only person to be irritated by engaged observers. Contemporaries found it difficult to understand the distance Erasmus maintained from his friend of many decades, Thomas More, when the latter was imprisoned in the Tower and later led out to the scaffold. Reason is, moreover, a very quiet passion that tends to express itself in irony, indeed cynicism, rather than in visible engagement. It was certainly not his choice, but nevertheless typical, that Karl Popper wrote his 'contribution to the war effort' (as he himself called it), his work on *The Open Society and its Enemies* in distant exile in New Zealand. Isaiah Berlin was well aware of having experienced the decisive period of the war far away from the front, in the comfort of the British embassy in Washington. Raymond Aron, too, was in exile. His young disputants, however, were more concerned with the fact that in 1968, when the *évènements de mai* began with the show of solidarity between the students of Nanterre and the workers of the Renault factory, he left on a lecture tour of America as if all this had nothing to do with him.

The people who remained in fascist countries confronted quite different impositions. Norberto Bobbio offers a good example. The uncontestedly liberal legal philosopher and later political theoretician soon came into conflict with Mussolini's fascist regime, and was arrested. He participated in initiatives of the intellectual resistance and then in groups preparing the liberal order after Mussolini. After the war, however, a letter turned up which the 26-year-old had written to the Duce in 1935 in support of his application for a first permanent position as lecturer. He wrote of the 'patriotic and fascist family' in which he had grown up and defended himself against 'accusations' of anti-fascism. On the contrary, his studies had helped him 'to consolidate my political opinions and to deepen my fascist convictions'. The scandal was enormous when the letter was published in 1992, although Bobbio was perfectly able to justify the need for such a pseudo-declaration. 'A dictatorship corrupts the souls of human beings,' he also said. Not even Erasmians are proof against it.

But I must restrain myself. It had been my intention to present a programme for future work, not a finished opus. At any rate, two things need to be outlined: what I myself intend to do with the Erasmians, and the extent to which they are still – or once again – important for understanding the period and for the future of freedom.

The 'short twentieth century', which (taking up and slightly varying Hobsbawm's approach) lasted from 1917 to 1989, was a time of testing for Erasmians and thus for liberals. Not many passed without fault. I have often considered awarding points for degrees of resistance to temptation, so to speak Erasmian points on a scale from 1 to 10. If we remain with the generation of the first decade of the last century: 10 points for Popper, Aron and Berlin; 8, perhaps only 7 points for Theodor Eschenburg, who defends conscious and controlled fellow-travelling in his autobiography; a similar score for Theodor W. Adorno, the observer without recognizable engagement, who always found the confrontation with reality embarrassing; 5, at most 6, points for those who succumbed to temptation for a while, but who then, like Manès Sperber, became convinced Erasmians; a still lower score for Arthur Koestler or Arnold Gehlen, who, although they forswore false gods, remained temptable by irrational and, in the case of Koestler, mysterious forces.

My adopted country, England, is particularly interesting in this connection. (I deliberately say England, not Scotland – although there were also Erasmians there; Indeed, the Scottish Enlightenment in the eighteenth century really supplied them with the theory – and certainly not Northern Ireland.) In the critical period of trial that was the twentieth century, England was really Erasmus country. It was not subject to temptation even when the liberal order was faltering almost everywhere. The few Red street fighters, like Oswald Mosley's blackshirts, were nothing more than '*Zeitgeistler*' driven out of the Labour Party without influence on government and society in England. Only in England could Erasmians feel completely at home. During the war, Raymond Aron enjoyed this and remained an Anglophile; Karl Popper and Isaiah Berlin made England their permanent home. We recall that even Erasmus of Rotterdam spent eleven years of his life in England, although he had not only praise for the country.

For the English themselves, Erasmus Land often tended to be too insipid. They set out in search of temptations in quite un-English social and geographical latitudes. Not all took their private protest as far as the Mitford sisters, of whom one, Unity, became an adherent of Hitler, a second, Diana, married the fascist leader Mosley, whereas a third, Decca, ran away to experience the Spanish Civil War among communists, and remained a communist all her life. Only Nancy Mitford, born in 1904, kept her head and wrote her often brilliant novels as an observer without engagement, of which she had seen too much in the family. The profoundly Erasmian George Orwell (born in 1903) repeatedly went in search of objects for his unquenched passions and came back – from Burma, from the slums of London and Paris, then from Catalonia – as someone who could not be enthralled by the temptations surrounding him. He revealed their grotesque and cruel aspects in *Animal Farm* and *1984*.

I shall be talking about such experiences when I follow the path taken by Erasmians through the century of temptations. The year 1984 has meanwhile come and gone without anything particular happening, and 1989 has for the time being put an end to all temptations. Is my interest therefore primarily historical? Or is there a current reason for it? In the course of a now pretty long life, I have learned to guard against a temptation other than those so far mentioned. Social scientists (sometimes even modern historians) occasionally have an unfortunate tendency to stylize ephemeral phenomena as the extraordinary, to suspect every excited gathering of being the source of the next revolution. This brings embarrassing errors of analysis, which are bearable only because they are themselves ephemeral and therefore swiftly forgotten.

Caution is hence advisable in asking whether there are new temptations that are once again jeopardizing the immunity of intellectuals and bringing Erasmians into play. With all due caution it should therefore be mentioned that there are signs of the spread of a new counter-Enlightenment. At the beginning of the twenty-first century, the loss of a sense of security, of commitment, which some believed they could perceive in 1933, indeed in 1917, is in evidence and, moreover, global. Many people have an unsatisfied longing for security which neither the old Churches nor the old State can fulfil. New fundamentalisms are taking their place. They may be Islamic, but also Protestant; some even speak, not quite unjustifiably, of market fundamentalism. The values and attitudes of which I have spoken are coming under pressure again. This may be a passing mood, perhaps even a fad. But there is good reason for vigilance among those to whom enlightened thought and the liberal order are dear. To recall that there were Erasmians in earlier periods of trial can do no harm at such a time.

Note

This is an edited version (translated from the German) of a lecture delivered at the Wissenschaftszentrum Berlin on 11 January 2005.

NOTES ON CONTRIBUTORS

Frank Adloff
Born in 1969 in Wuppertal (West Germany), Frank Adloff was awarded
his Ph.D. by the Free University Berlin. He currently works as an assistant
professor at the Institute for Sociology at the University of Göttingen.
Among his publications are *Im Dienste der Armen. Katholische Kirche und
amerikanische Sozialpolitik im 20. Jahrhundert* (2003); *Zivilgesellschaft.
Theorie und politische Praxis* (2005); and *Vom Geben und Nehmen. Zur
Theorie der Reziprozität*, edited with Steffen Mau (2005).

Ralf Dahrendorf
Lord (Ralf) Dahrendorf KBE, FBA is a social scientist and author. He is a
cross-bench member of the House of Lords and chairman of the House of
Lords Select Committee on Delegated Powers and Regulatory Reform. A
research professor at the Wissenschaftszentrum Berlin (WZB), Lord
Dahrendorf is a former director of the London School of Economics
(1974–84), a former Warden of St Antony's College, Oxford (1987–97)
and a former Pro-Vice-Chancellor of the University of Oxford (1991–97).

Hans Joas
Professor Hans Joas is Director of the Max Weber Center for Advanced
Cultural and Social Studies, Erfurt (Germany), and professor of sociology
and social thought at the University of Chicago. Among his publications
are: *G.H. Mead. A Contemporary Re-examination of his Thought*
(1985/1997); *Social Action and Human Nature* (with Axel Honneth)
(1988); *Pragmatism and Social Theory* (1993); *The Creativity of Action*
(1996); *The Genesis of Values* (2000); *War and Modernity* (2003);
Sozialtheorie (with Wolfgang Knoebl) (2004); and *Braucht der Mensch
Religion?* (2004).

John Keane
Born in Australia and educated at the Universities of Adelaide, Toronto
and Cambridge, John Keane is professor of politics at the University of
Westminster and a research professor at the Wissenschaftszentrum Berlin
(WZB). In 1989 he founded the Centre for the Study of Democracy.

Among his many books are *The Media and Democracy* (1991), which has been translated into more than twenty-five languages; *Democracy and Civil Society* (1988, 1998); *Reflections on Violence* (1996); *Civil Society: Old Images, New Visions* (1998); the prize-winning biography *Tom Paine: A Political Life* (1995); and a study of power, *Václav Havel: A Political Tragedy in Six Acts* (1999). Among his most recent works are *Global Civil Society?* (2003) and *Violence and Democracy* (2004). A member of the American-based Institutions of Democracy Commission, he is currently writing a full-scale history of democracy – the first for over a century.

Jürgen Kocka

Professor Jürgen Kocka is President of the Wissenschaftszentrum Berlin (WZB), professor of the history of the industrialized world at the Free University of Berlin, and Director of the Centre for the Comparative History of Europe (Free University and Humboldt University, Berlin). His publications include *Industrial Culture and Bourgeois Society – Business, Labor, and Bureaucracy in Modern Germany* (1999) and *Das lange 19. Jahrhundert. Arbeit, Nation und bürgerliche Gesellschaft* (2001).

Herfried Münkler

Herfried Münkler, born in 1951 in Friedberg, is professor of social science and political thought at the Humboldt University of Berlin. Among his publications are: *Machiavelli. Die Begründung des politischen Denkens der Neuzeit aus der Krise der Republik Florenz* (1982); *Im Namen des Staates. Die Begründung der Staatsraison in der Frühen Neuzeit* (1987); *Gewalt und Ordnung. Das Bild des Krieges im politischen Denken* (1992); *Der neue Golfkrieg* (2003); *The New Wars* (2004).

Paul Nolte

Born in 1963 in Geldern, Paul Nolte was professor of history at the International University Bremen from 2001 to 2005 and currently holds a chair in modern and contemporary history at the Free University Berlin. He has been a German Kennedy Memorial Fellow at the Center for European Studies, Harvard University, and a Fellow of the Wissenschaftskolleg Berlin. His most recent book publications are *Die Ordnung der deutschen Gesellschaft. Selbstentwurf und Selbstbeschreibung im 20. Jahrhundert* (2000); and *Generation Reform: Jenseits der blockierten Republik* (2004).

Claus Offe

Born in 1940 in Berlin, Claus Offe received his doctorate from the University of Frankfurt in 1968 and his habilitation from the University of Konstanz in 1973. He has taught at the Universities of Bielefeld (1975–89) and Bremen (1989–95) and served as visiting professor at academic institutions in the US, Canada, the Netherlands, Austria, Sweden, Italy and Australia. Currently he is professor of political science at the Institute for

Social Science, Humboldt University Berlin. His recent English-language book publications are: *Varieties of Transition* (1996); *Modernity and The State. East and West* (1996); and (with Jon Elster and Ulrich K. Preuss) *Constitutional Design in Post-Communist Societies. Rebuilding the Ship at Sea* (1998).

Shalini Randeria

Shalini Randeria is professor of social and cultural anthropology at the University of Zurich. She has been a fellow of the Wissenschaftskolleg zu Berlin and Max Weber Professor for Sociology at the Central European University Budapest. Her most recent publications include *Konfigurationen der Moderne: Diskurse zu Indien*, edited with Martin Fuchs (2004); *Worlds on the Move: Globalisation, Migration and Cultural Security* (Toda Institute Book Series on Global Peace and Policy), edited with J. Friedman (2004); and 'Scattered Sovereignties and the Cunning State: Sub-state and Supra-state Legal Pluralism in India', in B. Santos, ed., *Another Knowledge is Possible* (2004).

Sven Reichardt

Sven Reichardt studied history, political science, psychology and Italian studies at the University of Hamburg and the Free University Berlin. In 2000 he was awarded his Ph.D. by the Free University Berlin. In 2001–3 he was Research Fellow at the Wissenschaftszentrum Berlin (WZB), where he was a member of the working group 'Civil Society from the Perspective of Historical Social Sciences'. He is currently professor of contemporary history at the University of Konstanz. He is the author of *Faschistische Kampfbünde. Gewalt und Gemeinschaft im italienischen Squadrismus und in der deutschen SA* (2002) and co-editor of the volume *Zivilgesellschaft als Geschichte. Studien zum 19. und 20. Jahrhundert* (2004).

Dieter Rucht

Dieter Rucht is professor of sociology at the Wissenschaftszentrum Berlin (WZB) and co-chair of the research group 'Civil Society, Citizenship and Political Mobilization in Europe'. His research interests include political participation, social movements and political protest. Among his recent books are: (with Myra Marx Ferree, William Gamson and Jürgen Gerhards) *Shaping Abortion Discourse: Democracy and the Public Sphere in Germany and the United States* (2002); and (with Lee Ann Banaszak and Karen Beckwith, eds) *Women's Movements Facing the Reconfigured State* (2003).

Susanne-Sophia Spiliotis

Dr Spiliotis has been a lecturer in modern Greek history at the Free University Berlin (1998–99) and director of research at the German Business Foundation Initiative (2000–3). She is currently a researcher at the Wissenschaftszentrum Berlin (WZB). Her publications include 'The Merten

Trial (1957–1959) and German-Greco Relations', in Mark Mazower, ed., *After the War Was Over: Reconstructing the Family, Nation and State in Greece, 1943–1960* (2001); *Verantwortung und Rechtsfrieden. Die Stiftungsinitiative der deutschen Wirtschaft* (2003); and *Moral Responsibility and Legal Peace: The German Business Foundation Initiative* (forthcoming).

INDEX